"When I picked up Williams's *REFL*[illegible] what an astonishing, absolutely unique treasure I was about to read. I know Williams, and he (as flawed as we all are) practices what he preaches. The motivating problem is something that our vastly ignorant population simply does not get—that we all worship something and we become like what we worship. This is the scary and sober truth, and if people got ahold of this, they would think much more seriously about their ultimate source of transcendence and meaning. And Williams rightly identifies Jesus and the religion he founded as the only game in town. And he proves it by taking seriously the question, what if we really intended to become like Jesus in several key areas of his life and our lives. Williams draws on an impressive combination of scholarly works and popular culture, and he seems comfortable in both worlds. What results is a completely unique book that must receive a wide circulation. So, please, get a copy, and after you have read it, buy copies for your friends and get into groups to discuss the ideas contained therein. It will definitely be worth your time."

—**J. P. Moreland,** Distinguished Professor of Philosophy, Talbot School of Theology; author of *Love Your God with All Your Mind*

"Few people today, inside or outside the church, know who Jesus really is and what he actually taught. Williams's new book enlightens that darkness. Williams proves himself a worthy successor to the late Dallas Willard in emphasizing Christ's superior intelligence, his right emotion, his loyalty to the Scriptures, his servant leadership as the best form of power, and the significance of his death and resurrection. This is a book we've all needed for a long time!"

—**Howard Ahmanson,** President, Fieldstead and Company

"Williams has written a marvelous book that points readers toward authentic worship, faithful living, dedicated discipleship, and a love for Jesus Christ. Readers who take time to reflect on *REFLECT* will find a book that is brilliant, creative, wide-ranging, insightful, readable, challenging, and filled with wisdom. It is a genuine joy to recommend this outstanding book. I encourage readers to buy two copies and give one to a friend!"

—**David S. Dockery,** President, Trinity International University; coauthor of *The Great Tradition of Christian Thinking*

"Want to become more Christlike? Worship Jesus Christ. Why? Because we become what we worship. This logic fuels *REFLECT*, a winsomely written and thoroughly contemporary discipleship manual. At a time when our culture's authenticity obsession is leading individuals down find yourself dead-end paths, Williams rightly focuses our attention on Jesus, the source of everything truly authentic. This insightful and timely book reminds readers that becoming Christ-like is not about looking inside yourself or leaning on legalistic rules; rather, it's about getting to know, learning to love, and bowing the knee to the glorious Christ."

—**Brett McCracken,** author of *Hipster Christianity* and *Gray Matters*

"With trademark brilliance and wit, Thaddeus Williams turns his eye to the question of Jesus' identity, and its implications for, well, everyone."

—**Ross Andersen,** *The Atlantic*

"Williams is a renaissance man who loves Jesus and loves life. His wide-ranging passions are on full display in this exceptional new book, written with theological clarity, infectious curiosity, and an artist's touch. Featuring insights from Dorothy Sayers, Fyodor Dostoyevsky, David Foster Wallace, and many more, *REFLECT* paints a vivid picture of what it means to worship Jesus and why it matters. The book is a brilliant resource for twenty-first century people seeking to live meaningfully in a world where meaning is harder and harder to find."

—**Barry H. Corey,** President, Biola University; author of *Love Kindness*

"Williams convincingly and winsomely destroys the notion that a person can be non-religious, observing from historical testimony and everyday observation that everyone nurtures a god-concept, an all-important object of devotion that shapes all of life in significant ways. Not only are all people religious, all of life is religious, so it is crucial in our own lives to imitate the habits and practices of Jesus Christ. The book is beautifully written and gracious; the author knows how to write a page-turner with a father's warmth and scholar's insight. Along the way, he provides a more robust picture of Jesus, the God-man, than will have occurred to most of us. Yet Christ is revealed as much more than mere moral exemplar. Williams knows, and presents to us, the Jesus who is the Way, the Truth and the Life. It is my honor and delight to commend this unique and original work."

—**Joseph Boot,** Founder of the Ezra Institute for Contemporary Christianity in Canada; Director of the Wilberforce Academy, London UK; Senior Pastor, Westminster Chapel, Toronto

"Many works can raise the right questions; very few provide the right answers. And, even fewer do so in a way that provokes application and change. Williams practically grapples with and answers the defining issue facing the church and culture today: What is man? His answer is directional, yet not dogmatic; informed, yet not pedantic; fresh, yet not trendy; faithful, yet not frothy; joyful, yet not juvenile. Williams understands and communicates how our lives can reflect (and must reflect) Christ in the entirety of his integrated multi-faceted humanity. Far from being yet another generic collection of 'spiritual disciplines,' or pious admonitions, this volume basks in the glory of Christ, and this propels us (with

Williams' thoughtful nudging) to be transformed so that we become authentic transformers unto the Good, Beautiful, and True. This volume is at once sound, practical, doxological, loving, and encouraging, and shall be a prime resource for my university and graduate students."

—**Jeffery J. Ventrella,** Senior Counsel,
Senior Vice-President, Training, Alliance Defending Freedom;
author of *The Cathedral Builder: Pursuing Cultural Beauty*

"Williams speaks of a radical change in his life, how he 'slowly come to appreciate the wonderfully diverse ways in which creativity is part and parcel of what it means to bear the Creator's image . . . and to multiply the net beauty in the universe.' This book is a wonderfully diverse and creative example of how to imitate Christ, bearing the Creator's image, and thus to add to the beauty of the universe."

—**Peter Jones,** Executive Director, truthXchange; Scholar in Residence,
Westminster Seminary, California; author of *Capturing the Pagan Mind*

"*REFLECT* is a fascinating book of vignettes on values and key character traits. You will bounce back and forth hearing the many voices of people from an array of life's vocations who have reflected on life with care—and you will learn much."

—**Darrell L. Bock,** Executive Director for Cultural Engagement,
Howard G. Hendricks Center for Christian Leadership and Cultural
Engagement; Senior Research Professor of New Testament Studies,
Dallas Theological Seminary; author of *Jesus, the God-Man*

"Williams connects the dots between one of the church's most neglected practices—the imitation of Christ—and one of our generation's deepest questions—personal identity and meaning. *REFLECT* is a creative, winsome, and entertaining book that will help all different kinds of readers understand what it means to follow and worship Jesus in our current cultural moment."

—**Gavin Ortlund,** Associate Pastor, Sierra Madre Congregational Church (CA),
and writer for The Gospel Coalition

"No one can fathom the depths of Jesus' truth, wisdom, or virtue. Yet this book brings profound features of Jesus' character to bear on our existence. Those who want to live life the Jesus-way should read this rewarding work by Williams."

—**Douglas Groothuis,** Professor of Philosophy, Denver Seminary;
author of *Philosophy in Seven Sentences*

"This fine book on worshiping and imitating Christ is written with great verve and theologically informed insights drawn from art, film, literature, philosophy, science, and much more. It is a creative, clarifying resource that helps show what loving the Lord with heart, soul, mind, and strength looks like in today's world."

—**Paul Copan,** Professor and Pledger Family Chair of Philosophy and Ethics, Palm Beach Atlantic University; author of *A Little Book for New Philosophers*

"Williams understands that the greatest problem of humanity is a worship problem. We worship the wrong things and neglect or reject true worship of the one true God. With keen insight into human nature, philosophical precision, theological clarity, creativity, and humor, Williams leads the reader on an enjoyable journey of fruitful intellectual exploration. Atheists, skeptics, and believers alike, will benefit from this thought-provoking book."

—**Erik Thoennes,** Chair of Undergraduate Theology, Biola University; Pastor at Grace EV Free of La Mirada, CA; author of *Life's Biggest Questions*

"This is a remarkable addition to 'imitation of Christ' literature. Williams wants us to think, feel, act, love, elevate, create, and transform like Jesus. Behold! *REFLECT* is seriously thoughtful, emotive, active, loving, engaging, creative, and transforming. It is itself a model of his own thesis. It is on the top of my list of discipleship books, and I cannot recommend it highly enough."

—**Brian Mattson,** Senior Scholar of Public Theology, Center for Cultural Leadership; author of *Restored to Our Destiny*

"Williams has written a brilliant book that deftly weaves together theology, philosophy, history, science, art, literature and pop culture all with equal ease. Imagine Radiohead meets Jonathan Edwards! And he does all this while demonstrating that following Jesus Christ is not only of supreme worth but brings supreme satisfaction to the hungry soul. This book is both an apologetic for the Christian faith and a faithful guide to the all-encompassing enterprise of being a Christ follower. Read and *REFLECT*!"

—**Scott Christensen,** Pastor, Summit Lake Community Church (CO); author of *What about Free Will?*

"The term 'Christian' has come to connote a particular historical or theological persuasion that sometimes crowd out the original meaning, which Williams recovers and reanimates in this thoughtful, practical book. To be a Christian is not merely a static state but also a lifelong process of imitating Jesus. In this book, Williams shows us, quite simply, what it means to be—and to keep becoming—a Christian."

—**P. Andrew Sandlin,** Founder and President, Center for Cultural Leadership

"Williams has written a book of which I can give the highest praise possible: it made me want to be more Christ-like. In describing discipleship that is both thoughtful and emotional, rationale and aesthetic, Williams encourages a walk with God that will both bring joy to those following Christ and bring others to see the source of that joy. *REFLECT* provides an engaging and contemporary message for an authentic life lived for Christ, rooted in a long tradition of Christian reflection from Calvin to Bono. Readers will be richly rewarded by reading this unique perspective on reflecting Christ in all parts of life."

—**Myron S. Steeves,** Dean, Trinity Law School, Trinity International University

"Christians all agree that living like Christ is important, but it's hard to do when you don't know what that really means. Williams gives readers a comprehensive and captivating understanding of this call, one that engages every aspect of your being in the task of following Jesus."

—**Aaron Armstrong,** Brand Manager for The Gospel Project,
LifeWay Resources; author of *Awaiting a Savior*

"Williams lays out a masterful picture of Jesus that, like a prism, shows us Christ in dazzling Technicolor and what human life was always meant to be. I particularly appreciate that the author is refreshingly practical as he veers from the mere theoretical into the realm of knowing and mirroring Jesus in everyday life. This book offers us a banquet of sumptuous answers to those mystifying questions about the elusive meaning of life where those starving for clarity of purpose can gorge to their satisfaction. I recommend everyone to read this book. Those who do will forever be transformed."

—**Tyler Geffeney,** International Director, *Ratio Christi*

"*REFLECT* is both an insightful and enjoyable book. Williams has the rare ability of writing in a winsome and enjoyable fashion, but also with depth and clarity. I get to teach and speak to many students. *REFLECT* is going to be one of the top books I recommend for those who want to become the person God has designed them to be."

—**Sean McDowell,** Assistant Professor, Biola University;
author of *A New Kind of Apologist*

"Williams is one of the most exciting theological voices writing today. In this book his prodigious command of multiple disciplines, from literature to art to philosophy to law to theology, is on full display, all in service of equipping us to *REFLECT* Jesus in our everyday lives. For those seeking a resource to become better disciples themselves or disciple others, your search is over."

—**Gabriel N. E. Fluhrer,** Minister of Discipleship, First Presbyterian Church,
Jackson (MS); author of *Solid Ground*

"*REFLECT* is a book about the big questions in life—where we find our identity, our meaning, our purpose. While most people search within to find the answers,

Williams shows us that the answers we seek can only be found in the One who transcends us, created us, and came for us. All who want to grow in their understanding of how Jesus' life and character bear weight on our very own will enjoy digging into this very helpful and timely book."

—**Chris Poblete,** Pastor and Church Planter, King's Cross Church, Rancho Santa Margarita (CA); author of *The Two Fears*

"C. S. Lewis said that 'walking and talking are two very great pleasures.' I have walked and talked with Williams through the years. I have a sneaking suspicion that *REFLECT* will become just that for our meaning-seeking generation, a well-worn companion to walk and talk with through life. Williams's wide-ranging, integrated, and melodic treatment of everything from pop culture and the arts to philosophy, theology, and biblical exegesis will empower us to become more fully ourselves by beholding the beauty of Jesus. I invite you to grab a copy and a tasty beverage with your closest friends, pull up a chair and talk awhile."

—**Aron McKay,** Pastor and Church Planter, The Table, San Clemente (CA)

"*REFLECT* is a rollicking, sweeping survey of humanity's quest for meaning, featuring an eclectic collection of historic luminaries from philosophy, science, religion, and pop culture. Managing this troupe is literary ringmaster Thaddeus Williams, who's as comfortable quoting Bono as he is invoking apostle Paul. With equal parts logic, emotion, and humor, Williams directs his chorus—and in turn the reader—to reflect The Greatest Person in History. It's a fresh, challenging, and ultimately rewarding book—unlike any other I have ever read."

—**Stan Jantz,** Executive Director, Evangelical Christian Publishers Association; coauthor of *GodQuest*

"The Christian life is about Christ. Williams paints an attractive vision which understands that following him ought to be holistic and driven by love. Eminently readable, creative, and expansive in scope, this book is to be well recommended in introducing important themes in an accessible and integral way."

—**Gray Sutanto,** University of Edinburgh

REFLECT

Becoming Yourself by Mirroring the Greatest Person in History

Thaddeus J. Williams

WOOSTER, OHIO

REFLECT: Becoming Yourself by Mirroring the Greatest Person in History

Published by
Weaver Book Company
1190 Summerset Dr.
Wooster, OH 44691
weaverbookcompany.com

Cover design: Frank Gutbrod
Interior design: {In a Word}
Editorial: Line for Line Publishing Services

Library of Congress Cataloging-in-Publication Data

A CIP catalogue record for this book is available from the Library of Congress.

To Gracelyn, Holland, Harlow, and Hendrik,

each a gift from the Greatest Person in History

(and I don't mean Mom, although she comes in second)

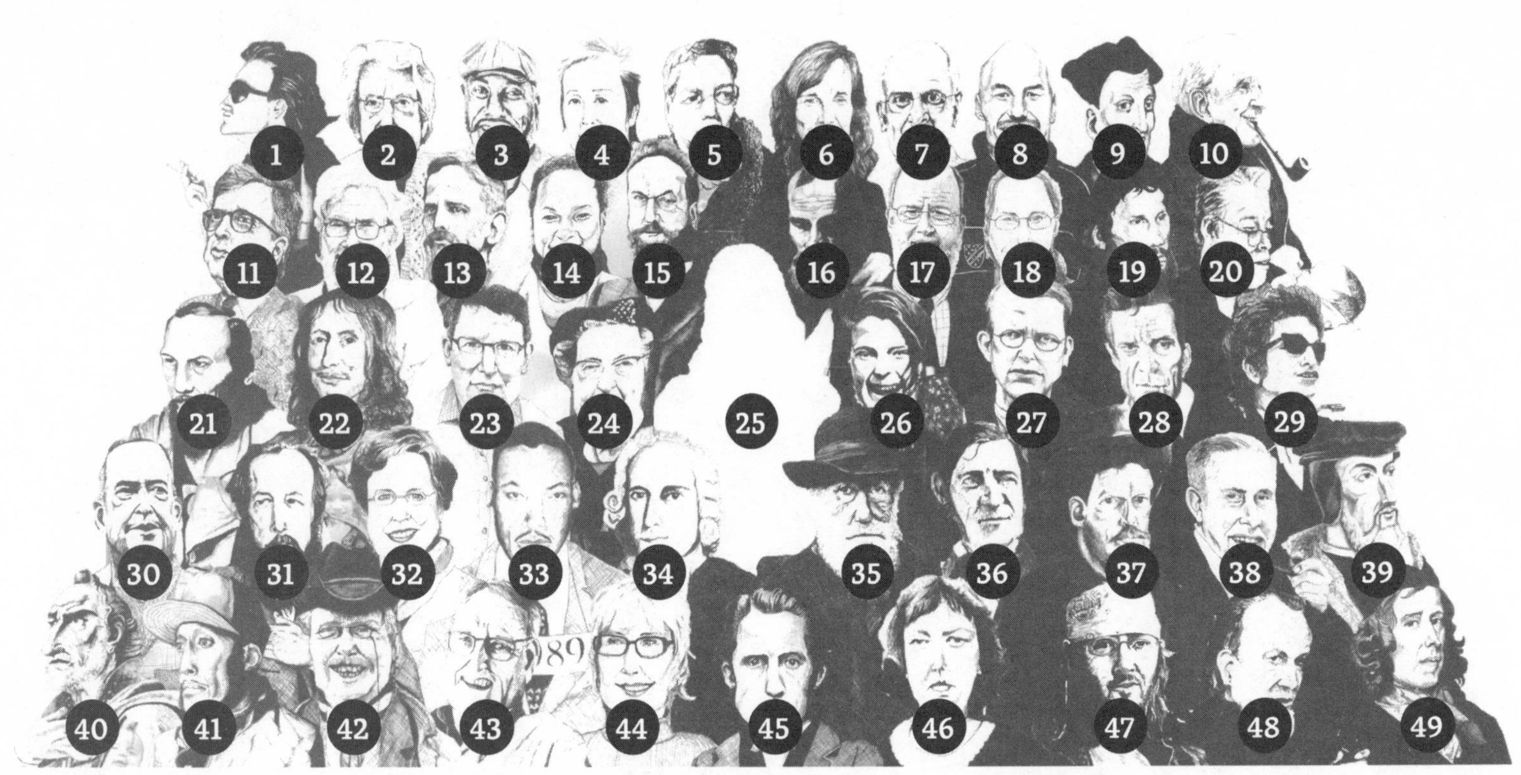
1
2
3
4
5
6
7
8
9
10
11
12
13
14
15
16
17
18
19
20
21
22
23
24
25
26
27
28
29
30
31
32
33
34
35
36
37
38
39
40
41
42
43
44
45
46
47
48
49

1. Bono, musician
2. Sister Ann Shields, evangelist
3. Thabiti Anyabwile, pastor
4. Joanne Jung, theologian
5. Dorothy Sayers, novelist
6. Rosaria Butterfield, author
7. Ajith Fernando, theologian
8. Francis Chan, pastor
9. Thomas á Kempis, monastic
10. J. R. R. Tolkien, linguist
11. Richard Lewontin, biologist
12. Leonardo Boff, humanitarian
13. Ernest DeWitt Burton, theologian
14. Trillia Newbell, author
15. Herman Bavinck, theologian
16. Paul, apostle
17. N. T. Wright, theologian
18. Evangeline Paterson, poet
19. Martin Luther, reformer
20. Jong-rak Lee (with baby), pastor
21. Fyodor Dostoyevsky, novelist
22. Blaise Pascal, mathematician
23. Andy Crouch, journalist
24. Corrie Ten Boom, author
25. The greatest person in history
26. Sophie Scholl, activist
27. Dietrich Bonhoeffer, pastor
28. Johnny Cash, musician
29. Bob Dylan, musician
30. C. S. Lewis, apologist
31. Alexander Solzhenitzyn, novelist
32. Nancy Pearcey, philosopher
33. Martin Luther King Jr., activist
34. Jonathan Edwards, theologian
35. Charles Darwin, biologist
36. Ralph Waldo Emerson, poet
37. Vincent Van Gogh, painter
38. Hans Rookmaaker, art critic
39. John Calvin, reformer
40. Augustine, theologian
41. Lecrae, rapper
42. G. K. Chesterton, humorist
43. David Wells, theologian
44. Joni Eareckson-Tada, artist
45. Abraham Kuyper, theologian
46. Flannery O'Connor, essayist
47. David Foster Wallace, novelist
48. Francis Schaeffer, philosopher
49. John Owen, theologian

CONTENTS

HOW TO MEET YOUR FUTURE SELF

They have mouths, but do not speak; eyes, but do not see. They have ears, but do not hear; noses, but do not smell. They have hands, but do not feel; feet, but do not walk; and they do not make a sound in their throats. Those who make them become like them; so do all who trust in them.

— PSALM 115:5–8

Imagine you are escorted through an underground laboratory into a controversial machine. You step inside a big silver cube and are told to think about whatever you love most in the world. A wall of glass rises out of the floor, dividing the cube into two equal chambers. Then everything goes dark. Your earliest memories project one after another on the glass. All of your firsts and all of your favorites, side-aching laughs, heart-palpitating joys, gut-punching rejections — all of it beams from your consciousness and onto the screen. On the opposite side of the glass all of the flashing rays of your personal movie reel seem to cluster together and take form. As the defining ideas, feelings, and choices of your life speed through the glass, your future self slowly materializes in the other chamber. Then the lights come up, the glass goes down, and you stand there, eye to eye with your future self.

REFLECT

1. EMERSON'S LAW

Blinking before you is the person you will become if all of your loves, hates, strengths, flaws, habits, and fears were to develop on course over the coming years. This is not a two-dimensional image doctored up with flattering filters. It is the real flesh-and-blood person you are becoming, for better or worse, staring back at you. In the up-close self-exposure of that machine, would you like the person your current character and choices have brought into existence? Would you see someone big-souled, caring, and full of life, or someone small, self consumed, and burned out? Someone flourishing or falling apart? Someone virtuous or vicious? Deep or dull? Who are you becoming?

There is no need to wait for future-self reflecting technology to answer those questions. There is one question that you can ask yourself now that, when answered honestly, can generate the same kind of future-unveiling insight. That question is, simply put: *What does your life say is the most important thing in existence?* If you were to stop and take honest stock of yourself—how you choose to spend your daily dose of breath and energy, which ideas occupy the most space in your thought world—what, more than anything else, moves you? Think about it. Be real with yourself. Whatever that ultimate something is for you now offers tremendous clarity about the person you are turning into. Poet Ralph Waldo Emerson helps us to see why:

> A person will worship something, have no doubt about that. We may think our tribute is paid in secret in the dark recesses of our hearts, but it will come out. That which dominates our imaginations and our thoughts will determine our loves, and our character. Therefore, it behooves us to be careful what we worship, for what we are worshiping we are becoming.[1]

Emerson makes two keen observations. First, that everyone worships something; and second, that those deities will shape our identities. Celebrated American novelist David Foster Wallace echoes: "In the day-to-day trenches of adult life, there is actually no such thing as atheism. There is no such thing as not worshiping. Everybody worships. The only choice we get is *what* to worship."[2] During his work as an economist, Bob Goudzwaard also came to the conclusion that everyone "absolutizes" something. We all serve god(s), take on the image of our god(s), then build society in our (that is, in our gods') image.[3] And long before Emerson, Wallace, and Goudzwaard it was Paul, the theologian, who opened a famous letter to Rome with the insight that whether it's the Creator or the creation, everyone worships.

For the poet, the novelist, the economist, and the theologian above, the question is not *whether* we worship. They took that to be an obvious fact. The real question is *what* we worship. With reverent hands trembling we all place something on that altar of empty space we find inside ourselves. These diverse minds converge on this point and encourage us to choose that sacred something with extreme care because, for better or worse, whatever we choose to worship will inevitably shape us.

2. THE THEIST AND THE ATHEIST IN EVERY HEART

Let us call this Emerson's Law: our deities shape our identities. We become like whatever we most love. Our objects of veneration define the scope and contours of our soul's formation (or de-formation). Consider a few examples:

If "we worship products," as Alexander Solzhenitsyn observed of American consumer culture,[4] then we slowly become more product-like ourselves. Like the latest trendy toy, we cease to be a deep, significant, and soul-filling presence in the lives of others. We become more artificial, more manufactured, and more plastic. If we worship our romantic partners, then we tend to lose our own identities and slowly morph into our partner's unimaginative clone. If we worship our children then we slowly become more childish, lacking the kind of wisdom and authority that should go with being a grown-up and a parent. If we worship other people's opinions, then we gradually lose ourselves and become exactly who we think others want us to be. If we worship the biological rush of sex for its own sake, reducing other people to a merely physical means to that end, then we become more soul-less, less able to connect with and meaningfully love other people for their own sake. If we worship sexual icons on a glowing screen, becoming pornography addicts who treat people as two-dimensional images, then we become two-dimensional ourselves.

But, the question arises: What about those who claim no deity whatsoever? Don't the many non-worshipers around the globe count as living, breathing proof against Emerson's Law?

That's a great question (I'm glad you asked). Consider how we express the impulse to worship even when we try to be our most anti-religious. It was the anti-religious Parisians of the French Enlightenment who hired a 14-year-old actress named Mademoiselles Candielle to dress up and play the Goddess of Reason. In the spring of 1792, wearing their Sunday best, they marched this blushing teenage girl along the Seine River banks and into Notre Dame Cathedral. There they sang hymns to their newly enshrined deity in a sacred ritual that would soon catch on in cities all over France. Religion did not fade away. The spotlight of human souls simply shifted to a new object of worship. Reason did not disprove God, so much as Reason *became* "God."

Read Carl Sagan, the brilliant and unapologetically atheist astronomer. You will meet a devout man, a worshiper on his knees before "the Cosmos" (which Sagan capitalizes). He wrote science books that read like hymnals — full of zeal, reverence, and poetry. His Voyager Golden Record and Pioneer Plaque, with greetings from and directions to Earth, were affixed to spacecraft and hurled into space like prayers. Sagan desperately hoped for answers from someone beyond what he called our "pale blue dot." The cosmos became a functional deity, a "God" for Sagan, where he looked for ultimate meaning and salvation.

In a meaningful sense, everyone is both an atheist and a theist at the same time.

Consider one of the most anti-religious regimes in history — the Soviet Union under Joseph Stalin. The Society of the Godless (also known as the League of Militant Atheists) took form. Russian churches and synagogues were bulldozed.[5] Atheism became a state-enforced dogma. Did this produce the godless utopia that the Soviet leaders dreamed of? On the contrary, worship was redirected to a new deity — Lord Stalin — while tens of millions of heretics who refused to bow were starved or executed. The Society of the Godless was anything but godless. As G. K. Chesterton observed, "Once we abolish God, the government becomes God."[6] In the act of abolishing religion in the traditional sense of the term, our own natures betray us and it becomes clear to others (if not to ourselves) that we remain on our knees, whether before Reason, the Cosmos, the State, or something else.

In addition to the cases of *religious* anti-religiosity above, we may add that, in a meaningful sense, everyone is both an atheist and a theist at the same time. I am an atheist about Kali, the Hindu goddess of destruction, just as Kali worshipers are atheists about the God I worship. There are stalkers who worship their celebrity crush, materialists who worship their car, narcissists who worship their mirror image, and North Koreans who worship their supreme leader. The majority of us, I would guess, are atheists about their chosen objects of supreme devotion. They worship something that we don't, just as the most important things to us are irrelevant to them.

I have taught college classes like History of Atheism for nearly a decade. I have conversed with hundreds of atheists. I have a great many friends who are self-described atheists or agnostics and whom I respect and love very much. Nevertheless, I have never known anyone who is not on his knees to something or someone. I am just as atheistic towards what many of my friends deem most important, as they are atheistic toward what (or rather who) matters most to me.

This way of seeing things takes us further than many of the broken record debates between theists and atheists over God's existence. There is a great deal that can be learned in that ongoing conversation (especially when it is a conversation rather than a shouting match). But the sooner we acknowledge that we are all theists *and* atheists simultaneously, that we are all supremely devoted to some things and undevoted to others, that we stake our meaning in places where others don't and vice versa, then the more we can move forward, thinking together about which of these different "gods" bring out the best and the worst in people.

3. THE UNHAPPY FATE OF CHARLES DARWIN

If anyone remains bothered by calling her objects of supreme devotion "god," if referring to that supreme devotion itself with the word "worship" annoys anyone, then that is all well and fine. We wouldn't want a semantic squabble to derail things. Bothered readers can simply substitute the G-word for whatever is most important to them, whatever they are most deeply moved for, their highest priority, or deepest love. We can then move forward to Emerson's deeper point, which is, how that all-important something for each of us shapes us in significant ways.

Consider Emerson's Law in the lives of two men. Charles Darwin was a gifted man who slowly evolved into that which he deemed most important in life. "My chief enjoyment and sole employment throughout life," said Darwin, "has been scientific work."[7] From this work, he added, "I am never idle," as it is "the only thing which makes life endurable to me."[8] One scholar observes, "Darwin became, in modern parlance, a workaholic. He felt emotionally secure only when he was at work."[9] What effect did elevating scientific work to the place of supreme importance have on the kind of person Darwin became? Hear it from Darwin's autobiography:

> In one respect my mind has changed during the last twenty or thirty years. Up to the age of thirty, or beyond it, poetry of many kinds . . . gave me great pleasure, and even as a schoolboy I took intense delight in Shakespeare. . . . But now for many years I cannot endure to read a line of poetry: I have tried lately to read Shakespeare, and found it so intolerably dull that it nauseated me.[10]

Darwin then describes the man he became in words that read heavy with remorse: "My mind seems to have become a kind of machine for grinding general laws out of large collections of facts," he says. "The loss of these tastes is a loss of happiness, and may possibly be injurious to the intellect, and more probably the moral character, by enfeebling the emotional part of our nature."[11]

We could weep for Darwin. An extraordinarily gifted man was turned into a scientific law-grinding "machine," a man whose love for great poetry turned to nausea, whose heart for art and music slowly turned to stone. What a nightmarish travesty to live through the petrification of your emotion, moral character, and intellect. Darwin came to see himself not as a robust soul bursting with life, full of years, wisdom, and joy, but as, in his words, "a withered leaf for every subject except Science" (which he saw as "a great evil").[12] If young Darwin could have stepped inside our machine and met the "machine," the "withered leaf," the unhappy man who emerged from the other side, would he have restructured his priorities? We can only wonder.

Consider Emerson's Law at work with radically different results in the life of another influential genius, a man who has been branded "America's first and best homegrown philosopher."[13] This celebrated philosopher (who will remain anonymous for now) offers the following autobiographical account of how his object of worship affected his soul over the years: "[It] brought an inexpressible purity, brightness, peacefulness and ravishment to the soul. In other words, it made the soul like a field or garden."[14]

Two gifted men. One became "a withered leaf" and the other a "garden." Where did our second genius find his chief enjoyment? What did he worship? Did different objects of ultimate devotion have anything at all to do with the very different kind of men these two became?

4. THE EX-PLANET'S ICY REVENGE

We move toward a better understanding of Emerson's Law (and the radically divergent results it can produce) with the help of the old word "glory." Much of the meaning of this word has been lost in our century. When Jews of the ancient Near East spoke of "glory" (or *kavod*, as they would say in Hebrew) they spoke of weightiness, fullness, and substance.[15] That is why Isaiah, the Hebrew prophet, talks about growing "lean," "withered grass," "dust on scales," and "empty wind," as the opposites of glory.[16] It is why Paul spoke of the "eternal *weight* of glory."[17]

While *kavod* meant heaviness — the opposite of light — the ancients also used "glory" almost synonymously with "light." The Hebrew prophet Ezekiel saw God's temple "filled with the *brightness* of the glory of the LORD," and Isaiah looked forward to a day when "the sun shall be no more your light by day . . . but the LORD will be your everlasting *light*, and your God will be your *glory*."[18] For the Bible's authors, God was not a distant flickering idea, but someone very real, luminous, and beaming.

How can this old word — *kavod* — help us understand the different ways in which deities shape identities today? Think of something both weighty and radiant that roughly half of the earth's population can observe at this very moment — the sun. The sun has enough *kavod,* enough weightiness and radiance, to be the center point of our solar system. It has enough gravitas to keep earth and the other planets spinning on their proper orbits. It is also luminous enough to keep our tiny blue planet teeming with warmth, beauty, and life.

What would happen, however, if Pluto, disgruntled and embittered by the 2006 International Astronomical Union vote that stripped him of planetary rights, took revenge on our solar system with a plot to overthrow and replace the sun? Pluto's cosmic coup would prove catastrophic. With a surface that is 98% frozen nitrogen and a mass less than a quarter of Earth's, Pluto is no match for the sun's *kavod.* The shift from a heliocentric to a plutocentric system would send the eight remaining planets spinning off their trajectories into chaos. The icy ex-planet's lack of mass and radiance would soon turn earth into a cold, lifeless sphere drifting through lonesome space.

The insight becomes clear if we move from astronomy to psychology, from the space around us to the space inside us. If we place something too small and too dim at the center of our lives, something that lacks *kavod,* then the planets in our soul's solar system — our creativity, intellect, emotions, moral sense, relationships, and so on — will tend toward a state of chaos and lifelessness. The lack of weight will cause many of those planets to drift into empty space, while the lack of light will turn any beauty on those planets into withered leaves.

If, however, the center of our souls, that which we glorify the most is, in reality, glorious, then our object of worship is massive enough to pull all the diverse spheres of human nature into a balanced orbit. There is also enough light to turn those different spheres inside us — our creativity, intellect, emotions, moral sense, relationality, and so on — into planets teeming with gardens, full of life and color.

5. THREE MARKS OF *KAVOD*

If we put Emerson's Law together with this ancient Hebrew idea of *kavod,* we reach something like this: everybody lives like something is the most weighty and radiant thing in the universe. If that something is, in reality, weighty and radiant, then our lives will take on something of that gravitas and glow. If we glorify inglorious things, however, then we ourselves become more weightless and shadowy, more like ghosts. Have you ever encountered a ghost in real life? In a sense, we all have. There are people whose lifestyles and spirits you could almost wave your hand through without bumping against anything solid.

There are see-through people and Technicolor people, with a thousand shades in between. The most vivid, substantial people you've ever met did not fall asleep one night as ghosts and wake up as sages. There is a backstory behind the best and worst of people. If you follow that backstory deep enough you will find something glorious that long ago began forming the most robust souls and something inglorious at the heart of every ghost. What, then, makes something glorious and, therefore, a center of weight and light in our lives, versus something that lacks *kavod*? Consider the following three marks of glory.

Glorious things are first things, not second

Consider the difference between first and second things. A partygoer who makes "fitting in" his first thing, for example, finds himself preoccupied with his social performance. Do you think he will fit in? Of course not. Constant self-analysis will leave him crucial seconds behind social cues. Our partygoer turns into the very oddball he dreads becoming. His efforts to fit in have made "fitting in" impossible. Why? He has mistaken a second thing for a first thing, a byproduct for a goal. If he put something else first, like caring about the people around him so much that he forgets to worry about himself, then he would likely find himself fitting in without even trying.

Life is full of these paradoxes. The most miserable people are often those who spend all their energy trying to be happy. People who become the most toxic in relationships tend to be the very people who hyper-obsess about finding the perfect mate. The person who spends all his brainpower getting everyone to like him ends up lonesome, too self-absorbed to be a true friend. C. S. Lewis points us to the principle behind these paradoxes: "Every preference of a small good to a great, or partial good to a total good, involves the loss of the small or partial good for which the sacrifice is made. . . . You can't get second things by putting them first. You get second things only by putting first things first."[19]

David Foster Wallace helps bring Lewis's principle out of abstraction into the real world, cataloguing some of the most popular second things that make for destructive gods:

> If you worship money . . . you will never have enough. . . . Worship your body and beauty and sexual allure and you will always feel ugly. . . . Worship power, you will end up feeling weak and afraid. . . . Worship your intellect, being seen as smart, you will end up feeling stupid, a fraud, always on the verge of being found out.[20]

This leads us to a second mark of *kavod.*

Glorious things are unbreakable, not brittle, things

I used to think that church songs where you could swap out all the God references with "baby" were evidence of a sappy romanticism in my own faith tradition. There may be truth to that. But perhaps the interchangeability of "God" and "baby" in church songs says less about church songs and more about love songs, less about how churches man-size God (which does happen) and more about a much broader tendency in the church and culture-at-large to God-size our romantic partners:

> Gonna build my whole world around you. . . .
> You're all that matters to me.
> —The Temptations, "You're My Everything"

> You know it's true, everything I do I do it for you.
> —Bryan Adams, "Everything I Do"

> If we believe in each other [there's] nothing we can't do.
> —Celine Dion, "Love Can Move Mountains"

> You're my religion, you're my church.
> You're the holy grail at the end of my search.
> —Sting, "Sacred Love"

> She tells me, "Worship in the bedroom."
> The only heaven I'll be sent to is when I'm alone with you.
> —Hozier, "Take Me to Church"

Back in graduate school I met "Jane." Jane was enjoying a new romantic relationship. She was the kind of person who was always in a relationship, with a list of exxes that seemed to roll on like the credits of a Peter Jackson film. After listening to Jane's story of break-up after brutal break-up, I saw a glint of hope in her eyes as she described her new special someone. She sounded like a psalmist describing Yahweh: "He's perfect in every way. He's so good to me. He's my rock, my breath of life, my *everything*."

Suddenly it became clear. Jane was not in a relationship; she was in a religion. She was looking to her boyfriend not to fill boyfriend-sized needs, but to fill God-sized needs. She was seeking nothing less than absolute perfection, and she was convinced that she had found it. What will happen, though, when reality chips away at that flawless statue, eventually crumbling the bigger-than-life effigy of her boyfriend that Jane built up in her imagination? Jane will be devastated, not because her boyfriend let her down, but because her "God," her functional deity, has failed her. Her whole identity built around her brittle idol comes crashing down. The boyfriend himself (as opposed to the one who existed only in Jane's imagination) will likely feel crushed under the burden of superhuman expectations that have been heaped on his shoulders.

What we are really talking about is proportions. When we see people as people rather than gods, then their faults appear in proportion to their size, that is, as *human* faults. If we blow people up to God-sized dimensions in our imaginations, then what are, in reality, finite faults will appear to us as infinitely huge faults. Faults that should merely hurt us end up apocalyptically destroying us. This superhumanity, that we often attribute to mere humans, is one reason people go from deifying to demonizing their romantic partners, children, and even celebrities (which is exactly what Jane ended up doing with her new boyfriend, who was soon added to her rolling credits).

Something worth worshiping must be superhuman and unbreakable, not just in our imaginations, but in reality. If we had an object of worship proportionate to our heart's massive needs, then the people in our lives would shrink back to their actual human proportions, and so would the cracks in their characters. The restless Jane in all of us would find freedom to love people realistically — as people — suffering finite hurt rather than infinite devastation *when* (not *if*) they let us down. We would also free the people we care about to really love us back, unburdened by the crushing gravity of our infinite expectations. Returning to Lewis's categories, we find the real joy in these second things only when we find our deepest meaning from a first thing. This leads to a third mark of something with enough *kavod* to worship.

Glorious things are suns, not spotlights

A spotlight sends out one long narrow cone of light, leaving everything outside that cone in darkness. A sun, however, fires out light rays in all directions simultaneously. Some of the things we choose to worship are more like spotlights than suns. Put academic accolades at the center of your life and your intellect may brighten, but your emotions and relationships will be left in the dark. Worship a romantic partner and some passion may light up, but your intellect will be left to the cold and the cobwebs. When we turn good things into ultimate things, they leave important spaces in our natures hidden in the shadows.

This helps us make better sense of Emerson's Law. If we worship money, then it's not that we become green and wrinkly, but that money lacks the necessary properties to really illuminate the intellectual, emotional, and relational spaces in our lives. Cash is too mindless, too heartless, and too loveless. Worship it long enough and the best things in us remain in the dark, and we slowly appear as dumb and uncaring as cold hard cash.

If we say that the product-worshiper becomes product-like himself, more plastic, then plastic is really a shorthand way of expressing a lack of intellectual, emotional, and relational light. Consumer products are inadequate gods because they are powerless to illuminate what is best in human nature. When malls become our churches and material things our objects of ultimate concern, then the best things in us are left in the dark. Shoppers in the cult of consumerism start looking more like the mannequins that they look to for meaning (they also become about as interesting to talk to). In the world of experience, the doctrine of the *imago Dei* is not optional. People will bear the image of their gods for better or worse, or, as the theologians of ancient Israel observed, people "went after false idols and became false."[21]

Consider your capacity to reason, feel, achieve moral greatness, love people well, help those in need, and create beauty. Imagine all of these powers of your humanity arranged around the primary light source in your life. Is that light source like a spotlight with its solitary cone fixed on a part of you while banishing the rest of you to darkness? Or is your object of worship like a sun, beaming warmth, clarity, and meaning on your whole being, leaving nothing to the shadows?

REFLECT OVERVIEW

Earlier we met an anonymous genius who grew to be a "garden." He was a valedictorian graduate of Yale, where he enrolled as a Latin-, Greek-, and Hebrew-fluent 12-year-old.[1] He was instrumental to America's First Great Awakening. He preached meticulously logical sermons that were cut short more than once when the volume of "piercing and amazing cries" from affected crowds overpowered his famously weak voice.[2] He served as president of Princeton University. He defended Native American rights and inspired one of the first schools in America that gave women educational parity with men. His books became required reading throughout the Ivy League for more than a century. He remains a beacon in twenty-first-century academia, influencing entire schools and fields of study that didn't exist until he inspired them.[3] He was also an adoring husband to his teenage sweetheart and wife of more than thirty years, with a full quiver of eleven deeply loved children. One study traced the bloodlines of "one U.S. Vice President, three U.S. senators, three governors, three mayors, thirteen college presidents, thirty judges, sixty-five professors, eighty public office holders, one-hundred lawyers, and one-hundred missionaries" back to his Massachusetts home.[4] That garden of a man was Jonathan Edwards.

Long before Edwards's success as a philosopher, theologian, revivalist, pastor, and family man, he believed that he had found true *kavod.*

At age 19, while drafting seventy personal "Resolutions" in his journal, Edwards divulges his object of lifelong worship: "Resolved . . . to cast and venture my soul on the Lord Jesus Christ, to trust and confide in him, and consecrate myself wholly to him."[5] This glimpse into the center of young Edwards's solar system is essential to making sense out of the man he later became, a man whose "sense of divine things gradually increased, and became more and more lively," a man whose soul became "a flower . . . low and humble on the ground, opening its bosom to receive the pleasant beams of the sun's glory."[6] We can't understand how Edwards became a garden if we ignore the Sun that nourished his soul over the decades.

This brings us to the central thesis of this book. *Jesus is the most glorious being in existence.* He is the most massive and radiant person our lives could possibly orbit around. He is the First Thing. He is indestructible. The good things we enjoy in life are, in Edwards's words, "scattered beams, but he is the sun."[7] Jesus is more reasonable, more passionate, more virtuous, more loving, more gracious, more creative, and more powerful than anyone or anything else. When we enjoy any true reason, passion, goodness, love, grace, beauty, or power in anyone or anything else, he is the Sun we discover if we trace those beams back to their true Source. He can shape, expand, illuminate, and grow us in ways that no amount of money, power, lovers, chemical rushes, or any other conceivable object of worship can. Whether or not we worship him will make the crucial difference in what kind of people we can expect to step out of the future self-reflector.

Jesus specializes in healing idol-a-holics.

But isn't Edwards a fluke? What about those who claim to worship Jesus yet live inglorious lives? That's the beauty of Emerson's Law. It calls our bluffs. Our lives are dead giveaways to any perceptive observer of what we really worship, regardless of our publicly claimed deities. If we are really worshiping Jesus as he really exists, and not some figment of our imaginations or a religiously conceived fictional character called "Jesus," then our lives will reflect something of the real Jesus' glory; not perfectly of course, but perceptibly.

R-E-F-L-E-C-T structures our exploration of what it would look like if we actually worship and, thereby, became more like Jesus. In chapter 1 we look at *Reasoning* like Jesus, developing his intellectual virtues. Chapter 2 turns to *Emoting* like Jesus, feeling joy at the things that bring him joy and outrage at the things that get his blood boiling. With chapter 3, we look at *Flipping* our upside-down attempts to live meaningfully to align with the holy actions of Jesus. Chapter 4 looks at *Loving* like Jesus, and cultivating his relational depth. Chapter 5 moves to *Elevating* people; mirroring the grace of Jesus, who pulls us up out of darkness and despair. Chapter 6 brings us to *Creating* beauty like the artistic Jesus, whose imagination brought us everything from sunsets to the spots on ladybugs. Lastly, in chapter 7, how do we *Transform* so that the fruit of his intellect, emotion, goodness, love, grace, and creativity grow in and out of us?

For many, "Christlikeness" is little more than a cliché, a spiritual buzzword for people who speak the strange tribal dialect of Christianese. Press people on its meaning and you find that "Christlikeness" is vaguely synonymous with being nice. Becoming like Jesus means *so* much more than that, and that is the focus of this book.

All of this is coming from a man who has bowed his knee to many finite gods — intellect, religion, romance, status, jobs, children — a man who continues to prove John Calvin right when he said that the human heart is "a perpetual factory of idols." Thankfully, this is not a book about me, a recovering idol-a-holic. It is about Jesus.

And Jesus specializes in healing idol-a-holics.

1

REASON

Mirroring the Profound Thinking of Jesus

Jesus answered them, "You are wrong, because you know neither the Scriptures nor the power of God. For in the resurrection they neither marry nor are given in marriage, but are like angels in heaven. And as for the resurrection of the dead, have you not read what was said to you by God: 'I am the God of Abraham, and the God of Isaac, and the God of Jacob'? He is not God of the dead, but of the living."

— MATTHEW 22:29–32

> Testing his categorical assertions by centuries of experience, [we] find his thought more clearly verifying itself as true, we accept him today, not only as Lord and Christ, to whom we owe the allegiance of our wills, but as first among the thinkers of the world, teacher of all teachers, leader of the world's best thought.
>
> ERNEST DEWITT BURTON

As we ponder what could happen to our intellectual lives if we really worshiped and became more like Jesus, let us begin with a twenty-five-foot-long, sixteen-foot-high fresco called *The School of Athens.* At the center of Raphael's masterpiece, a balding Plato strolls alongside his star protégé Aristotle. Plato points up with one hand, clutching a copy of his book *Timaeus* in the other. Plato's vertical finger (like his argument in *Timaeus*) calls us beyond the world of our senses, above the shadows of the material world into a glowing heaven of ideas, a perfect world of abstraction, logic, and numbers. So great was Plato's love for mathematical ideas that the warning *ageometretos medeis eisito* — "None but Geometers may enter" — hung over the entrance to his Athens Academy.

No such warning hung over the Lyceum, the school that Aristotle founded in Athens. Raphael's Aristotle extends one hand horizontally with his palm down, with his famous *Nicomachean Ethics* held sideways in his other hand. He motions us downward, to the world of our senses, the material, the empirical, the scientific.

What would Jesus be doing if he were painted into Raphael's canvas? Would he be pointing up with Plato, beckoning us into the invisible world of logic? Would he gesture downward with Aristotle, encouraging us to the concrete world of science? Would he be holding a King James Bible in the air poised to beat Plato and Aristotle over the head for being too rational and scientific? Would he stand with outstretched arms, blindfolded, inviting us to take a leap of faith? How are we to understand the role of reason in our lives if we look to Jesus for answers? How might our own intellectual lives change if we worship and become like him? The answers may surprise you.

What kind of hope does the Jesus of Jerusalem bring to consumer spaces, the hills of academia, and the temples of spirituality in our day?

We will be asking in a fresh way a very old question: "What does Athens have to do with Jerusalem?" When Tertullian posed this question nearly 1,800 years ago, he was questioning the connection between the Christian faith ("Jerusalem") and non-Christian philosophy ("Athens"). We will slightly tweak Tertullian's question. In "Jerusalem" our focus will be on Jesus himself in a very specific instance on the temple steps where we see his mind in action. In "Athens" we will make three stops: there is the Agora — the city's consumer marketplace; the Areopagus — an elevated marble slab where ancient knowledge-seekers would gather to dispute the day's intellectual trends; and the Acropolis — the sacred religious summit of the city. What we are really asking then is this: What kind of hope does the Jesus of Jerusalem bring to the consumer spaces, the hills of academia, and the temples of spirituality in our day?

1.1 JESUS IN JERUSALEM

We begin in Jerusalem on the steps of the temple. It is the Tuesday before Jesus' execution. A lawyer asks him to define the greatest of the 613 commandments from the Jewish Law. Jesus answers, "You shall love the Lord your God with all your heart and with all your soul and with all your mind."[1] Jesus cares enough about our minds to include them in his first and greatest commandment.

But what does it mean to love God with all of our minds? Jonathan

Edwards provides an important clue. In Jesus, says Edwards, "is found the greatest spirit of obedience to the commands and laws of God that ever was in the universe."[2] Jesus not only *talked* the greatest commandment, he *walked* it better than anyone. The greatest commandment is best understood, therefore, not as an abstract principle, but in the flesh-and-blood Jesus as he walked the earth. How, then, did history's Greatest Keeper of history's greatest commandment love God with his mind?

Moments before answering the lawyer's question, Jesus demonstrates what a mind that fully loves the Father looks like in action. The Sadducees, a group of politically savvy Jewish thinkers, confront Jesus on the crowded temple steps to test his mind. As the historian Josephus tells us, the Sadducees "think it an instance of virtue to dispute with those teachers of philosophy whom they frequent."[3] These veterans of debate pool their collective genius to construct a clever logical trap for Jesus. They begin with a sad story. A woman loses her husband. The dead husband's brother steps in to marry and support her. He dies too, and she marries yet another brother-in-law. The sad story repeats down to the seventh and last brother. Finally, the widow dies.[4] Like a Shakespearian tragedy, the Sadducees' story concludes with everyone dead on the stage.

Jesus does not retreat, cop out, or bully.

With this grim tale of seven weddings and eight funerals, the Sadducees have pulled back the steel teeth of their logical trap. Then they lay the bait and carefully set the trigger with a simple question: "In the resurrection, therefore, of the seven, whose wife will she be? For they all had her."[5] To appreciate how skillfully the Sadducees had constructed this intellectual trap, it is helpful to look at its logical structure. The Sadducees were forcing Jesus into the middle of what philosophers call a "destructive dilemma."[6] The logic of a destructive dilemma goes like this:

1. If *x* is true, then either *A* or *B* must also be true.
2. *A* and *B* are both false.
3. Therefore, *x* is also false.

If that seems abstract, the dilemma becomes clear when we fill in the blanks with the specifics of the Sadducees' argument. The *x* they were trying to prove false is Jesus' belief in life after death. As Josephus tells us, "The doctrine of the Sadducees is this: That souls die with the bodies."[7] Their destructive dilemma against Jesus' belief in the afterlife runs like this:

1. If (*x*) the dead will one day rise, then the woman will either (*A*) be married to all seven when she resurrects, or (*B*) she will only remain married to one of the seven when she resurrects.

2. (*A*) is false because a woman married to all seven brothers would violate marriage as a monogamous institution, and (*B*) is false because it would be totally arbitrary for the woman to remain married to only one of her seven husbands.

3. Since *A* and *B* are both false, *x*—Jesus' belief that the dead will rise—is also false.

The Sadducees knew that if Jesus answered with either *A* or *B* then his credibility as a rabbi would be left bleeding and twitching for all to see. There seemed to be no way out.

What does a mind that fully loves the Father do in such an intellectual fix? Does Jesus say, "Hey! What's that over there!" and run to hide in a nearby cave? Does he condescendingly pat them on the head and say, "Quit asking silly questions, close your eyes, and take a leap of faith with me"? Does he threaten to smite them with fire from the sky for questioning him? None of the above. Jesus does not retreat, cop out, or bully.

He answers, "For in the resurrection they neither marry nor are given in marriage, but are like angels in heaven."[8] Jesus instantly dismantles the Sadducees' trap. He exposes a hidden assumption of their argument, their false assumption that resurrected people will be married. Since the resurrected will "neither marry nor are given in marriage," there is no need to worry about whom the widow will call "sweetheart" for eternity. Jesus articulates what philosophers call the *tertium quid*, meaning the "third thing," not the false *A* or the false *B*, but the true *C*.

Having exposed the fallacy of the Sadducees' anti-life-after-death argument, Jesus sets forth his own pro-life-after-death argument: "And as for the resurrection of the dead, have you not read what was said to you by God: 'I am the God of Abraham, and the God of Isaac, and the God of Jacob'? He is not the God of the dead, but of the living."[9] Jesus recalls a well-known scene from the book of Exodus where God tells Moses that he is the God of three men whose hearts had long stopped beating. How does this support Jesus' belief that physical death is not the terminus of human existence? In short, if the God of the living *is* the *present-tense* God of Abraham, Isaac, and Jacob, then they must still, in some sense, be alive. Follow the logic of Jesus:

1. If (*x*) "souls die with the bodies" then (*A*) God could only say that he *was* (past tense) the God of three dead men, or (*B*) God is the God of the dead.

2. (*A*) is false because God says in Exodus 3:6 that "I am" (present tense) the God of three dead men, and (*B*) is false because God is not the God of the dead, but of the living.

3. Since *A* and *B* are both false, *x* — the Sadducees' belief that "souls die with the bodies" — is also false.

Do you see the brilliance of a mind that keeps the greatest commandment? Jesus used the same style of logical trap that had been set for him — a destructive dilemma. Only there was no escaping Jesus' logic without embracing the reality of life beyond the grave. The scholars blushed.[10] The crowd that the scholars had hoped would be astonished by a blundering Jesus is astonished by something else altogether — his sheer brilliance.[11]

Dallas Willard adds, "'Jesus is Lord' can mean little in practice for anyone who has to hesitate before saying 'Jesus is smart.' He is not just nice, he is brilliant."[12] This exchange with the Sadducees helps us to appreciate at least nine features of Jesus' brilliance. As we circle around Jesus on the temple steps to explore his mind from these different angles, we see a living blueprint emerge for how the mind that worships him takes on new shape and dimensions.

1.2 JESUS IN THE AGORA

Having met Jesus in Jerusalem, we turn next to Athens. We enter the Agora, the marketplaces of the twenty-first century. The sights and sounds of our society's consumer spaces are largely the legacy of Leo Burnett. Burnett was the Chicago ad-man whom *Time* magazine branded "the Sultan of Sell," ranking him among the top 100 most influential people of the twentieth century. According to *Time*, Burnett "was obsessed with finding visual triggers that could effectively circumvent consumers' critical thought." This mastermind behind the Jolly Green Giant, the Pillsbury Doughboy, the Marlboro Man, and Tony the Tiger hailed the triumph of "visual form" over "carefully reasoned argument."[13] Advertising has been famously defined as "the science of arresting human intelligence long enough to get money from it."[14] Leo Burnett was the Isaac Newton of that science. What was Burnett's secret? "Make it simple. Make it memorable. Make it inviting to look at. Make it fun."[15]

To grasp the scope of Burnett's legacy on the modern Agora, take a guess at how many advertisements the average American is exposed to within a typical 24-hour period? 100? 1000? 10,000? In the late 1990s researchers found the number — 16,000![16] That was nearly 6 million simple, memorable, inviting, and fun things each year clamoring over the voice of reason.[17] And that was before the global explosion of social media and the smartphone revolution. Today, you can hardly check in on your friends without being bombarded by ads for magical supplements that promise an Olympian body without the inconvenience of exercise, or a million other snake oils you simply *must* consume to have a life worth living.

This ubiquitous "I consume, therefore I am" culture can be infertile soil for the cultivation of intellectual virtue.[18] What lessons might we learn from Jesus on the steps of the Jerusalem temple for developing our minds in the consumer Agora? Consider these three.

A Colorful Mind: Jesus Creatively Tells the Truth

It is instructive that when his beliefs about the afterlife are questioned, Jesus doesn't respond with a mind- and wallet-emptying slogan — "A shekel today keeps the hellfire away." "Cast your rusting silver down and bejewel your heavenly crown." "When your coin in the coffer rings, the soul from purgatory springs." No. Jesus does not arrest the intelligence of his challengers or circumvent the critical thought of the temple audience. He was not the Leo Burnett of the first century.

To see the way Jesus engages our minds consider the concepts of "hot" and "cool" media. The famous communication theorist Marshall McLuhan coined these terms to describe a spectrum of effects that different communication mediums can have on an audience. On one reading of McLuhan, hot communication tends to be linear, analytic, quantitative, and cerebral. It speaks to your intellect. Cool communication is more artistic, imaginative, symbolic, and multisensory. It taps more directly into your emotions. A nutritionist's lecture on the health benefits of green bean consumption would be on the hot end of the McLuhan's communication thermometer. Burnett's Jolly Green Giant striking a super hero pose in a canned veggie ad would be on the cool end. Cool media has become the medium of choice in the Agora of twenty-first-century culture, from how we sell food, phones, and automobiles to how we peddle politics and religion.

Is Jesus a hot or a cool communicator? Perhaps the best way to answer that question is to think of a popular product used around the world to sooth aching muscles. When you rub it on your skin the menthol triggers an immediate sensation that is both icy cold and burning hot at the same time. Icy Hot™ is the perfectly oxymoronic brand name for this product that can take two seemingly contradictory sensations and make them one. Jesus is an Icy Hot communicator. He speaks to the whole person.

That day at the temple, right before he speaks truth to the logical mind, he speaks truth to the senses and the imagination with a series of vivid parables. He compares his coming kingdom to a joyous wedding party. When asked about the meaning of loving your neighbor, he doesn't answer, "Obey the Categorical Imperative whereby you rationally universalize the action of helping another morally relevant agent whose intrinsic dignity can be metaphysically anchored in her volitional autonomy." Rather than a hot lecture in Kantian meta-ethics, Jesus tells a cool story of a battered stranger shunned by the religious elite and saved by an unlikely hero.[19]

Sociologist Mike Featherstone notes how advertising "is able to exploit and attach images of romance, exotica, desire, beauty, fulfillment, communality, scientific progress, and the good life to mundane consumer goods such as soap, washing machines, motor cars, and alcoholic drinks."[20] Today's cool communicators use the big and extraordinary to sell the small and the mundane. The creative genius of Jesus uses the small and the mundane — dirt, mustard seeds, salt, lamps — to freely offer us something big and extraordinary, life in his kingdom.

A Logical Mind: Jesus Builds Sound Arguments

Unlike the six-million-plus ads we face each year, every one of Jesus' icy images is simultaneously hot with meaningful content. Jesus tells the truth by constructing compelling syllogisms just as easily as by painting vivid multisensory pictures. Logic is part of how a mind that fully loves God functions.

There is not only the logical heat of his afterlife argument with the Sadducees. Jesus deploys a wide array of intellect-igniting arguments throughout the Gospels.[21] When the Pharisees accuse him of casting out devils by Satan's power, he uses the logic of *reductio ad absurdum* to reduce their charges to absurdity.[22] He uses *argumentum a fortiori* ("argument from the stronger [reason]") to prove that it is lawful to heal on the Sabbath, and that the Father will give good things to those who ask.[23] He uses *modus ponnens* ("the way of affirmation") to vindicate his messianic claims.[24]

We get our word "logic" from the Greek word *logos*, which is, not accidentally, one of the famous titles for Jesus from the pages of the New Testament.[25] In being logical, Jesus was simply being himself. As Dallas Willard concludes, "We can learn from him to use logical reasoning at its best."[26] (That is no small statement coming from the distinguished professor of philosophy for nearly half a century at the University of Southern California.)

Willard adds, "Jesus' aim in utilizing logic is not to win battles, but to achieve understanding or insight in his hearers."[27] Today's Agora is not about achieving understanding and insight, but maximizing profits. Mirroring the mind of Christ will make us less dupe-able, less susceptible to the ploys of cool communicators. We become more discerning, more immunized to commercial, political, and religious propaganda. Yet, Jesus is able to exercise our heads without ossifying our hearts. He values and revitalizes the whole person. As we are shaped more and more by the mind of Christ, we ourselves become increasingly Icy Hot thinkers and communicators.

A Factual Mind: Jesus Cares about Evidence

That is not all. Jesus offers truth to the hands as well as to the head and the heart. He cares about good evidence. He doesn't demand a blind leap, but invites a reasonable step.

Just three days after their public debate with Jesus, the Sadducees contrive another strategy against him. They had already attempted a logical case to prove that Jesus was a phony and death was the final word. That attempt had failed miserably. Perhaps, then, an empirical case — making a permanent corpse out of Jesus — would settle the question. And so they argue for his execution before the Roman authorities, thinking that a bloody Friday would be the end of him. A long and deathly silent Saturday seemed to prove them right.

Jesus extends his hand horizontally, offering a scarred palm for a doubter's inspection.

Sunday morning, however, the Sadducees find that their conclusions on the fraudulence of Jesus and the finality of death have been challenged again, not by a logical argument this time, but by an empty tomb. Jesus himself became the empirical proof for everything he had proven logically just days before. He became the walking, talking case that he is, in fact, all of the extraordinary things he claimed to be, and that death is not the final chapter of the human drama.

Over the following forty days Jesus makes public appearances. He presents his body to the scrutiny of a crowd of more than five hundred eyewitnesses (whom Paul encouraged his Corinthian readers to consult for a fact-check).[28] One witness testifies, "We did not follow cleverly invented stories when we told you about the power and coming of our Lord Jesus Christ, but we were eyewitnesses of his majesty."[29] Another describes the resurrected Jesus in unmistakably empirical terms — "that which we've heard," "seen with our eyes," "looked upon," "touched with our hands," and so on. (While beyond the scope of this book, I point readers to the landmark work of scholars N. T. Wright and Gary Habermas for the most comprehensive historical evidence for Jesus' resurrection.)[30]

In Raphael's *School of Athens,* Aristotle's outstretched hand becomes a symbol for the value of facts and evidence. In the New Testament Jesus extends his hand horizontally, offering a scarred palm for a doubter's inspection. Jesus cared about facts and evidence, and if we worship him, so will we.

1.3 JESUS IN THE AREOPAGUS

What happens if we ascend from the Agora to the Areopagus, from the marketplace to the centers of higher learning? The fruits of intellectual inquiry, wherever we find them, grow from the conviction that truth exists and can be known. Take an axe to the existence of truth and you no longer have education, you have propaganda. Ideologies that deny the very possibility of truth can be found in many (thankfully, not all) fields of education. I am not talking about healthy academic skepticism, the kind that questions and opens itself to the universe with a humility that says, "I might be wrong." Healthy skepticism does not reject but rather *requires* the existence of truth, some North Star visible enough to determine whether we've veered off course.

I am talking instead about a skepticism that erases the stars. It denies any objective truths above us. The mariners themselves — the academics, that is — then become their own reference point, making it impossible for them to ever know if they've gotten lost. Instead of a jagged and rewarding journey of aligning and re-aligning our ideas with reality, we drift under an empty sky to nowhere in particular. "Truth" becomes a language game that the seafarers play amongst themselves to pass the time. As postmodern philosopher Richard Rorty quips, truth is simply a matter of whatever your colleagues will let you get away with saying.[31] With no truth to seek or discover, we are left with only social constructs to endlessly dream up and deconstruct.

To those cynical members of the intelligentsia and the students under their influence, Jesus poses a hopeful challenge.

In the words of one lamenting Harvard graduate, "The freedom of our day is the freedom to devote ourselves to any values we please, on the mere condition that we do not believe them to be true."[32] When the very idea of truth is considered so out-of-fashion, schools turn from the pursuit of knowledge to the business of data transfer, indoctrination, and diploma-printing.

This creates a conundrum in the Areopagus. Students file into classrooms seeking knowledge only to be told in so many sophisticated terms that there is no truth to be known. Expecting future generations to take their intellectual lives seriously while teaching them that there are no truths, only constructs, is like teaching courses in animal mythology and expecting students to pursue careers as unicorn and Pegasus veterinarians.

To those cynical members of the intelligentsia and the students under their influence, Jesus poses a hopeful challenge. Below are three ways that he opens up fertile vistas for the human intellect to flourish.

An Inspirational Mind: Jesus Stimulates Knowledge

Three days after his exchange with the Sadducees, Jesus stands trial before Pilate and explains the reason he was born: "For this purpose I was born and for this purpose I have come into the world — to bear witness to the truth."[33] Pilate shrugs with the cynicism of a postmodern academic — "What is truth?" Jesus' word for "truth" — *aletheia* — carries a sense of objective reality. *Aletheia* is not about what your colleagues will let you get away with, what is socially trending, or what has won the approval of the ideological gatekeepers. Truth is about what *is*. A quintessential goal of Jesus' stated life mission is to help minds grasp *aletheia* — aligning our thinking with what is. Another word for that is "knowledge," which also happens to be the goal of good education.

"Hold on," comes the welcome skeptic's question. "Since when is Christianity about stimulating knowledge? Isn't Christianity about filling auditoriums with a hyper-suggestible mob to listen to an ordained hypnotist until everyone's brainwaves flatline?" Sure. A host of "isms" claiming Christian pedigree — for example, Montanism, pietism, fundamentalism, televangelism — have not exactly been at the vanguard in the forward march of knowledge against ignorance. They have often rallied from the other side of that front line. What would happen, however, if those who claim his name actually took their intellectual marching orders from the Jesus we meet in the New Testament?

We don't have to speculate. It has happened before. It was people seeking to love God with their minds as Jesus commanded who gave us the modern university — a Christian invention from the Middle Ages. St. Andrews, Oxford, Cambridge, Harvard, Princeton, Yale, and many more world-class institutions of higher learning were founded by and flourished under Jesus' followers. Belief in the mission of Jesus led directly to the introduction of written languages in cultures that had none. It led to the flowering of modern English, French, and German. It led to globally unparalleled literacy rates.[34]

Christians gave us the Royal Society — the first professional society of modern scientists — with its charter that advanced scientific inquiry "to the glory of God and the benefit of the human race." It was the Irish chemist Robert Boyle, believing that "science is a religious task, the disclosure of the admirable workmanship which God displayed in the universe," who made massive strides forward in physics and chemistry. Then there was the German mathematician whom Carl Sagan branded as "the first astrophysicist"[35] — Johannes Kepler. Kepler, with his belief that "God ever geometrizes," gave us the laws of planetary motions, without which there would have been no Space Age. It was "the father of modern observational astronomy" — Galileo Galilei — who confessed, "I don't believe that the same God who endowed us with sense, reason, and intellect had intended for us to forgo their use."

Christology inspired them to become giants on whose shoulders we stand to peer further into the cosmos.

The list could go on,[36] but it should be clear that Jesus' imitators seeking to love God with their minds have passed on a rich intellectual legacy to humanity. They believed that a rational God made the rationally structured cosmos and called it "good," then equipped us with the rational minds to recognize and relish that structure. Jesus made the material world. He was born into the material world. He built chairs and framed houses in that world. He died in that world, not to bid it farewell forever, but to rise again bodily as a profound validation of physical existence. Matter matters to God, so it mattered to the scientific revolutionaries. Their Christology inspired them to become giants on whose shoulders we stand to peer further into the cosmos.

But aren't there also Christian giants who huddle over us to block out the sky and leave us in intellectual darkness? Sadly, yes. And yes, both kinds of giants — those who open and those who close intellects — claim to follow Jesus. But which giants sound more like the Jesus we meet in the actual accounts of his life and mission? Which hold the more credible claim to the legacy of the Jesus who engaged the Sadducees at the temple, offered empirical evidence, and crafted the cosmos?

A Teleological Mind: Jesus Tells Us Why

There is something else profound that the Jesus of Jerusalem offers the Areopagus of Athens. Recall that Jesus escapes the Sadducees' destructive dilemma with his claim that when the dead rise the current institution of marriage will become obsolete. Why did Jesus believe that marriage-as-we-know-it will cease to exist? The answer can be found in the New Testament idea of marriage as "the profound mystery." The meaning of that mystery is found not within the human institution of marriage itself, but in something far bigger, something transcendent — namely, Jesus' infinite affection for his people.

The Bible begins with the small wedding of Adam to Eve. It ends with a big wedding of Jesus to his cherished bride. In the last marriage ceremony ever, a multitude of people from every tongue, tribe, and nation will walk down the aisle in radiant white toward the joyfully misty-eyed Jesus. When those final "I do's" are exchanged, there will no longer be a need for what we now know as marriage. When the dream destination has been reached, the travel brochures, no matter how picturesque, can be left behind. They offer stunning images, but the real thing is just that much better. In other words, it is in Jesus himself that we find not the *only* meaning but the most *ultimate* meaning of marriage. He is what marriage exists *for* not just in this home or in that society but in the grand story of the entire cosmos.

Not only marriage but *everything* exists *for* him, according to the New Testament. He is not only the *Logos*, but also the *Telos*, the Goal—the Final Point where all lines converge. "But isn't that such a strange and invisible conclusion? What happened to all that talk about Jesus inspiring science?" This confusion clears with a moment's reflection on the meaning of the word "for." Most of us use this three-letter preposition every day when we want to express the teleology of something, that is, its purpose, *why* it is. "*Why* are there lawnmowers, Daddy? What are they made *for*?" "Well, my boy, lawnmowers are *for* mowing lawns." Dad has offered Junior a teleological answer. If Junior asks, "What are lawnmowers made *of*, Daddy?" then Dad faces a very different question. This question calls not for a teleological but a material answer, something to do with motors, wheels, and steel blades.

We know more and more about matter but less and less about why matter matters.

We know more about something when we know what it's made *of* and what it is made *for*. *Both* are important to knowledge-seeking. Imagine Junior again asking his dad why lawnmowers exist and Dad responds, "Well, son, lawnmowers have plastic wheels, metallic frames, steel blades." "Hmmm. Ok, but *why* are there lawnmowers?" 'Well, once upon a time there was a simple single blade at the end of a stick called a sickle. Eventually three or four blades were twirled together around an axle with two wheels. Then came two more wheels, a metal frame, a motor, and eventually we got the lawnmowers we have today. Get it now?" Junior scratches his head. He wasn't asking what lawnmowers have been made *of* through the centuries; he was after their meaning. If this goes on long enough, a lawnmower's meaning will be buried under an ever-growing pile of knowledge about a lawnmower's mechanics.

Ignorant of a lawnmower's actual meaning Junior might as well make up his own. One blistering summer day, he props one up sideways in his room, fires up the motor, and gets the blade whirling as a makeshift fan. A few missing fingers and a minced housecat later, the lopsided-ness of Junior's education becomes clear. For all of his encyclopedic knowledge of lawnmower mechanics, he has become too teleologically thick-headed to realize that lawnmowers and their sharp blades were never designed for indoor cooling.

The moral of the story is that it is possible to be an expert and a blockhead about something simultaneously.[37] Before the seventeenth century, before Galileo, Kepler, and Newton, a fixation on meaning questions often left our understanding of the material world dragging woefully behind. In the era following the Scientific Revolution, we have come to understand the mechanics of the universe better than ever before. And yet, it appears more meaningless to us than ever. We know more and more about matter but less and less about why matter matters.

It is not as if we carried out an open-minded investigation and finally reached a scientific consensus that there is no meaning out there.[38] No scientist's list of material facts, no matter how long, could ever warrant a philosopher's conclusion of cosmic meaninglessness. Rather, we presuppose meaninglessness for non-scientific reasons. We wear anti-teleology goggles into the laboratory, then look under the microscope and exclaim, "Behold, it's meaningless!" Evolutionary biologist Richard Lewontin explains,

> We have a prior commitment, a commitment to materialism. It is not that the methods and institutions of science somehow compel us to accept a material explanation of the phenomenal world, but, on the contrary, that we are forced by our *a priori* adherence to material causes. . . . Moreover, that materialism is an absolute, for we cannot allow a Divine Foot in the door.[39]

Such close-minded materialism has ushered us into a kind of teleological Dark Ages. We have become just as naïve about the meaning of the universe as the medieval alchemist was about the mechanics of the universe. But the meaning void left swirling at the center of a materialist's cosmos will be filled with something. The human heart, like nature, abhors a vacuum.

Dr. Loyal Rue offered the American Academy for the Advancement of Science[40] three possibilities for filling the void. (1) Each individual can become the center point of meaning for his own universe of personal fulfillment. Rue calls this "the madhouse option," which abandons all hope for social cohesion. (2) The State can make itself the center point of meaning in an otherwise meaningless cosmos. Rue calls this "the totalitarian option," where all individuality and freedom are lost. (3) We can say that the universe has meaning even though it doesn't. Rue calls this "the Noble Lie," which "deceives us, tricks us, compels us beyond self-interest." In Rue's bleak trilemma, either the Me destroys the We, the We destroys the Me, or the Lie saves them both, but only by destroying the Truth. (Rue himself defends option 3 since "without such lies we cannot live.") Alex Rosenberg offers a fourth option in the concluding line of his book, *The Atheist's Guide to the Galaxy*: "Take Prozac or your favorite serotonin reuptake inhibitor, and keep taking them till they kick in."

So take your pick: Would you rather live in Rosenberg's Pharmacy of chemically induced meaning, Rue's Church of the Noble Lie, the totalitarian's Prison of State-imposed meaning, or the relativist's Madhouse of self-made meaning? But those are not our only options if (and it is a massively hope-filled "if") Jesus is, in fact, the *Telos*. What if he really can break into our teleological Dark Ages and cast infinite beams of meaning on everything? "But wouldn't that plunge us backward into some kind of scientific Dark Age?" some might worry. Why be so pessimistic? The last time people took Jesus seriously as the *Telos*, a scientific revolution happened. If everything exists *for* him, then we have all the more reason to explore what things are made *of*. Probing the mysteries of the natural world is no longer a matter of what Nietzsche called "staring into the void," but of Kepler's "thinking God's thoughts after him."

A Musical Mind: Jesus Puts Melody to Education

There is still more that Jesus brings to the Areopagus. He brings a certain melody to education. We could understand Handel's famous oratorio *Messiah* as 259 sheets of paper with 252,794 black dots generating 152-minutes of mucous membranes vibrating around a frequency of 210Hz while hot air is expelled from bent metal, felt balls strike a dead cow's skin, and horsehair drags across stretched catguts. But it is possible to understand what Handel's oratorio is made *of* without really understanding Handel's oratorio. Something is lost if we leave out why Handel composed the *Messiah*, what it is *for*. So that we are not left guessing, Handel inked the letters S.D.G. (*Soli Deo Gloria*, that is, "For God's Glory Alone") at the bottom of the final score. We fail to understand and appreciate this sonic masterpiece as what it really is if we fail to hear the millions of sound waves all moving toward the same ultimate goal — that is, worship.

A famous author recounts the first time he tapped into the *Telos* of Handel's *Messiah* at a London symphony: "The event came, quite unexpectedly, not just a performance, but a kind of epiphany. . . . I felt able to see beyond the music to the soul of the piece. . . . I had a glimpse of the grand sweep of cosmic history. All of it centered on the Messiah who came on a rescue mission, who died on that mission, and who wrought from that death the salvation of the world."[41]

To understand the cosmos as particles expanding in a vacuum, a horse as a quadrupedal *Equus ferus*, a human being as a bipedal primate, is to understand the universe, animals, and people, without actually understanding the cosmos, animals, and people. We miss "the soul of the piece." With the "striking revelation" of what it's all *for*, the tumblers fall into place, the door of knowledge swings open, and we join in the Hallelujah chorus.

There were times in the history of education that joining in the pursuit of knowledge was to join in the Hallelujah chorus. At the founding of the first universities and Ivy League schools there was a unity underneath all the diverse fields of study, a unity captured in the words of Harvard's 1650 motto, "In Christi Gloriam" ("For the glory of Christ"). Christ was the melody on top of which every discipline could add its distinctive harmonies, making the university itself a kind of symphony of knowledge.

The modern university, however, functions more as a mere "versity." The unity has been lost. Without a shared *Telos* behind truth in different fields, there is little reason to expect any harmonious picture of reality to emerge.[42] Each discipline, then, sets its own key and tempo. Knowledge is no longer like an inspiring Handel symphony, with its unifying themes unfolding in layered harmonies. Instead it becomes a disconnected John Cage cacophony. No key. No melody. No meaning.

This dissonance drives some students to tune out completely. Many cope with the noise by specializing — that is, limiting their pursuit of knowledge to a single department. There may be no symphony, but at least some coherent tune emerges as the other disciplines fade into silence. This lack of a unifying *Telos* under every field of knowledge, however, does not inspire many Renaissance men and women, but tends to produce what John Updike called "brains no longer conditioned for reverence and awe."[43] It churns out the kind of specialists who, as the saying goes, know more and more about less and less until they eventually know everything about nothing.

Contrast this with the Jesus we meet in Jerusalem. Jesus was not a one-dimensional thinker. He can engage people poetically, philosophically, empirically, historically, and theologically all at once. He can turn slackers and specialists into Renaissance men and women — wide-eyed truth-seekers who can sing with the psalmist, "How precious to me are your thoughts, O God! How vast is the sum of them!"[44] Every "logy" in its truest form — cosmo*logy*, psycho*logy*, bio*logy*, anthropo*logy*, kinesio*logy*, and so on — becomes a branch growing from the living trunk of Christology. How does the *Logos* understand that anomaly in space, that quirk in the human psyche, that cardiovascular system? All truth becomes Christ's truth. Education becomes an act of worship, like Handel's *Messiah*.

Some think that such a Christocentric view of knowledge would send us into a free fall back to the Stone Age. But we must not forget: it was people seeking to think Christ's thoughts after him who made fresh footprints up the peaks of mathematics, astronomy, physics, chemistry, genetics, medicine, philosophy, history, psychology, architecture, literature, art, and, of course, music.

1.4 JESUS IN THE ACROPOLIS

We have seen the imagination, logic, evidence, inspiration, meaning, and harmony that Jesus offers the Agora and Areopagus. What about the Acropolis? What hope does Jesus offer the temples of twenty-first-century spirituality? Most people today simply do not consider deep thinking to be a spiritual activity. This is nothing new. Long ago, Plato drove a wedge between the spiritual and the rational. He celebrated the holy "madness" of the oracles — temple priestesses who would inhale mind-altering vapors, fall into a trance, and babble "spiritual" insight. "Madness is superior to a sane mind," wrote Plato, "for the one is only human, but the other of divine origin."[45]

This holy madness is still revered in today's Acropolis. Many still slay their God-given intellects on the altar of faith.[46] There is what historian Mark Noll calls "the intellectual disaster of fundamentalism," which offers no fundamentalist philosophy, no fundamentalist science, no fundamentalist aesthetics, history, literature, jurisprudence, sociology, and so on.[47] In the trance of our twenty-first-century temples, it never occurs to us that analyzing a complex philosophical argument, probing the enigmas of physics, unraveling the riddles of history, learning Greek verb paradigms, reading the literary classics, or thinking hard about the roots of poverty, can all be profoundly spiritual activities. Jesus, again, subverts the status quo, helping us recover the kind of spirituality that is robust enough to include a vigorous mental life. Here are three ways he does so: by giving us an invitational, relational, and biblical mind.

An Invitational Mind: Jesus Builds Belief-Bridges

Under the spell of the twenty-first-century Acropolis, we gradually lose our ability to reasonably connect with anyone beyond our own faith-tribe. Jesus, by contrast, knew what people different from himself believed. He could dig down and excavate meaningful points of contact from deep within people's different worldviews, helping them discover new levels of insight.

For example, Jesus could have easily bombarded the Sadducees with Old Testament passages that speak unambiguously about life-after-death.[48] But he doesn't. Instead, he builds a logical destructive dilemma from a seemingly more obscure passage in the book of Exodus. Why? Not only did Jesus detect in their question just how seriously they took logic (and, in particular, their fondness for destructive dilemmas). He also knew that the Sadducees only accepted the first five books of the Hebrew Bible (which includes Exodus).[49] He cared enough about people — in this case, the very people seeking his public demise — to discern the contours of their embedded belief structures and custom tailor his insights accordingly.[50] He was not so black-and-white as to think that his opponents had it *all* wrong. By making real contact with their convictions, Jesus turns

Jesus is not about religious bullying.

what could have easily become a shouting match into an offer of genuine insight (even if the Sadducees snub the offer).

Jesus is not about religious bullying: "I believe *y* and *z*. You better too, or else." Rather, Jesus' arguments take a winsome form that elicits genuine insight: "You believe in *x*. Great, me too. Can you see how our belief in *x* is the bud that logically blooms into *y* and *z*?"[51] Such an invitation treats people like minds worthy of real respect. If we develop this aspect of the mind of Jesus, then we bring something to the twenty-first-century Acropolis that is sorely lacking — not a threat of blind authority but an invitation to experience firsthand the blossoming of intellectual consistency.

A Relational Mind: Jesus Loves by Thinking

Prior to his dialogue with the Sadducees, Jesus said something that casts that entire exchange in a new light. He said, "He who sent me is with me. He has not left me alone, for I always do the things that are pleasing to him."[52] Follow the logic: If (*x*) Jesus *always* does what pleases the Father, and (*y*) Jesus engages the Sadducees with intellectual rigor, then what is the *z* that logically blossoms from *x* and *y*? Think about it.

There is no way to separate Jesus' vibrant intellectual life from his reverent connection to his Father. For him, thinking is relational. It is spiritual. It is another way of "pleasing" the Father. If Jesus were in the school of Athens we might picture him on his knees with arms outstretched to the Father he loves. This sheds more light on why Jesus offers the Sadducees the passage from Exodus rather than one of the more obvious afterlife passages. As the Sadducees were well aware, Exodus 3 is all about God deepening his covenant relationship to the Jewish people. As the Sadducees fixate on a covenant to a dead woman, Jesus reminds his Jewish brothers of their covenant with the living God. In this way, Jesus' logical argument for life-after-death becomes a deeply relational argument too.[53] His logic is not about leaving his foes vanquished on an intellectual battlefield, but offering them new life as God's beloved sons and daughters. This comes as no surprise since Jesus is not only the *Logos* but also the *Agapetos* — the Beloved.[54]

The New Testament also identifies Jesus as the *Aletheia* — the Truth.

This means that truth is found not only in propositions, but most ultimately in a Person. Truth is not just for believing, but also for loving, and obeying, and enjoying. It breathes. Truth has a pulse. It pursues. When we seek It, It (or rather He) seeks us back. If truth were only a social construct, then we can deconstruct it at our leisure. We're in control. We're safe. If truth is just a series of facts about nature, then we can comfortably peer into truth without the threat of it peering back into us. If, however, truth is a person who constructs us and knows us, then our jig is up. Truth is not only something to take hold of, but Someone who can take hold of us. It is only when truth is a person, Someone who snaps us out of the illusion of control, that thinking transcends thinking to become also an act of love and worship.

A Biblical Mind: Jesus Knows Scripture

This leads us to a final challenge that Jesus brings to the Acropolis. His opening line to the Sadducees is *planasthe!* — "You are wrong." Where had their thinking gone wrong? Jesus answers, "You know neither the Scriptures nor the power of God."[55]

After decades of data gathering, the pollster George Gallup concluded, "Americans revere the Bible — but, by and large, they don't read it. And because they don't read it, they have become a nation of biblical illiterates."[56] Gallup's grim conclusion is hard to avoid when faced with the facts. The American Bible Society's 2014 State of the Bible Report found that half of the country "strongly agrees" that "the Bible contains everything a person needs to know to live a meaningful life." For all of this lofty regard for the Bible, research reveals that more than 50% of graduating high school seniors think that Sodom and Gomorrah were husband and wife, 12% of Americans think that Joan of Arc was Noah's wife, more than 50% cannot name the four Gospels, and a meager 4% of Christians polled believe poverty to be an issue of primary responsibility for the church. Many respondents even credited the Sermon on the Mount to Billy Graham.[57] "You don't know the Scriptures" is an indictment of more than the Sadducees.

What Gallup calls a "record low" in biblical literacy finds an embarrassing contrast in Jesus himself. His conversation with the Sadducees reveals that loving the Father with all his mind included studying the verb tense and theological gravity of Exodus 3:6. Throughout the Gospel narratives, Jesus skillfully cites Scripture no less than seventy-eight times. His biblical literacy did not occur by osmosis. In his early years, he frequented the Jewish temple, "sitting among the teachers, listening to them and asking them questions." He "increased in wisdom."[58] To take the Bible seriously is to keep the greatest commandment the way that Jesus did.

At the age of 18, Jonathan Edwards mirrored his master well when he wrote: "Resolved, to study the Scriptures so steadily, constantly, and frequently, as that I may find, and plainly perceive, myself to grow in the knowledge of the same."[59] Yet there is an important warning to stamp on Edwards's resolution. The Bible is not just another book to study. It is the only book in history that is always read in the presence of its Author. If we don't move from knowing about God into knowing God, then we miss the book's main point.[60] We become like blind astronomers who can wax eloquent on the science of space, but whose hearts never race from watching the stars come out in the mountains. The Sadducees' problem was not only that they didn't know the Bible, but also that they were oblivious to "the power of God." As Jesus warned first-century Bible scholars, "You search the Scriptures because you think that in them you have eternal life; and it is they that bear witness about me, yet you refuse to come to me that you may have life."[61]

Those times when I fail to find any intimacy or awe in the text (which are far more frequent than I care to admit), I find three primary culprits: I'm not reading it often, I'm not inviting the Author into my reading, or I'm not bothering to do what I read. When any of one of those three occurs, the Bible quickly becomes a dusty textbook. For those who find no joy in the Bible, I offer the following suggestions (and for those who don't care to, I offer the following challenges): (1) Try "examining the Scriptures daily to see if these things were so," like the Bereans did.[62] (2) Ask with the psalmist, "Open my eyes, that I may behold wondrous things out of your law."[63] (3) Take James's advice to "be doers of the word, and not hearers only, deceiving yourselves."[64] Read it, ask the Author for a sense of wonder, do what it says, and watch what happens. You might experience something like Rosaria Butterfield, who, as a university English professor, viewed the Bible as outmoded literature from superstitious dead people. Then she read it with an open mind and, in her own words,

> saw for myself that it had a holy Author; I saw for myself that it was a canonized collection of sixty-six books with a unified biblical revelation. . . . The fog burned away. The whole Bible, each jot and tittle, was my open highway to a holy God.[65]

1.5 LIFE TO THE MIND

This concludes our brief tour of Jerusalem and Athens. In the Athens of twenty-first-century culture, the mantra has become, in the famous words of Harvard's Timothy Leary, "Death to the mind!" The Jesus of Jerusalem offers exactly the kind of intellectual resurrection we need. To imaginatively, logically, and factually deprived consumers in the Agora he cries, *"Life to the mind!"* To uninspired, meaning-starved, fragmented intellects in the Areopagus he shouts *"Life to the mind!"* To narrow, dazed, biblical illiterates in the Acropolis he sings *"Life to the mind!"*

✷

We began this chapter with the question: What would Jesus be doing if he were painted into Raphael's *School of Athens*? We might picture him pointing upward, like Plato, to signify the importance of logic. Then again, as the incarnate *Logos* he could simply point to himself. To express the importance of the empirical world we could picture him next to Aristotle, with his arm stretched out horizontally. Only his open hand reveals something profound — the scars of his resurrected body and all the hope they represent. Perhaps he would be holding out an open and well-worn Bible, expositing its insights with a grammarian's precision and a poet's imagination. Or maybe his arms would be stretched out in a 'V' worshiping the Father, or in an upside-down 'V' inviting his critics into a reasonable conversation and a relationship more profound than anything they've ever fathomed.

REFLECT

So which is it? Perhaps it is for the better that there is no Jesus among the fifty-eight thinkers whom Raphael chose to immortalize in his fresco. No single, static, two-dimensional pose could possibly capture the living, dynamic, multidimensional genius of Jesus. As we worship and become more like him, may our lives express his mind with more color, depth, and beauty than a fresco ever could.

A PRAYER TO REASON

Jesus, help us to follow your lead in loving the Father with all of our minds. Resurrect our imaginations. Make us logical. Help us care about evidence. Inspire our hands to explore the universe you made and called "good." Open our eyes to see the Meaning all around us. Unplug our ears to hear the Melody under every pursuit of knowledge. Turn our thinking into an ongoing act of love, an expression of worship. Help us to read, relish, and do what you say in Scripture. Amen.

2

EMOTE

Mirroring the Just Sentiments of Jesus

And Jesus entered the temple and drove out all who sold and bought in the temple, and he overturned the tables of the money-changers and the seats of those who sold pigeons. He said to them, "It is written, 'My house shall be called a house of prayer,' but you make it a den of robbers." And the blind and the lame came to him in the temple, and he healed them.

— MATTHEW 21:12-14

> The people who hanged Christ never, to do them justice, accused him of being a bore — on the contrary, they thought him too dynamic to be safe. It has been left for later generations to muffle up that shattering personality and surround him with an atmosphere of tedium.
>
> DOROTHY SAYERS

If Plato, Aristotle, Augustine, and a mix of our ancestors from virtually any age of human history were crammed into a time machine and hurled into the twenty-first century, there is something normal to us that they would find totally bewildering. I am not referring to space travel, the worldwide fame of a cartoon mouse, or even technologies that put all human knowledge at our fingertips that we use to watch cat bloopers, bizarre as all of that would seem. I am referring, instead, to the sacred, unquestioned authority granted to feelings in our day.

Western culture has been through a so-called Age of Faith and an Age of Reason. We live in what Princeton's Robert George calls "the Age of Feeling."[1] Canadian philosopher Charles Taylor prefers the moniker "the Age of Authenticity"[2] to describe how staying true to your feelings, whatever they may be, has become the highest virtue of our day (unlike historic virtues in which certain feelings could and should be chastened). Without appreciating the strangeness of this feature of modern life, it is difficult to see anything significant about the emotional life of a first-century rabbi.

Most of our human ancestors thought that some feelings were valid and others were not. The difference, for them, was whether or not the feeling corresponded to the world beyond the feeler. Feeling awe at a night sky, for example, would be valid, not merely because you feel it, but because the night sky is truly awesome. For Plato, feelings were about a "just distaste [for] the ugly" and "delighted praise to beauty."[3] Aristotle called them "ordinate affections."[4] Augustine called it the *ordo amoris*, ordering our loves to match the actual love-worthiness of things. Early Hindus called it *satya*. Chinese tradition called it the *Tao*.

The past half century has taken a sharp detour from that long-traveled road. In our age of feeling the only condition required for a feeling to be valid is simply that it be felt, not that it conform to the world beyond us. Nowadays, a feeling can no more be invalid than a circle can be unround; a circle is round just by being a circle and a feeling is valid just by being felt. This all seems very liberating. But before jumping on the new cultural wagon and leaving our ancestors forever in the dust, we might pause to ponder the implications: Doesn't progress require us to move from erroneous feelings to more noble and virtuous feelings? If we hail every feeling as sacrosanct and authoritative, is it even possible for us to make real progress anymore? And if we can no longer quest upward to reach better feelings, are we left to drift sideways on a never-ending plateau of equally valid feelings?

> *Doesn't progress require us to move from erroneous feelings to more noble and virtuous feelengs?*

Is the world really that flat? How might Jesus open us up to a more layered and mountainous terrain of life where it is again possible for us to embark on a meaningful quest toward more worthy emotions?

2.1 THE *GREEN BOOK* AND THE BOMB

First, consider the strange way in which we came to live in the age of feeling. Picture yourself in a beautiful city where the skyline is made of towering trees instead of steel high-rises. People live and work in this vast network of living redwoods, sycamores, oaks, and maples — buildings that grow and change colors with the seasons. At the base of the Redwood Skyline stands the Painter's Museum. Here, paintings aren't framed as much as the paintings frame you. In the Van Gogh Room you can sip a coffee with the dark silhouettes at the Café Terrace. You can get lost trying to navigate through the three-dimensional paint splatters floating around the Pollock Room. Or, you can defy physics climbing up the stairs that lead to the floor of the Escher Room.

Across from the Painter's Museum stands the Musician's Louvre. Every level of this grand pyramid features live music — a floor for folk, blues, jazz, rock, and classical — all the way up to the apex, which houses an open window aviary. This is where songbirds flock together and broadcast melodies all over the city. At the Poet's Arboretum, statues of history's most moving wordsmiths stand like a forest of terracotta soldiers. With a touch, each comes to life and recites for you. Shakespeare recites Shakespeare, Bradstreet recites Bradstreet, Austen recites Austen. I wish there was time to tell you about the Edible Art District, or all the other hidden wonders of this sublime city. Unfortunately, we must get to what happened there less than a hundred years ago.

> *If the only things allowed to count as facts are physical facts . . . then a smile and a shudder are equally valid, equally unjustified, equally meaningless.*

One day, a low-pitch hum could be heard from the horizon. It got louder and louder until you couldn't hear the songbirds from the apex of Musician's Louvre anymore. A B-52 bomber came into view. Its engine's rumble shook the skyline as its shadow glided across the city like a black albatross. Its aluminum belly opened slowly and a small green book dropped out, falling in a fluttering zigzag toward the earth. Then came a blinding flash, followed by the deafening sound of a single, kick drum boom. The aesthetic city was gone and a flattened, scorched, radioactive wasteland had taken its place.

Something not unlike this took place in Great Britain around the middle of the twentieth century, moving us one step closer to the age of feeling. C. S. Lewis recounts the event in his short book, *The Abolition of Man*. *Abolition* begins as a book about a book, a book with ideas that, in Lewis's estimation, threaten to annihilate our noble species. What book did the Oxford don consider so sinister? Hitler's *Mein Kampf*? Mao's *Red Book*? LaVey's *Satanic Bible*? No. It was a children's book of grammar. What ideas could anyone (especially a world-class professor of literature) possibly find in a children's grammar book that could inspire doomsday?

The so-called *Green Book* by "Gaius and Titius" (pseudonyms supplied by Lewis)[5] relays a famous story of Samuel Taylor Coleridge about a waterfall. A tourist beholds the waterfall and exclaims, "It's sublime!" Gaius and Titius explain to British children that this seems to be a statement about the waterfall, but it only *seems* that way. What masquerades as a factual observation about a waterfall's aesthetic power is really nothing but a subjective declaration about some tourist's arbitrary feelings. Or so say Gaius and Titius. "That waterfall is sublime" has been deconstructed to mean, "I have sublime feelings." Lewis adds,

> The schoolboy who reads this passage in the *Green Book* will believe two propositions: firstly, that all sentences containing a predicate of value are statements about the emotional state of the speaker, and secondly, that all such statements are unimportant.[6]

What is really at stake here is every young Harry's and Nigel's belief in what Lewis calls "just sentiments," that is, feelings that do justice to the object felt. Feeling awe at a waterfall's sublimity, for example, is one of the just sentiments we can have toward it. Feeling that "It is ugly and I want to fill it with toxic trash" is not. Feeling grief at the news of a public shooting rampage is a just sentiment; it reflects the actual grievousness of the event. Laughing and celebrating such news is not. We would shudder at a man's happy reaction to such a horrible headline. Why? Because we see at once, and on a very deep level,[7] the injustice of his sentiment, that his twisted smile contradicts the frown-shaped reality of lives lost.

All connection between feelings and facts, any finger-interlocking intimacy between the hand inside us and the world reaching toward us, all feelings of awe for the truly awesome, gratitude for the truly undeserved, horror for the truly horrible, courage for the truly worth fighting for, laughter for the truly hilarious — that is what the *Green Book* has torn apart. The unsuspecting schoolboy came to have his head filled with a lesson in English grammar. Instead, he finds himself anesthetized to beauty, staggering bare-backed, stitched, and half-dazed off an operating table where his heart has been removed from his chest. Lewis argues that Gaius and Titius have made it that much more difficult for the generation under their scalpel to look at a waterfall and see anything more than H_2O molecules obeying gravity, or stare into the mirror and see anything more than what Louis-Ferdinand Celine called "packages of tepid, half-rotted viscera."[8]

If the only things allowed to count as facts are physical facts — the waterfall is blue; it is cold; it is over there; that person is male; he is five feet tall; he's got dandruff — then a smile and a shudder are equally valid, equally unjustified, equally meaningless.[9] In this way, the grammar lesson becomes a metaphysical bombshell. The old, aesthetic city — beautified layer by layer, century by century by master craftsmen, maestros, moral heroes, and poetic prodigies — gone in a flash.

2.2 FROM JUST SENTIMENTS TO *JUST* SENTIMENTS

Where has the dropping of the green bomb left us? Has all beauty and emotion been nuked out of existence, leaving us to stagger around like zombies? Surprisingly not. In fact, something like the opposite has occurred. Somehow the modern assault on feelings has ushered us into the Age of Feeling. But how?

We understand the surprising aftermath we live in if we play a short language game with Lewis's term "just sentiments." For Lewis and the long tradition he represents, the term meant sentiments that do justice to the object felt. The dropping of the *Green Book* reduces the ancient city of just sentiments to a rubble of *just* sentiments, as in *merely* sentiments, emotions that amount to nothing because they tell us nothing about the "real world." The adjective "just" in this case is a dig, as in the sentence, "You're *just* a kid," or "He's *just* a freshman." Those are *just* sentiments.

Over the past half century, however, this second meaning has unexpectedly spawned a third way to understand the phrase. In this third way, "just" no longer means un-important, but all-important. Who do you pledge your life to? *Just* you. Who do you worship? *Just* Allah. What do you listen to? *Just* classic rock. How do you define reality? What's the basis of your life choices? How do you know what's right? *Just* feelings. "Just" here signifies exclusivity. On this meaning, all sentiments become sacred and unquestionable. The only thing required for a feeling to be just in this view is, again, not that it correspond to anything beyond the feeler, but simply that it be felt.

Why the move from the second to the third meaning, from "just" as in *unimportant* sentiments to today's "just" as in *all-important* sentiments, and why does it matter? Imagine two rooms. In one room we can find everything that the *Green Book* (and the modern spirit it represents) will allow us to count as facts — waterfalls as H_2O obeying gravity, stars as burning balls of gas, humans as decomposing meat, and so on.[10] In the other room we find all sentiments, the feeling of awe toward the waterfall, humility at the night sky, love for people, and so on. You are told that there is no window or door connecting one room to the other. Your feelings can never touch the facts. An impenetrable wall divides them. Now you must make a choice: In which of the two rooms would you rather spend the rest of your life?

This is the ultimatum posed by the *Green Book*. Though posed to convince schoolboys to snap out of fantasy and join the grown-up world of facts, the dilemma backfires. The surgery goes all wrong. The scalpel slips. The attempt to make what Lewis called "men without chests" results in men without heads, people who live almost entirely in a world of feelings with little regard for facts. The reason is this: most people, if pushed into such an ultimatum, would opt for life in the feeling room. The fact room seems too bleak and boring. We'd prefer lovers to rotting carbon shells. We'd rather live clueless about a sunflower's chemistry than live in a box where we could never know that a sunflower is beautiful. Who wants to stare at Seurat's painting, *Sunday Afternoon on the Island of La Grande Jatte*, and see nothing more than three million dots of oil and zinc chromate on a seven-by-ten-foot rectangle?

After modern thought constructed a wall between the facts and our feelings, and the majority made its choice between the two, the feelings room became the entire world to us. In that quarantined world it is impossible to fact-check any of our feelings, so all feelings become equally valid, unfalsifiable, and all that really matters.[11] This third meaning of "just sentiments" comes very close to how most people today, unlike most people through history, think about our feelings. Compared to theirs, our new world, where every feeling finds validation, seems much more freeing, limitless, and empowering, at least at first. But sooner or later, like Jim Carrey's Truman on his voyage toward the open blue horizon, we crash into the painted clouds. Sure, we are free to feel whatever we want, but only within the small space of an artificial human construct, cut off from the great big world beyond us. David Wells describes our predicament well:

> The proud and erect shaper of life first remakes reality and then finds that what has been remade has no existence outside his or her private consciousness. . . . The self, now left completely to itself, cut off from God and from the outside world, began to disappear. Once severed from the larger frameworks of meaning, people became increasingly introspective, and what they gazed upon looked increasingly weightless.[12]

In other words, we went looking inside ourselves expecting to find omnipotence only to find ourselves with a bad case of claustrophobia. Anyone who has seriously tried to follow the twenty-first-century mantra of looking within for ultimate answers will know what I mean. That supposedly infinite space within ourselves very quickly becomes a prison. The cell walls of our solitary confinement have only been painted to look like an open horizon. The freedom is an illusion.[13]

Maybe we chose the wrong room. But, then again, life in the fact room of Gaius and Titius is no more freeing, especially if the only facts we think we can find there are the ones that can fit inside a calculator. What we need is a wrecking ball, someone to smash through the artificial wall between facts and feelings. We need someone to crash into the lonesome subjectivity of the twenty-first century and free us to feel not just sentiments or even just sentiments, but *just* sentiments, the rush of the sublime, and tragic, and glorious world not only inside but all around us? This, as you may have guessed, is where Jesus comes in.

2.3 DEMOLITION MAN

What hope does Jesus offer for our modern predicament (or our post-modern predicament, depending on which of the two rooms we choose)? Just like in the first century, he does not come as a man-of-the-times to preserve and champion the *zeitgeist*. He won't be boxed in by our cultural ideologies. He does not visit our day to validate every feeling and whim. He loves us far too much to do that. What he does is far better for us.

The first thing he does is blow the roof off the modern fact room and let the light in. He pries open reality. He makes the world bigger. He shows us a cosmos that is layered and spacious enough to include both truths that fit into calculators and truths that cannot. The old fact room was too small for facts like "People are worth more than money," "Exploiting the poor is a terrible injustice," "Self-righteousness is ugly," "Love is our utmost duty," and ten million other truths that we know to be true despite our inability to spot them on the Periodic Table. In this new expansive world of facts (which has really been there all along) waterfalls can be seen as H_2O obeying gravity *and* for all their gushing sublimity. People are Celine's "tepid, half-rotted viscera" and Shakespeare's "beauty of the world." William Wordsworth said, "There's more to the flower than the botanist can study." That breathtaking "more" is what Jesus encourages us to see in the world, and without discouraging us from the sacred task of botany. The world he opens to us is plentiful enough for both scientists and poets to coexist and thrive.

He leads us over the rubble and shows us, by example, what merits our joy, what to rage at, what to grieve, what to be grateful for.

The second thing Jesus does, having blown the roof off the fact room, is smash through the wall between that vast, multilayered world of facts and our claustrophobic feelings room. This act of demolition frees us up to say, "That is sublime!" "That is tragic!" "That is awesome!" and actually be saying something meaningful about more than our own emotional states. How is this new freedom possible? Because his robust world is a place where sublime things, and tragic things, and awesome things actually exist (and existed before we could even feel them). In Lewis's words, this world is a place where "objects do not merely receive, but can *merit*, our approval or disapproval, our reverence or our contempt."[14] "Just sentiments" in the original sense of the term become possible for us to feel again.

This leads us to the third thing Jesus does. Once he has blown the roof off modernism's fact room, and once he has smashed down the walls of postmodernism's feeling room, he leads us over the rubble and shows us, by example, what merits our joy, what to rage at, what to grieve, what to be grateful for. He *incarnates* the just sentiments, showing us what they look like not in the black-and-white abstractions of a philosopher's book, but in the vivid existential colors of human life.

Then, there is a fourth thing he does to restore just sentiments for us. It is fantastic and, I dare say, miraculous, but that must wait. First, let us ponder how Jesus exemplifies the just sentiments for us.

2.4 OUTRAGE, COMPASSION, AND JOY

Let us join eighty to a hundred thousand religious pilgrims on their trek to the sacred city to worship at the Jewish temple. It is Passover week. In order to participate in the traditional temple offerings, we need doves or pigeons. Since worshipers need these birds, they were sold at the temple at a premium price. You could get a more economical bird outside the temple courts or lug one from home through the hot desert. However, every bird used in temple rituals had to pass the rigid purity standards of the temple's in-house animal inspectors. Only inflated temple-sold birds had the guaranteed certification of the scrupulous inspectors. In this way, the house of prayer had become a classic case of what economists call a "captive market."

But that is not all. Temple-certified pure birds could only be purchased with temple-certified pure money. Crowds of traveling worshipers with all their Roman, Greek, Syrian, and Persian currency had to swap out their dirty silver, graven with kings' heads, for the temple's only acceptable currency. The faceless sacred shekels could now be sold to the faithful at a gouging exchange rate. You are charged a one *maah* fee for every single coin exchanged (roughly, one-fourth of a day's working wage per coin), then another *maah* if you wanted any change back in an uneven transaction. You had to spend your money just to buy the right kind of money with which to buy their already overpriced birds. You had to get swindled in one captive market just for the honor of being swindled in the next.

One historian estimates that "a pair of doves [that] cost as little as nine pence outside the temple [cost] as much as fifteen shillings within the temple."[15] That's a 2,000% markup, like having to pay $40 for a drink you could get for $2 just outside the sports arena.[16] And so the sound of worship echoes through the courtyards of God's house — Cha-ching! Cha-ching![17]

Outrage

Those are facts that any historian could tell you. Jesus saw something more. He enters the scene like a fireball. Matthew's eyewitness account of the event tells us that Jesus "drove out all who sold and bought in the temple, and he overturned the tables of the money-changers and the seats of those who sold pigeons."[18] Around the money-changers' and bird sellers' upside-down tables were beggars with broken bodies who assembled daily at the gates of the temple courts.[19] Jesus could see extreme need literally steps away from extreme greed. It wasn't merely that the greedy failed to lift up the needy. The greedy lifted themselves higher by pushing them into deeper poverty. Poor worshipers couldn't afford goats, lambs, or oxen,[20] so they were the social class most heavily exploited by the temple's monopolized bird market.

He teaches us to fume when profit takes priority over people, greed over need, revenue over reverence.

According to the Jewish Scripture Jesus cites in his rage, the temple was to be "a house of prayer" where outcasts could gather to enjoy God.[21] Jesus saw that it had become instead a monument of corruption and oppression, "a den of robbers."[22] An old Jewish proverb says: "Whoever oppresses a poor man insults his Maker."[23] Given his profound solidarity and identification with the poor and exploited, God was being insulted in his own house. Jesus could see that and it boiled his blood. Outrage was his just sentiment; it fit the outrageousness of what temple had become.

What in today's world could evoke this same kind of just sentiment? Over the years I have received hundreds of letters from poor worshipers, mostly from South America. The story is usually the same. Some destitute village has a small transistor radio piping in the airwaves of American televangelists who wear custom suits, live in sprawling mansions, and drive luxury sedans. Their promise of the so-called hundredfold financial blessing echoes through mud and straw huts: "Give $10 and receive $1,000; give $1,000 and receive $100,000."[24] When a week's wage is measured in pesos and your children are looking to you with hunger-hollowed eyes, the promise of a hundredfold financial blessing sounds irresistible (especially when it comes from rich Americans claiming to be the very voice box of God on earth).

If she accrues enough hard-earned wages from enough third-world families then that first-world televangelist can have more spending cash for her Florida shopping getaway. She can take one of five, yes *five*, ministry-owned jets for that much-needed getaway from her 6 million dollar, 18,000 square-foot, crystal-chandeliered, fully staffed residence in Tarrant County, Texas.[25] It could also help her husband (also a televangelist) achieve his dream of buying his wife a Cessna 10 super-jet to match his own (20 million dollars each).[26] That way they can race each other at just under the speed of sound in side-by-side flying palaces to their next third-world speaking tour. When they land there to a rock star's welcome, the donor families will still be hungry. That hundredfold blessing never came. They are told that they didn't sow their last seed with enough faith, so they had better sow again. And they will. More fuel for the Cessnas; Cristal for the champagne flutes; wax for the Bentleys; and all in the name of Jesus. Is your blood boiling like his yet?

The New Testament tells us to "be angry," with the important caveat, "and do not sin."[27] Aristotle observed, "Anyone can become angry — that is easy. But to be angry with the right person, to the right degree, at the right time, for the right purpose, and in the right way — that is not easy."[28] Jesus breaks us out of ourselves and shows us how to be angry in the right ways. He teaches us to fume when profit takes priority over people, greed over need, revenue over reverence. Following him will make us angry when we see religion that's supposed to give people an "open door"[29] to God turned into a never-ending series of toll booths toward some divine blessing dangled like a sacred carrot in front of weary-souled travelers. *Jesus, teach us to rage at the outrageous things done in your name.*

Compassion

If we peer underneath Jesus' table-flipping rage at the temple, we find a still deeper emotion to reflect. Matthew's account tells us that immediately after protesting the poor-oppressing, God-mocking temple system, "the blind and the lame came to him in the temple, and he healed them."[30] What a beautiful moment. In it we see that Jesus was outraged not *in spite of* his care for people but precisely *because* of it. The very people marginalized and trampled under the religious power structure are brought into the spotlight and elevated by Jesus. (He has a way of doing that.) He didn't take anything from them or treat them like chumps in a captive market. He gave them vision and sound bodies. He treated them like the intrinsically valuable human beings they each were — and all for free.

He blows the roof off modernity's fact room so that people can again be esteemed as more than their bodies.

While Jesus was busy helping people amidst scattered coins and damaged furniture, the temple business of selling and slaying animals for people's sins had grinded to a halt.[31] Not only did he single-handedly shut down the sacrificial system that day; he was also known to walk from town to town offering people free-of-charge, on-the-spot forgiveness and direct access to God. Here was a scandalously free alternative to the captive markets of the temple's booming forgiveness business. He was becoming to people everywhere everything that the temple should have been all along. His very being was making the old building obsolete.

This threatened its revenue stream and its leaders' privileged position as God's middle men. This painted a big red target on Jesus' back.[32] But it didn't matter to him. He knew the consequences. People were worth it. His just sentiments valued people's freedom over a cushy, pain-free existence.

This moves us to the emotion that Jesus was said to feel more often than any other emotion recorded in the narratives of his life — compassion. The Greek word for compassion — *splanchnizomai* — describes the interior state of Jesus with more frequency than any other emotional term in the Gospels.[33] In Greek, *splanch* meant your guts. First-century Jews often located the deepest physical core of your emotions down in your guts. (Anyone who has ever felt the abdominal churning of extreme anxiety or that losing-your-stomach-on-a-rollercoaster rush of extreme joy can understand why.)

The *splanchnizomai* that Jesus so often felt was nothing short of a gut-twisting emotional reaction to other people's suffering. His guts twisted for hungry people, for sick people, for blind people, for people grieving a lost loved one, for people who were spiritually harassed, lost, and exhausted.[34] In every single New Testament instance of *splanchnizomai* the twisting guts inspire action. Jesus feeds, mends, comforts, and teaches the starving, sick, sorrowful, and spiritually confused. When Jesus tells his famous parable of the good Samaritan, it was twisting guts — *splanchnizomai* — for the battered, half-dead stranger that propelled the heroic Samaritan to action. *Splanchnizomai* set him apart from the calm-bellied religious villains of the story.[35] In his parable of the prodigal son it is again *splanchnizomai* that sends a father running for the horizon to embrace and kiss the son who had abandoned him.[36]

All of this shows us that, to Jesus, people are far more than "self-compulsive bundles of 126 instincts" (William Costello), "an aggregate of trillions of cells" (Jean Ronstand), or "digestive tubes" (Pierre Cabanis). For him, there is much more to people than what the biologist or neurologist can study. He blows the roof off modernity's fact room so that people can again be esteemed as more than their bodies (while valuing and mending their bodies too). *Jesus, teach us to feel compassion for people in all of their irreducible value and twist our guts to action when that value is trounced.*

Joy

As we learn just sentiments from Jesus, not only does our blood start to boil and our stomachs turn, he also shows our hearts how to beat with real joy. There is a stereotype floating around that says that Jesus and the faith he represents are about cold-hearted duty, doing the right thing at the expense of our happiness. There are enough grim-faced moralistic systems out there that brandish the name of "Christianity" to keep the stereotype alive. They have more in common with the philosophy of Immanuel Kant than with the kingdom of Jesus. The day after he stormed the temple, Jesus returns to the same temple courts to announce that his kingdom is like a big party, and everyone is invited; not a boarding school, not a boot camp, not a chain gang, but a party.[37]

Jesus' entrance into the world was announced as "good tidings of great joy." He came "eating and drinking," and was accused of being "a glutton and a drunkard"[38] (a strange accusation if Jesus was a dull kill-joy you'd avoid at a party). Princeton theologian B. B. Warfield spent his entire academic career studying the life of Jesus and concluded that "if our Lord was 'the Man of Sorrows,' he was more profoundly still 'the Man of Joy.'"[39] We need Warfield's reminder, especially those of us who have come to think of faith as an unhappy chore, while the world out there has all the fun.

We come to feel things most truly when we feel them in light of God's existence.

When we get a real sense of Jesus' joy, all of the hedonistic buzz-seeking of our culture seems lackluster and dull. "We are half-hearted creatures, fooling about with drink and sex and ambition when infinite joy is offered us," says Lewis, "like an ignorant child who wants to go on making mud pies in a slum because he cannot imagine what is meant by the offer of a holiday at the sea. We are far too easily pleased."[40] Jesus was joyful, but not easily pleased. He did not settle for mud pies, and if we worship and become more like him, neither will we.

Where then did Jesus find his source of joy? Not where we are told to find it today. He never pursued the posh lifestyle of a business mogul, rock star, or televangelist. He was homeless.[41] He didn't stake his joy in winning everyone's approval. John 6 ends with many people turning their backs and rejecting him. John 7 does not begin with, "And then Jesus threw a big pity party about why everyone didn't like him." He didn't find joy by looking inside himself either. Jesus found joy outside himself, and in infinite abundance. His "heart was glad" and "his tongue rejoiced." Why? Because the Father was "always before him."[42] Proverbs 8:30 shows us Jesus "rejoicing always" in the presence of the Father. The Father anoints his head with "the oil of gladness" in Hebrews 1:9. And it is that same joy

— what David Brainerd called "the only soul-satisfying happiness" — that Jesus prays for us to experience the way he does.[43]

This moves us to the deepest source of just sentiments. We have already seen that we can look at a waterfall with an unjust sentiment — "It's ugly and I want to turn it toxic" — or with a just sentiment — "It's sublime!" Yet, there is a way to feel a waterfall even more justly. Picture Jonathan Edwards at the misty base of the falls. Listen to the kind of sentiments Edwards expresses:

> The appearance of everything was altered; there seemed to be, as it were, a calm sweet cast, or appearance of divine glory, in almost everything. God's excellency, his wisdom, his purity and love, seemed to appear in everything; in the sun, moon, and stars; in the clouds, and blue sky; in the grass, flowers, trees; in the water, and all nature.[44]

It is just to have your feelings touch the sublimity of a waterfall; it still more just — still more in synch with reality — to feel something of the sublimity of God in the sublimity of the waterfall.

The Dutch-American philosopher Cornelius Van Til argued that our intellects can know things, and even know things truly, but we come to know things *most* truly when we know them in light of God's existence.[45] Extend Van Til's point to our emotions: our hearts can feel things, and even feel things truly, but we come to feel things *most* truly when we feel them in light of God's existence. That is the light that pours down on everything when Jesus tears the roof off the modern fact room. The whole world starts to look and feel different when it is seen and felt for what it really is — God's world.

People in the dark can grope around and describe what they feel. In the modern dark room we feel around and determine people's shape and calculate their value from their size, their skin, their stature, their sex, the size of their wallet. The roof comes off, our eyes adjust, and we cup our mouths. We have been surrounded by image-bearers of an infinitely valuable God the whole time, objects of divine affection — black, white, rich, poor, big, small, male, female — each one a masterpiece. Everyone starts to feel different. You start to feel different. Waterfalls start to feel different. *Jesus, teach us to enjoy the Father the way you did, and in him to enjoy what is truly joyous in everything else!*

2.5 BECOMING AUTHENTIC

We have come to better understand, with the help of Gaius, Titius, and Lewis, how we came to live in the age of feeling. We have come to see how Jesus can save us from it, how he can restore just sentiments like outrage, compassion, and joy. This leaves us with two hanging questions. First, how do we actually come to feel just sentiments the way Jesus did? Second, why Jesus' feelings? Can't we learn just sentiments from the emotional lives of Gandhi, or Mother Teresa, or Rosa Parks? Or from that friendly janitor, that caring co-worker, or that self-giving mother? Or perhaps even from Homer's Ulysses, Tolkien's Aragorn, or J. K. Rowling's Harry? Aren't there a billion admirable feelers, real and fictional, who show us what life can look like beyond the confines of the modern fact box and the postmodern feeling box?

The answers to the first question can be found in the answers to the second. The short answer to the second question is yes, of course, there are volumes upon volumes of just sentiments that can be learned from all kinds of people in all kinds of times and places. In history books we can be inspired by university students, like Sophie Scholl and her brother Hans's defiant courage against the Third Reich. In hardbacks and on the big screen we can learn from the priest's candlestick-bestowing mercy on Jean Valjean in Victor Hugo's *Les Miserables*. In daily life there are just sentiments to be learned all around us, if we're looking for them — that waiter's infinite patience, that toddler's sense of wonder, that friend's light-hearted ability to be un-phased by an insult.

Many can inspire just sentiments; Jesus can infuse them in us.

This partially answers our first question too. How do we come to feel just sentiments? They are more effectively caught than taught. We come to feel them for ourselves when we intentionally surround ourselves with noble feelers. We can put ourselves in close proximity to people who exude the affections we need more of. We can use history to transport us through time to interlock arms with the Selma marchers. Film and fiction can whisk us off to find courage and compassion through the wardrobe of Narnia, on the battlefields of Middle Earth, or in the halls of Hogwarts.

All of this can help us to feel more just sentiments. But there is much more to it, especially when Jesus is part of our emotional odyssey. A case could be made that all heroes, real or fictional, dramatic or mundane, relate to Jesus the way sunbeams relate to the sun. If we really think about it and trace Parks's, Potter's, or that waitress's just sentiments all the way back to their most radiant Source, we are led right back to Jesus. That case could be made. I am after something even more extraordinary here, that miraculous fourth thing I hinted at earlier. Jesus not only opens us to a world bigger than the modern fact room; he not only breaks down the isolating walls of the postmodern feeling room; he not only leads us over the rubble to show us by example how to feel more justly. He goes further. He reaches into our chests and creates just sentiments there.

If he is indeed who he claimed to be, then Jesus has a direct, hands-on ability to electrify our affections in ways that no one else can. He has unique, unrestricted, intimate access to human hearts. In Francis Turretin's words, his Spirit "glides into the inmost recesses of the soul, [and] reforms the heart itself, healing its depraved inclinations and prejudices."[46] Augustine experienced it in a pear orchard. C. S. Lewis experienced it in a motorcycle sidecar on his way to the zoo. Bob Dylan experienced it in an Arizona hotel room. Jonathan Edwards experienced it during a thunderstorm, on nature hikes, and in his bedroom.[47] I have experienced it myself (and I suspect many of my readers have too). Many can *inspire* just sentiments; Jesus can *infuse* them in us. Many can challenge us from the outside in; Jesus can change us from the inside out.

✳

This chapter began by pointing out the strangeness of our age of feeling and authenticity. "Authenticity" has come to mean staying true to your own feelings, whatever they may be. But isn't it more authentic to acknowledge that our feelings are not the unquestionable and sacred standard, to acknowledge that we very often get angry at the wrong things, love some things too much and others too little, enjoy some of the wrong things and yawn at some of the most joyous things, fail to be moved like we should for hurting people around us? Isn't it more authentic to acknowledge how broken our hearts really are and that we can't fix ourselves to feel what we ought to feel? Arrogance says, "All my feelings are right." Authenticity says, "I need a Heart Surgeon."

A PRAYER TO EMOTE

Jesus, teach us to feel the way you feel. Do your heart surgery. Go deep and remove unjust sentiments. Heal the torn parts, thaw the frozen parts, and spark new life into the clogged and dead parts. Take your scalpel to our self-centered sentiments. Help us rage at the outrageous. Make our guts quick to twist at suffering and our hands swift to relieve it. Connect us to the Father as our nonstop flow of satisfaction and joy. Take our mangled hearts and make them just, like yours. Amen.

3

FLIP

Mirroring the Upside-Down Action of Jesus

Jesus, knowing that the Father had given all things into his hands, and that he had come from God and was going back to God, rose from supper. He laid aside his outer garments, and taking a towel, tied it around his waist. Then he poured water into a basin and began to wash the disciples' feet and to wipe them with the towel that was wrapped around him.

—JOHN 13:3–5

> I am finished with low living, sight walking, small planning, smooth knees, colorless dreams, tamed visions, mundane talking, frivolous living, selfish giving, and dwarfed goals. . . . My road is narrow, my way is rough, my companions are few, my Guide is reliable, and my mission is clear. . . . I am a disciple of Jesus.
>
> SISTER ANN SHIELDS

Worshiping Jesus not only reshapes our thinking and feeling, but also our doing. Jesus cares about meaningful action. If we're honest with ourselves, we all care about and even crave meaningful action. We want what we do to count for something. Deprive our actions of meaning, said Dostoyevsky, and we "go stark, raving mad."[1]

3.1 POWER, PLEASURE, AND PURITY

The madness starts to set in when one of three things is taken away from our actions — power, pleasure, or purity. Think about it. If nothing we did made any difference, brought us zero satisfaction, and was jaded by guilt, then we would find ourselves one step closer to the madhouse.

What if I told you that, as we seek to live more meaningfully, there is a kind of sanity that will drive us mad and a kind of madness that will make us sane? There is a way we seek power that seems perfectly reasonable. But it leaves us whimpering. There is a widely assumed way to harness pleasure that leaves us hollowed out inside. There is a mainstream way to feel pure that, from time immemorial, has left us riddled with corruption. Yet we trudge these same worn pathways again and again, century after century, as if we'll be the first to find some luscious paradise rather than a lemmings' cliff at the end of the road. There is a word for that kind of behavior — "insanity" — which has been defined as "doing the exact same action over and over again while expecting a different result."

Thankfully, there is another way. It is not the "wide road." It breaks long-cherished human traditions. It seems not only implausible, but downright crazy at first glance. It is, as you may have guessed, the way of Jesus. Frankly, this is where many get Jesus wrong. Nietzsche famously thought of the call of Jesus as a call to totally divest ourselves of power,[2] to trade in our superman capes for cowbells. Many still think of Christianity as the religion of choice for those who would rather "moo" along with a herd than live powerfully.

Then there is what we might call the *Footloose* understanding of what Jesus was about, the idea that Christianity may be pro-power, but is fundamentally anti-pleasure. As in the classic 1984 Kevin Bacon film, *Footloose*, Christianity is a club for killjoys and curmudgeons who gather every Sunday to shame youth out of 1980s dancing and any other damnable sins they might enjoy. Like Bacon's character, many believe that real pleasure requires rebellion against all things Christian (or in its Christianized version, that real Christianity requires rebellion against all things pleasurable).[3]

Then there is an opposite but equally inaccurate view of what Jesus was about. The Pharisees accused Jesus not of being anti-pleasure, but a "glutton and a drunkard" inspiring an anti-purity movement. Why else would he shun their high purity standards and surround himself with hooligans and scoundrels?

Logically, Nietzsche, Bacon, and the Pharisees cannot all be right about Jesus. In fact, they each in their own ways had Jesus all wrong. As we will see, Jesus' extreme way to power makes Nietzsche's supermen look like sedated cows; his extreme way to pleasure makes a bobbing and weaving Bacon look like an uptight church lady; and his extreme way to purity makes the Pharisees' holy cloister look like a seedy brothel. If we are really after meaningful action, Jesus is where the real power, the real pleasure, and the real purity are found.

3.2 HOW NIETZSCHE GOT POWER WRONG

We turn first to power.[4] In his influential book *Will to Power*, Nietzsche sees that power is a much bigger motivator than we realize.[5] It is not just CEOs, aspiring presidents, and movie villains; we are all power-seekers. Nietzsche's disciple Michel Foucault says that we often try to mask it as something else, but "there is no escaping from power."[6] Nietzsche also had the insight to question the common assumption that power is all bad, something to be shunned rather than celebrated.

Nietzsche makes a big assumption about how power works, and we, often unwittingly, make the same assumption. "This world," through Nietzsche's eyes, is "a firm, iron magnitude of force that does not grow bigger or smaller, that does not expend itself but only transforms itself . . . increasing here and at the same time decreasing there."[7] Simply put, we live in a zero-sum universe. For me to gain a thousand more units of power I must take a thousand power-units from someone else. Stooping down to lift others would be certifiably crazy in such a universe. The only mathematically possible way to live more meaningful lives in a zero-sum universe is to lift ourselves up by pushing others down.

That is the kind of universe the disciples believed they were living in the night before the crucifixion. A dispute breaks out around the dinner table over which of them would be the greatest in Jesus' kingdom. Then Jesus does something bizarre that opens their minds to a very different kind a kingdom, an inverted world where cows soar across the sky and Nietzsche's supermen are the ones who chew grass.[8]

Watch how John sets up this world-flipping action: "Jesus, knowing that the Father had given all things into his hands . . ."[9] Hands were a symbol of power in the first-century Jewish world (much like Michelangelo's famous *David* statue with disproportionately large hands to convey power). Holding "all things" would require huge hands. It is John's way of telling us that Jesus held absolute power.

What did he do with so much power? He "rose from supper. He laid aside his outer garments, and taking a towel, tied it around his waist."[10] Was Jesus making some kind of a fashion statement? Why a towel? Today, power roles come with specific attire that make power statements. A green blazer says, "I have the power to win the Masters golf tournament." Silver chevrons on your shoulder say, "I have the power to command armies." The same was true of the first century. A suit of armor, a toga, or a crown would have fit nicely into the kingdom the disciples expected. But a towel? In what inverted dream world does the King with absolute power dress like a house slave?[11]

Jesus takes it further: "Then he poured water into a basin and began to wash the disciples' feet and to wipe them with the towel."[12] Picture that scene in your mind's eye for a moment. The disciples, who were bickering over which of them would be greatest, extend their dirty feet. Then there is Jesus, wearing the uniform of an oppressed social class, bowing low to scrub. Whom do you sense to be the most powerful person in the room? The answer is as upside down as it is obvious. Andy Crouch explains,

> We often retell that story [of Jesus washing feet] as if it involves Jesus "giving up power," as if power were the opposite of humility and servanthood. But . . . servanthood, ensuring the flourishing of others, is the very purpose of power. . . . The foot washing, like John's whole Gospel, is shot through with signs of power.[13]

The fact that we almost instinctively read the foot washing as "Oh, how nice of Jesus to give up power that way" reveals just how hypnotized we have been by Nietzsche's zero-sum philosophy. If we let John's Gospel speak for itself, then we snap back to reality. We begin to see Jesus washing feet for the incredibly powerful action that it is.

Immediately after washing feet, Jesus adds: "You call me Teacher and Lord, and you are right, for so I am."[14] Crouch clarifies, "There are no more powerful roles in the disciples' world than *rabbi* ["teacher"] and *kyrios* ["lord"] — the titles given to Jewish leaders and the lordship ascribed to Caesar himself. Jesus claims them both."[15] In fact, if you were a citizen of ancient Rome then, once a year, you would have to burn a pinch of incense and shout for Caesar, "Worthy art Thou, my Lord and God!" John uses this power language to tell us that Jesus, not Caesar, is Lord.[16]

These two ways to be "Lord" could not be more antithetical. They come from opposite worlds. In Caesar's world, power enslaves. In Jesus' world, power becomes a slave to elevate others. In Caesar's world, there is always the nagging fear that someone else will try to gain power by taking yours. To remain "Lord" in that world, Nero "showed neither discrimination nor moderation in putting to death whomsoever he pleased."[17] He slayed his own mother, his first wife, and (by some accounts) his second wife on the altar of his own power. He impaled and ignited Christians as human lampposts in his imperial courtyard.

In Jesus' world power has no need to be paranoid or pernicious. Ten of the toes that Jesus washed that night belonged to Judas, who Jesus knew was conspiring with his executioners that very night.[18] If he was "Lord" by the standards of Caesar's world, Jesus would have had the saboteur's throat slit. Instead, he washed his betrayer's feet.[19] In doing so, Jesus rehearsed his death the following day. He died not for loyalists but for enemies. His power is so utterly sure of itself that it does not dehumanize, but dignifies and even dies for its enemies. That is real power.

Whose world, then, is the real world—Jesus' or Caesar's? Our answer to that question is an important predictor for how powerful (or pathetic) we will become. Thankfully, there is a kind of test, a totem to help us discern reality from the dream world. It comes from Lewis's observation that if we turn second things into first things, we will lose not only first, but the second things too.[20] In the will-to-power-world of Nietzsche and Nero, power is indeed the first thing. But as David Foster Wallace observed, "Worship power, you will end up feeling weak and afraid."[21] Nero committed suicide. Adolf Hitler (a big fan of Nietzsche's "will to power") ended up weak and afraid, chewing a cyanide capsule in a Berlin bunker. Two days later Benito Mussolini fell powerless before an executioner's machine gun in a small Italian village. Saddam Hussein was found disheveled and alone, hiding in his underwear in a hole in the desert.

Some of our best fiction echoes this truth about power. Tony Montana, better known as *Scarface* from Oliver Stone's celebrated 1983 gangster drama, is a true Nietzschean superman. Scarface asserts his "will to power" to become kingpin of the Miami underworld.[22] In the final shot [spoiler alert], the Cuban Caesar lies facedown in a bloody fountain in the foyer of his mansion. His neon globe that reads, "The World Is Yours," glows ironically over his floating corpse. It is the same truth that J. K. Rowling tells us as "Lord" Voldemort [spoiler alert] curls up in fetal position, withered, small, and helpless at the end of *Deathly Hallows*. It is the same truth that Vince Gilligan tells us in the *Breaking Bad* finale as [spoiler alert] Walter White, who prides himself as being not only in the meth business but "in the Empire business," loses his family, his freedom, his fortune, his only friend, and finally his life.

These stories remind us that when we break the structure of reality, reality has a way of breaking us back. Nietzsche himself suffered multiple mental breakdowns in his quest to become a "superman."[23] It is always a tragedy to see great minds that could have soared like rocket ships nose-dive into the ground and be reduced to shrapnel. That is what happens if we fly through life with an inverted horizon, mistaking up for down.

When Jesus washed feet he showed us the true horizon. We can see how the best bosses are powerful precisely because they empower their employees to succeed. The best parents are powerful because they empower their children to flourish. The most positively powerful people in your life are powerful because they lift you up. Each in their own ways, they have become towel-clad foot washers, and, therefore, powerful.

John's Gospel gives us a profound insight into why power works this way. He begins his book by showing us Jesus, there "In the beginning," creating the universe.[24] The Jesus doing powerful things in the world — washing feet, empowering people to walk and see — is the *Logos* who made the world. When we follow John's clue back to Genesis, we see that Jesus was not an imperialistic power-hog when he made the world. He made people in his own image and told them to do something like he did. He tells them to be powerful creators, filling voids and multiplying life and power and beauty all over the world.[25] Real power has been empowering others since the very beginning.

There is no such thing as neutral living. Our every action says either "Caesar is Lord!" or "Jesus is Lord!"

Then the deceiver enters the Genesis story to convince Adam and Eve that God is trying to keep them down.[26] As Nietzsche would argue millennia later, God issues commands to make us weak. But God does not play zero-sum power games. His commands empower.[27] He commands us to tell the truth because he knows that lying will take away our power to be taken seriously. He commands Sabbath-resting because he knows that we will fizzle and burn out from nonstop work.[28] He commands us to worship only him, not only because he is infinitely worthy of our worship, but also because he knows that idolatry will make us powerless. (As the psalmist says, idols are powerless to hear, feel, walk, or talk and "those who make them become like them.")[29] Saying "no!" to God's commands is not the Superman's liberating declaration of power. It is a "moo!" uttered by those opting for a powerless existence.[30]

A choice must be made. Whose world will we live in? The serpent's or the Creator's? Caesar's or Christ's? Nietzsche's or the footwashing Jesus? The truth is that we have already made that choice. We make it again a thousand times a day in the way we treat our families, the way we work and spend money, the way we do politics, and the like. There is no such thing as neutral living. Our every action says either "Caesar is Lord!" or "Jesus is Lord!" We become like whichever "lord" we bow to, a power who oppresses or a Power who empowers. We can either become fruit-takers or fruit-makers, subtractors or multipliers in our homes, our workplaces, our communities, and culture. The one thing we cannot do is *not* bow.

3.3 THE PLEASURE PARADOX

This brings us to a second thing we need for our actions to take on new meaning. In addition to power, we need pleasure. Pleasure is a lot like power in that we all want more of it and we can't help but want more of it. Some of history's greatest students of the human psyche from Aristotle to Augustine recognized this universal appetite. Though it was Blaise Pascal who put it most famously:

> All men are in search of happiness. There is no exception to this. . . . So while some go to war and others do not the same desire is in both but from different viewpoints. . . . This is the motive for men's every action, even those who are going to hang themselves.[31]

Pascal realized that even when it seems like we are saying no to pleasure it only *seems* that way. We could interpret resisting the cupcake or slogging through a painstaking assignment as saying no to pleasure. On a deeper read of ourselves, we are actually saying yes to pleasure, yes to the pleasure of a less bulbous mid-section, and yes to the pleasure of a higher grade or paycheck. So, just like power, the question of pleasure is not so much "to seek or not to seek?" but "*how* we will go about gratifying our irrepressible appetites?"

Right after washing his disciples' feet to show them what power looks like, Jesus says this about pleasure: "If you know these things, blessed are you if you do them."[32] "Blessed," from the Greek root *makar,* describes a state of profound happiness. *Makar* happiness is very different from modern happiness. The difference becomes clear if we ponder for a moment what shopping has come to mean in our world:

> **Shopping:** An autonomous individual's attempt to gratify his subjective pleasure-preferences in a space contrived to minimize pain and maximize options.

I move from store to air-conditioned store, website to user-friendly website, with one driving question on my mind: What do *I* want? In a superstore world with 27 varieties of Crest toothpaste to choose from (versus a meager 25 varieties of Colgate), 74 iterations of Campbell's condensed soup, 9 styles of Tropicana Orange Juice (each available in 8 size-options), there is no shortage of ways for us to express our pleasure-preferences.[33]

"Shopping" is not just a word for how we attain toothpaste and Tropicana. It describes what has become a total life-orientation.[34] Out of the dizzying array not only of cereal options but creeds, ideologies, and lifestyles swirling around us, just pick (or mix-and-match) whatever makes you feel happy. Who is the final authority on what makes you happy? You are, of course. That may seem sane enough. Indeed, the freedom to choose what makes us happy is *far* better than living under some regime that wields an iron cookie cutter. (No one risked their lives to break *in* to East Berlin, just as no one risks rafting the Pacific waves to break *in* to Cuba.) Yet, as we have increasingly reinterpreted the "the pursuit of happiness" as the right to do whatever makes my three best friends — me, myself, and I — happy, we find reason to doubt the consumer view of happiness.

From 1988 to 2011 the U.S. Centers for Disease Control charted a 400% rise in antidepressant use.[35] The numbers become even more unnerving if we extend the time range back to the 1960s, when gratifying our subjective pleasure-preferences came to be publicly embraced and celebrated as a comprehensive worldview. In *The American Paradox*, psychologist David Myers carefully documents how from 1960 to the turn of the twenty-first century, America doubled its divorce rate, tripled its teen suicide rate, quadrupled its violent crime rate, quintupled its prison population, sextupled out-of-wedlock births, and septupled the rate of cohabitation without marriage (which has been established as a significant predictor of divorce).[36]

Whereas shopping lures us into spaces meticulously arranged by trend experts and feel-good specialists, a quest pushes us out of our comfort zones.

It is no coincidence that the cultural crescendo of unhappiness since the 1960s corresponds with the steep rise of autonomous happiness seeking as a defining mark of the American experience. Social science has gradually caught up with something that theologians have been talking about for millennia — "the paradox of hedonism." That is, the more we seek happiness the more miserable we tend to become. Here, again, pleasure and power look like twins. As the mainstream way to seek power leaves us powerless, so what seems like a perfectly sane way to seek pleasure leaves us profoundly unhappy.

Perhaps real pleasure, like real power, is found in the opposite direction of the mainstream. As power comes not from subjugating, but from serving others, could it be that pleasure comes not from shopping, but from its opposite? What, then, is the opposite of shopping? The opposite of shopping, I suggest, is *questing*, the very thing Jesus invited his disciples into after washing their feet.

What does it mean to quest? Questing remains familiar to us with the help of Hollywood. There is the Jedi's quest to defeat the Sith, Frodo and Sam's quest to the fires of Mount Doom, and Hermione, Harry, and Ron's quest to destroy horcruxes. Unlike shopping, there is a great urgency to a quest (a contrast that breaks down every Black Friday and Christmas Eve). Whereas shopping lures us into spaces meticulously arranged by trend experts and feel-good specialists,[37] a quest pushes us out of our comfort zones. It carries massive consequences, from the crowned glory of success to the mortal doom of failure. That risk is worth it since a quest is always about something bigger than the quester. It is predicated on the existence of real moral goods worth dying for (whereas, shoppers, by and large, are not willing to die for their favorite cereal or shoe brand). A quester also needs old travelers who have journeyed farther and have hard-won wisdom to pass on. Shoppers, however, need no Gandalf, Obi-Wan, or Dumbledore to commission and guide their efforts.[38] They need only their own impulses, and perhaps a photo-shopped supermodel to guide them toward the hottest fashions.

But the most important contrast between shopping and questing, for our present purposes, is the kind of pleasure that each generates. A quest generates *makar,* something that infinite lifetimes worth of self-gratification could never achieve. *Makar* is closer to what William Wilberforce (played by Ioan Gruffudd) feels in the closing scene of the historical drama, *Amazing Grace*. After eleven years of hard questing, the good news comes: British slavery has been legally abolished! Parliamentarians rise in thunderous applause to congratulate Wilberforce for his exhausting and finally victorious efforts. *Makar* is what beams from his humbled, teary-eyed face. It is the pinnacle of happiness that the autonomous self, weighed down with all of its wanting and consuming, can never attain.

It is this *makar* that Jesus offered his disciples in the first century. It is the same happiness that he offers weary shoppers in the twenty-first century. This offer is attached to a commandment to "do just as I have done for you."[39] What exactly are we to do as Jesus did? It is not a call to ritualistic foot hygiene. It is an invitation to a quest. The distinguishing marks of a quest are all right there in the text.

Every good quest has four marks: a sage, a catharsis, a risk of mortal doom, and a promise of *makar*. It is no mystery who the Sage of this quest is. John 13 identifies Jesus as "Lord," "Teacher," "Master," and "Sender." Quests also include a catharsis, a process by which the quester experiences some kind of deep inner cleansing. This text is just such a cathartic moment. The Greek word *catharsis* itself appears in the text of John 13 three times. (What exactly that cleansing means will be the question of our following section.) Then there is the risk of mortal doom. The foot washing foreshadows what Jesus would do the following afternoon in fulfillment of his quest, that is, giving up his life to abolish death and overthrow a dark lord's tyranny over the earth. Indeed, later that night, Jesus tells his disciples to follow his lead by laying down their lives for one another.[40] As Dietrich Bonhoeffer, who gave up his life questing to save people from the Third Reich, put it, "When Christ calls a man, he bids him come and die."[41]

If the situation called for it, this quest could mean literally dying for someone (as it did for Bonhoeffer and countless others). It could also mean a million and one different actions.[42] It could mean some magnanimous act — resisting a dictator, tackling a shooter, parenting. It can also mean what David Foster Wallace calls "sacrificing for [others] over and over, in myriad petty little unsexy ways"[43] — moving furniture, changing the diaper, picking up the bill, taking the insult without lashing back, and so on.[44] As we learn from Jesus the art of dying daily for others, we also find ourselves raised up into real *makar*, just like our Sage, "who for the joy that was set before him endured the cross."[45]

So it would seem that we stand at a crossroads between Madison Avenue and the Via Dolorosa. In one direction our search for pleasure will look like a self-guided shopper's air-conditioned search for whatever fits her subjective style. In the other, we look more like questers trudging defiantly up some deadly summit for the good of others.[46] *Makar* is found along only one of those roads. If we're after real happiness, then it is time to put down our shopping bags and pick up our crosses.[47]

3.4 CATHARSIS

We cannot stop there or we will become the villains of our own quests. There is something we need in addition to power and pleasure. We find it in the words of Jesus to Peter. Peter tells Jesus, "You shall never wash my feet," to which Jesus answers, "If I do not wash you, you have no share with me."[48] Jesus' answer only makes sense if he is talking about something more than feet. Otherwise, we are left with a strange gospel of salvation by podiatric hygiene. What, then, needed washing?

To answer that question, consider the curious case of Joseph-Marie Lequinio. Lequinio held the job title of "representative on mission" for the French revolution. He traveled town to town evangelizing his countrymen with the Enlightenment gospel of reason. In November 1793 (or year 2 in the month of Brumeire by the revolutionaries' new calendar), Lequinio's mission took him to the French port town of Rochefort. He entered what had been a Catholic cathedral until the revolutionaries forcibly tossed out the priest and refurbished it as the "Temple of Truth." Lequinio ascended the pulpit to deliver a secular sermon. His theme? How to live a happier life. "Happiness," Lequinio declared, "does not exist in *jouissances personelles*," that is, "personal pleasures." "Where must we search for happiness?" the French preacher asked his congregation. "In self-abnegation, in work, in the love of others. This is the secret." The truly happy man is the "man who has made a sacrifice of himself. . . . [he] lives entirely for the happiness of others." He would even face death for others and "mount [the scaffold's] steps with firmness."[49]

We tell ourselves we're doing something noble and enlightened when we're really being nasty and brutish.

That might sound familiar. Lequinio's happy man sounds a lot like the kind of men Jesus inspired his disciples to become at the foot washing.[50] There is something troubling about Lequinio's sermon. Shortly after preaching self-sacrificial love, he penned a report to his fellow revolutionaries in Paris to celebrate his success "finding in Rochefort more men to operate the guillotine than needed." He quickly put his newly recruited executioners to work, and "dozens of heads fell in the city" before Lequinio moved on to Brest, La Rochelle, and the Vendee, where he boasted of "'blowing the brains out' of several prisoners himself."[51] The same Lequinio who preached about living "entirely for the happiness of others" became infamous for forcing French children to walk through the puddles of their beheaded parents' blood.

This grim tale helps us better see why Peter needed to be washed by Jesus himself. The truth is that there is a Lequinio in all of us. We tell ourselves we're doing something noble and enlightened when we're really being nasty and brutish. It is not merely our feet, but our hearts that need washing.

But isn't this kind of inner purity something that only so-called religious people care about — the Catholic in the confessional booth, the Muslim on his knees facing toward Mecca, the Hindu plunging into the Ganges? No. You don't have to be religious in the traditional sense to want that inner voice of conscience to tell you, "You're clean!" University of Texas philosopher J. Budziszewski has researched the human conscience for decades. He has reached the same conclusion about purity that Foucault and Pascal reached about power and pleasure. Budziszewski has found that what we think of as traditionally religious steps to purity — remorse, confession, atonement, reconciliation, and justification — cross over religious-secular lines and crop up in every society and indeed every soul on the planet.[52] The need for purity is every bit as irrepressibly human as our needs for power and pleasure. We all seek catharsis somehow.

Here again the mainstream way-up only leads us downward. We try to feel pure by shifting blame. I've seen my own children willing to believe that stuffed animals came to life when no one was looking (like in *Toy Story*) to hide in our stroller and escape the evil corporate toy store. With age comes a new flock of scapegoats. "The devil made me do it" is a favorite religious option. "My genes made me do it" is often its secular alternative. We prefer a comfortable binary conversation about nature versus nurture because it relieves us of that inconvenient third factor — as a morally responsible choice-making agent, *I* did it. We turn contributing factors into determining factors because it is always easier to say "Mommy culpa," or "Daddy culpa," or "serotonin deficiency culpa," than to utter those dreaded words, "mea culpa."

We might express our deep need to feel pure by playing the comparison game. "I'm not as bad as so-and-so." So-and-so will tell you he's not as bad as what's-his-name, and so on.[53] If blame passing and comparison aren't enough, there's always the power of redefinition. When death camp soldiers couldn't cope with the damning reality that they were destroying innocent lives, they told themselves that the Jews weren't human after all. As an SS propaganda pamphlet put it, the Jew "only looks human, with a human face, but his spirit is lower than that of an animal. . . . [He represents] unparalleled evil, a monster, subhuman."[54] If systematic murderers could change the meaning of words and convince themselves that they were really just glorified rat exterminators, doing the dirty but noble work of purifying their beloved nation from some deadly subhuman scourge, then perhaps they could sleep a little better after a long day of dropping Zyklon B canisters into the death chambers.[55]

What unites the many strategies we use to make ourselves feel blameless is that none of them actually work in the long run.[56] This is where purity, again, looks a lot like power and pleasure. The more honest we are with ourselves, says Foucault, we find "fascism in all of us, in our heads and in our everyday behavior, the fascism that causes us to love power."[57] Pascal found that there is not only a power-seeking fascist, but also a pleasure-seeking hedonist living in our heads. There is also a shady defense attorney living inside us. He zealously pleads for our not-guilty sentence and has no qualms with bending the facts in our favor. He works long hours to convince both the jury of our peers and the judge of our own conscience that our hands are clean, even when they aren't.

What good is it to stay true to ourselves if we are so easily self-deceived?

These, then are the voices in our heads: "You want power? Elevate yourself!" "You want pleasure? Gratify yourself." "You want purity? Justify yourself." In reality, self-centered power-seeking makes us weak, and self-centered pleasure-seeking makes us miserable. Likewise, self-centered purity-seeking makes us corrupt. The worst villains are often those with the most elaborate justifications for why their actions are necessary and even noble. I'm sure Lequinio could tell you all about his great intentions with a twinkle in his eye, even as heads were falling at his feet.

Herein lies the real danger of today's gospel to believe in ourselves and trust the voice within. The "voice within" has a pathological tendency to lie. We often paint our ugliest motives in a saintly light. What good is it to stay true to ourselves if we are so easily self-deceived? What Lequinio needed, what Peter needed, what *we* need, therefore, is true catharsis. We need purified hearts.

Here, again, Jesus invites us into a flipped world. Serving others seems like a free fall toward powerlessness. In Jesus' world, it sends us soaring upward like supermen. Questing for the good of others seems like a descent into a dungeon of pain. In Jesus' world, we find ourselves rising up into *makar*. Likewise, fessing up to our need to be cleaned seems like it would send us tumbling into a pit of shame and damnation. In Jesus' world, we find ourselves lifted up guilt-free and spotless.

3.5 DEAD LIZARDS, LIVING HORSES

We have now moved beyond thinking and feeling into doing. We have seen three irrepressible needs behind what we do. The question is not *whether* we will pursue power, pleasure, and purity. We already are. The question is, whose world we will live in? Will our actions be at home in the fascist's world of subjugating others, or Jesus' world where power comes from serving others? Will we live in a hedonist's world where all of life becomes one long shopping spree, or Jesus' world where we find real happiness questing for the good of others? Will we live in a defense attorney's world of tiring self-justifications, or Jesus' world where we stop defending ourselves and our guilty hearts find their true catharsis?

It is not as if we float between worlds and must choose which to call home. We are already citizens of one world or the other — breathing its air, walking by its gravity, shaped by its rules. But what if we find the allure of the world we were born into wearing off? The zero-sum power game starts to look absurd. Its best players look like children fighting each other for Boardwalk and Park Place in a game where all the paper money and plastic hotels eventually end up in the same dusty box. As our eyes adjust, the world's glitzy consumer spaces, with all their glowing promises of pleasure, look more like a joy-less wasteland. Our ears play tricks too. All that propaganda to "follow our hearts" and "just believe in ourselves" starts to ring hollow. We're getting tired of having to feel so wonderful about ourselves all the time.

It would be a mistake to try to modify our behavior when what is really needed is an all new behaver.

What I am describing is an experience shared by millions over the millennia. There are many ways to describe it — words like "disillusionment," metaphors like "waking up," theological terms like "regeneration." Paul described it like the world dying to us and us dying to the world.[58] John described it like being "born again."[59] Ezekiel described it like a heart transplant in which a divine Surgeon replaces the stones in our chests for beating hearts of flesh.[60]

These images help us to see that it is not enough to say, "Ok, I'll try to implement some more of Jesus' inspirational ethics into my weekly routine. Maybe I'll try to serve more, do more for the good of others, and say 'sorry' more." No. It is not about doing more nice things in the old world; it is a matter dying to the old upside-down world, being reborn for life in the right-side-up world where Jesus lives. It is about receiving new hearts like his to survive and thrive in that world. As Martin Luther King Jr. preached:

> By opening our lives to God in Christ, we become new creatures. This experience, which Jesus spoke of as the new birth, is essential if we are to be transformed nonconformists. . . . Only through an inner spiritual transformation do we gain the strength to fight vigorously the evils of the world in a humble and loving spirit.[61]

King is telling us that it would be a mistake to try to modify our *behavior* when what is really needed is an all new *behaver*. The fascist, the hedonist, and the defense attorney living inside us must not be given another self-help sermon or TED talk, they must be given a good old-fashioned crucifixion.

The New Testament has a name for our inner fascist, hedonist, and defense attorney. Paul called them "the flesh," or "the old self." And this is Paul's advice for dealing with them: "And those who belong to Christ Jesus have crucified the flesh with its passions and desires."[62] In his letter to Rome, he echoes, "For if you live according to the flesh you will die, but if by the Spirit you put to death the deeds of the body, you will live."[63] As John Owen put it in his classic work, *The Mortification of Sin*,

Indwelling sin is compared to a person, a living person, called the old man, with his faculties and properties, his wisdom, craft, subtlety, strength; this (says the apostle) must be killed, put to death, mortified; that is, have its power, life, vigor, and strength to produce its effects, taken away by the Spirit.[64]

There is an unexpected beauty in the death described by Paul and Owen. C. S. Lewis gives us a glimpse of this beauty in *The Great Divorce*. In Lewis's fictional account of a flying bus trip to the afterlife, we meet a tired man with a red lizard living on his shoulder. The red lizard (which Lewis tells us represents lust) has a chain shackled around the man's neck and whispers orders into the man's ear. It is a strange image, no doubt, but not half as strange as what happens to the lizard. The shackled man finally breaks down and gives an angel permission to strike the protesting lizard dead. The angel obliges and the red lizard falls to the ground, gasping and writhing in agony. Surprisingly, the dead lizard starts to twitch and twirl, and unfurl until it rises gloriously, stamping and neighing on all fours. The dead lizard resurrects as a magnificent horse. The grateful man leaps onto its back and rides off into the horizon toward heaven.

It is a testament to Lewis's theological brilliance that the man is not left asexual after his long-cherished lizard of lust is struck dead. Rather, the man's sexuality rises up as something beautiful and noble, moving him heavenward. When we turn our heads, close our eyes, and ask God to slay our inner fascists, hedonists, and defense attorneys, we are not left without power, pleasure, and purity. To remove these drives would leave us less human. They are so deeply intertwined with human nature that any attempt to remove them altogether would leave the patient flatlined. Rather, as the fascist on our shoulder writhes and dies, the real power of a Servant rises in us. As the hedonist gasps for air and falls motionless, the real pleasure of a Quester sparks to life. As the defense attorney falls silent, the real purity of a Saint begins to shine. Jesus does not remove our desires for power, pleasure, and purity. He redeems them.

✴

There is a biblical word for what rises from the ground when God has done his flesh-slaying work in us — "holiness." In fact, holiness is what we have really been talking about this entire chapter.

Scholars will tell you that holiness means separateness, distinction, otherness. They are right. But we should not reduce that otherness to a list of behavioral axioms, "Don't smoke, chew, or go with those who do." It goes much deeper. Holiness in Scripture has to do with otherness in how we pursue power, pleasure, and purity. Don't blend in to a system that promises power by self-elevation, pleasure by self-gratification, or purity by self-justification. Be nonconformists. "Be holy as God is holy."[65] Be powerful by empowering others. Find pleasure working for the joy of others. Find purity from Jesus himself. It may seem upside-down, but that is how we find real meaning.

A PRAYER TO FLIP

Jesus, make our actions meaningful like yours. Flip us so we can live in your right-side-up world. Kill the self-elevating fascist inside us, and make us powerful servants who lift others up. Crucify the self-gratifying hedonist inside us, and resurrect real joy in us as we quest for the good of others. Silence the self-justifying attorney in us. We confess our sin, and ask for the purity that only you can give. Wash us. Amen.

4

LOVE

Mirroring the Radical Relationality of Jesus

I do not ask for these only, but also for those who will believe in me through their word, that they may all be one, just as you, Father, are in me, and I in you, that they also may be in us, so that the world may believe that you have sent me. The glory that you have given me I have given to them, that they may be one even as we are one, I in them and you in me, that they may become perfectly one, so that the world may know that you sent me and loved them even as you loved me. Father, I desire that they also, whom you have given me, may be with me where I am, to see my glory that you have given me because you loved me before the foundation of the world.

—JOHN 17:20–24

> Love is real and genuine because we were created by a God whose very character is love. The Bible teaches that there has been love and communication between the members of the Trinity from all eternity. Love is not an illusion created by the genes to promote our evolutionary survival, but an aspect of human nature that reflects the fundamental fabric of ultimate reality.
>
> NANCY PEARCEY

So far, we have seen that we become like what we worship, and that worshiping Jesus makes our intellects more reasonable, our emotions more just, and our actions more holy. But to think and feel and act in isolation, without community, is to miss the point of Jesus' mission. To paraphrase Paul, "If I have the intellect to join MENSA, the emotion to inspire revolutions, and the meaningful action to win a Nobel Peace Prize, but I have not love, then I am nothing."

4.1 "LONELINESS IS SUCH A DRAG"

In the song "Without Love," the great baritone crooner, Johnny Cash, echoes Paul's insight. Without love, Cash sings, he is just a machine, barely human. "I will die without love," he concludes. These were lyrics that Cash could sing with credibility.[1] In the fall of 1967, the country star crawled deep into Nickajack Cave in the Tennessee country and laid down in the blackness to die alone. As the Man in Black later recounted,

The absolute lack of light was appropriate, for at that moment I was as far from God as I have ever been. My separation from him, the deepest and most ravaging of the various kinds of loneliness I'd felt over the years, seemed finally complete.[2]

That complete loneliness was something like what rock legend John Lennon experienced between booze-fueled escapades on his self-described "Lost Weekend," Lennon's two-year hiatus from his wife Yoko. It was during that time that Lennon wrote "Scared." The first verse opens with, "I'm scared," repeated eight times for emphasis. Verse 2 adds a single letter — "I'm scarred." In the final verse Lennon laments how he is "tired of being alone." This is, of course, the same Lennon who gave us one of the most anthemic lines in the history of rock with "All You Need Is Love."

Famous thrill-seeker and counterculture icon Chris McCandless questioned whether all we need is love. "You are wrong if you think Joy emanates only or principally from human relationships," McCandless wrote a friend. "God has placed it all around us. It is in everything and anything we might experience."[3] Practicing what he preached, he set off "into the wild" (as the book and movie based on his life were titled). He wanted to experience the pure rush of life in the Alaskan bush. After more than two months without human contact, he opened his journal and scribbled in all caps, "HAPPINESS ONLY REAL WHEN SHARED." It was one of his final entries. Chris McCandless died the following month, alone in a broken-down bus, miles from civilization. A handwritten S.O.S. was posted to the bus with the haunting words, "I am all alone. This is no joke. In the name of God, please remain to save me."

We rarely feel so effortlessly and happily ourselves as when we are deeply in synch with others.

What Cash, Lennon, and McCandless realized, each in his own way, was something that God said at the dawn of humanity. Genesis 2:18 reads, "It is not good for man to be alone." God sees a solitary Adam and speaks the very first malediction in the Bible (*malus*, meaning bad, and *dictio*, meaning speech or word).[4] The Bible begins as a series of benedictions, or good words, spoken over creation. The heavens, the earth, day, and night. It is good. Sky, water, clouds. It is good. Oceans, land, trees, flowers, fruit. It is good. Stars, seasons, the moon. It is good. Fish, birds, wildlife. It is good. But a man all by himself in a garden, or in a Tennessee cave, or in a Los Angeles bar, or in the Alaskan wild — "It is *not* good for man to be alone."

Why does this ancient verse ring so true? Why is it that "loneliness is such a drag," to quote the great philosopher Jimi Hendrix? Why is a grandparent with little human contact beyond the talking images on a television, an ex-lover withdrawn after a broken relationship, an odd theologian who exerts more effort on books than people — why are these are all tragic figures? Why do prisons punish their most unruly inmates with solitary confinement? What makes "the hole" so chilling? Why do we sing, dance, and write so much about love, the invigorating power of it, the yearning desire for it, the lamenting loss of it?[5] And just as closed physical systems tend toward a state of entropy, why do our psyches, cut off from relational energy outside ourselves, tend toward a state of disorder and eventually collapse? With too much time and space from others, we go start to fray and become strange, even to ourselves. Yet we rarely feel so effortlessly and happily ourselves as when we are deeply in synch with others.

Harvard researcher Robert Putnam found that "if you belong to no groups but decide to join one, you cut your risk of dying the next year *in half*."[6] One famous study even found that relationally well-connected people with bad health habits — smoking, poor diet, and heavy drinking — consistently outlive isolated people with healthy habits. Relationally disconnected people were *three times* more likely to die than connected people![7] Why are we such profoundly social creatures?

4.2 HOW RADICAL IS LOVE?

One possible answer to these questions is that to be without love is to be cut off from reality itself because love is, quite simply, the most radical thing that exists. The word "radical," from the Latin *radix*, describes the fundamental nature and source of something, getting to its very root (hence, the word "radishes" for the red roots we put on salads). John's Gospel is, among other things, a stunning revelation that love is far more radical than we knew.

Mark begins his Gospel of Jesus' life with a quote from the book of Isaiah. Matthew starts his story even farther back, tracing Jesus' genealogy to Abraham. Luke goes even farther, tracing Jesus' roots all the way back to Adam. If Matthew and Mark are radical in a Jewish way, telling their Jesus stories from deep within Israel's history, and Luke is an anthropological radical, telling his Jesus story from the roots of the human race, then John is a cosmological radical.[8] He starts at the origin of the universe itself, borrowing the opening line of the entire Bible — "In the beginning." But John is even more radical than Genesis. Genesis 1 merely takes us to the beginning of the heavens and the earth. John 1 goes back even farther when he tells us that "the Word" — the *Logos* — existed even before the cosmos sprang into being.

Greek philosophers (the Stoics in particular) had their own *Logos*, not a "He" but an "It," an impersonal rational principle that explains the logical order of the universe. John's *Logos* is not a principle but a Person. Before Isaiah, Abraham, and Adam, and even before the heavens and the earth, there existed a Personal Being, not a something but a Someone. That Someone, John tells us, "was God." Moreover, this divine Someone did not create the world out of lonesomeness or boredom. Rather, the *Logos* who "was God" was also "with God." There is a diversity of persons in the unity of God, not a single Someone, but *Someones*. Interpersonal relationship was, therefore, possible even before anything or anyone else sprang into being.

From there, John moves beyond a philosophy word, *Logos,* to a family word, "Son." The *Logos* is not just a divine Someone, but the divine Son. There is a reason that Christians throughout history have never described God as Uncle, Nephew, and Holy Spirit, or Boss, Employee, and Holy Spirit, or President, Citizen, and Holy Spirit. None of these images would capture the depth of interpersonal love that has always existed in the very being of God.

John then takes us deeper into this love as the language of *with-ness* is eclipsed by the language of *in-ness*: "I am in the Father and the Father is in me," says Jesus.[9] Then, by the time we get to John 17, we get to eavesdrop on a conversation between the beloved Son and his loving Father.

We overhear one of the most radical statements in the entire Bible. Jesus prays: "Father . . . you loved me before the foundation of the world."[10] What is older than Abraham, than Adam, than even the heavens and the earth? What is the most radical thing in existence? Love. The doctrine of the Trinity — one God who exists eternally as Father, Son, and Holy Spirit — means that love is more radical than war, than heartbreak, than hate, than loneliness.

Theologians have long talked about *creatio ex nihilo* — a Latin phrase signifying God's creation of the universe "out of nothing." God is not like a painter who needs pre-existing brushes, paint, and canvas to create beauty. When he said, "Let there be" things came to be that, prior to that creative command, were not. We should affirm right along with *creatio ex nihilo* the truth of *creatio ex amor* — creation from love. Our universe was not spoken into existence by a lonely or bored deity seeking company or entertainment. God was already enjoying intimate relationship when he said "Let there be."[11] Because John traces the genesis of everything to this God of love, relationality is written into the very structure of creation, and the very structure of our own hearts.

John has offered us a captivating cosmic picture of why "it is not good for man to be alone." But why should we, in the twenty-first century, care about the radical views of a first-century Gospel author? I offer two reasons. For the first, consider Denmark's most celebrated wordsmith, Søren Kierkegaard. Kierkegaard's poetry, for all of its brilliance, is notoriously confusing. If you come to understand the Danish poet's first love, his passionate affection for a woman named Regine Olsen, then his cryptic work takes on a new light. His poems make more sense. Likewise, the poem of creation as a whole and our individual lives, like lines in that poem, find their deepest meaning only in light of the Poet's first love.

The modern world's view of love is not nearly radical enough.

That is one reason to care about John's radical view of love: if he is right about the pre-cosmic love between Father, Son, and Spirit, then that revelation sheds new light on the whole universe and our entire lives. A second reason is that the modern world faces a real crisis with the meaning of love itself. Philosopher Francis Schaeffer explains:

> Modern man quite properly considers the conception of love to be overwhelmingly important as he looks at personality. Nevertheless, he faces a very real problem as to the meaning of love. Though modern man tries to hang everything on the word *love*, love can easily degenerate into something very much less because he really does not understand it. He has no adequate universal for love.[12]

For Schaeffer, the modern world's view of love is not nearly radical enough. It lacks metaphysical depth. Take Johnny Rotten's famous definition in which "love is two minutes and fifty-two seconds of squishing noises." Without any reference point beyond our own biology, emotions, and cultural fictions — without what Schaeffer called an "adequate universal for love" — "love" becomes little more than an endorphin rush, a sentimental buzzword, or a marketing slogan.

Schaeffer saw a radical alternative. "Love," he said, "existed between the persons of the Trinity before the foundation of the world. This being so, the existence of love as we know it in our makeup does not have an origin in chance, but from that which has always been."[13] Here, in the Trinity, Schaeffer saw the great hope for modern man. He believed that by getting back to the root, to "that which has always been," love will blossom forth with meaning and color. We can see far more to love than the slender categories of a modern worldview allow us to see. And in the Trinity, Schaeffer believed, we can experience love on deep levels to which modernism has long restricted access.

Below we will focus on one of the primary passages where Schaeffer learned his radical Trinitarianism. John 17 records a prayer from Jesus to the Father. In it we will see three ways that the love between Father, Son, and Spirit deepens what it means to love in our lonesome century.

4.3 LOVE'S SHAPE: "THAT THEY MAY BE ONE"

One of the first things we discover about love when we start with the Trinity is that real love means unity and diversity. False love is what happens when either unity devours diversity or diversity devours unity.

One or Many?

To see the difference, consider a very old problem that perplexed the Greek philosophers, a problem that seems bizarre if not altogether pointless to a twenty-first-century mind. When trying to make sense out of the world, some ancient Greek philosophers became corporeal monists, which is to say that they tried to explain the world by reducing everything to one physical element. For Thales, all is water. For Anaximenes, all is air. For Heraclitus, all is fire, and so on. Then came the corporeal pluralists, championing diversity over unity. For Anaxagoras, reality is made up of infinite physical particulars. For Empedocles, reality is earth, wind, and fire moved by the forces of Love and Hate. For Democritus, it is all just atoms falling in the void. So on the one side you had Greeks like Thales who were so big on unity that they left little room for meaningful differences in the world, while others, like Anaxagoras, were so big on diversity that their world became hopelessly fragmented.

Thales or Anaxagoras? The One or the Many? Unity or Diversity? It is an ancient problem. Isn't their problem our problem too? Isn't it *the* problem behind the problems we face in the twenty-first-century world of romance, family life, politics, and spirituality? Picture two couples. First, there is Bob and Mary. Bob and Mary's food and entertainment choices, conversation topics, social circles, and even their home décor are almost entirely one-sided, expressions of Bob's dominant personality. Mary has slowly become Bob's soul-less clone. Her identity has totally dissolved into his. Unity has devoured diversity, and we are dealing with something less than love. Next, there is John and Layla. John and Layla are so independent, guarded, and uncompromising that there is very little, if anything, holding them together as a couple. Diversity has devoured unity.

Picture two families. The Smith family has an all-unity-no-diversity home. Every family member is forced into a steel cookie cutter that severs off some of their most beautiful edges and distinct gifts. In the Jones home, by contrast, everyone does his own thing. There is no overlapping vision of what is true, good, and beautiful. There is no real connection beyond a shared last name, some common DNA, and the same roof over sleeping heads.

Think of two nations. In one nation we find the totalitarian drive, what Dostoyevsky described as the push "to unite all in a common, harmonious, and incontestable ant-hill." This "need of universal unity is," according to the Russian novelist, "the last torment of men,"[14] a point made chillingly clear by the dehumanizing regimes of the past hundred years. The world has had its share of Soviet Unions and North Koreas, nations where citizens find their individuality minced through the meat-grinder of some authoritarian State. Then there are nations that are so fiercely individualistic — each citizen marching to the tempo of his own desires — that social fragmentation, tribalization, and loneliness run rampant.[15] There is little to no sense of unity. The ironically titled *United* States of America comes to mind.[16]

Consider two religious devotees. An Eastern monk sits in lotus position pondering Brahman, that is, "the One" at the root of all existence. From this oneness it follows that "divisions are imaginary lines drawn by small minds," as Yogananda put it. *The Teachings of Buddha* echoes, "apparent distinctions exist because of people's absurd and discriminating thoughts."[17] If unity is more fundamental than diversity, then the more enlightened our monk becomes, the less room there will be in his world for apples as apples, dogs as dogs, good as good, evil as evil, me as me, or you as you. Rather, "this world is only an illusion," says Siddhartha; "good and evil are one and the same," says Vivekananda; "Hate is not a different thing than love," says Rajneesh; "all individuality dissolves into universal undifferentiated oneness," says Capra. "Let, therefore, no man love anything," the Buddha concludes.[18]

We have a way, often subconsciously, of re-enacting our origin stories.

A religious devotee may lose sight of love in the opposite direction, that is, by making diversity more fundamental than unity. Take the ancient Marduk worshiper. According to an ancient Mesopotamian creation myth called *Enuma Elish,* our world came not from oneness but from division, the god Marduk's battle with the snake god Tiamat. Marduk slays Tiamat and filets her corpse in two, making the heavens and the earth. Conflict is, thus, the most radical thing in our world.

It's no surprise, then, that such polytheisms have been forces of division throughout history, with the devotees of one tribal deity warring against the devotees of another tribal deity. By splitting, competing, and warring, these worshipers were doing unto others what their gods had been doing to each other in the ages before humankind. Something similar can occur in the modern West when people trace the origin of our species to a bloody struggle where the fit survive and the weak are eaten alive. For better or worse, we have a way, often subconsciously, of reenacting our origin stories, and embodying whatever we think is the most radical thing in existence.

Thales's problem is Mary's problem is the Smith family's problem is North Korea's problem is the Eastern monk's problem: How do we have oneness without erasing important differences? In the other direction, we find the problem that haunted Anaxagoras, Layla, America, and the Marduk worshiper: How do we preserve important differences without leaving everything and everyone hopelessly torn apart? This is not an abstract brainteaser à la the sound of one hand clapping, the plot holes in time travel movies, or Schrödinger's Cat. How we approach the question of unity and diversity — whether we side with Team Thales or Team Anaximander — is an existential question with real-life consequences. It has everything to do with how we love, and whether we are actually loving others when we think we are.

Oneness

This is where Jesus' John 17 prayer comes in. Jesus prays for his followers, "that they may be one" just as he and the Father "are one." Jesus wants his followers to show the cracked world what radical unity looks like, the kind of unity that existed long before loneliness, hatred, or war. But Jesus is *not* praying for the oneness we find in lop-sided romances, rigid homes, totalitarian states, or eastern ashrams. He is not seeking a unity that wipes out our individuality. Jesus prays for a unity that *enhances*, not erases, diversity, oneness that makes us *more*, not less, our selves.

We know this because the oneness enjoyed between the Father and the Son makes each of them *more*, not less, themselves.[19] God the Father is who he is — God *the Father* — only because of his relationship with the Son, and vice versa. Take the beloved Son away and the Father is no longer God *the Father*; take away the loving Father and the Son is no longer God *the Son*, which is to say that God would not be God. God is Unity *and*

Diversity; as British theologian Colin Gunton clarifies, "The persons do not simply enter into relations with one another, but are constituted by one another in the relations. Father, Son, and Spirit are eternally what they are by virtue of what they are from and to one another."[20]

If we lose sight of these eternal relationships we are left with an altogether different deity. We may be left with the disinterested Clockmaker, who winds up the universe, then lets it tick away while he retires to a posh galactic golf course to polish his short game. Or the Lonesome Bachelor, who likes Labradoodles and long sunset walks, desperately seeking human affirmation. Or the Magical Life Force, the Cosmic Killjoy, the Fearsome Dictator. The revelation of God as Father and Son comes jolting like an earthquake through our stone pantheon of competing gods. It turns to rubble and dust any concept of the divine in which love and relationship are not at the eternal core of God's being. The God who is Father and Son shows us that a loving relationship of unity and diversity is what makes God quintessentially God.

We don't have to either erase all distinctions to get to some more fundamental Unity or rip everything apart to get at some more fundamental Diversity.

One immensely freeing implication of this God's existence is that, as we try to get at ultimate reality, we are not forced to choose between Thales or Anaximander, Mary or Layla, North Korea or America, Brahman or Marduk. We are freed from the false Either-Or. We don't have to *either* erase all distinctions to get to some more fundamental Unity *or* rip everything apart to get at some more fundamental Diversity. "That which has always been" — the love between Father and Son — means that both Unity and Diversity existed before the universe. Both are eternal, primal, and fundamental. So Jesus prays for us to enjoy that beautiful kind of oneness that does not erase but makes us more truly and uniquely our selves, something like the oneness he and the Father have always enjoyed.

How can something be more utterly itself by being one with something other than itself? Imagine that you are walking down a vacant street and are struck by a disturbing sight. There, on the sidewalk, lies a mysterious lone eyeball, apparently plucked from someone's poor, staggering body. Totally disconnected, it would hardly be an eyeball in the most meaningful sense. It couldn't see or be truly what it is. If a friendly opthamologist salvaged the eyeball and reunited it with the owner's body, would the eyeball suddenly lose its eyeball-ness? On the contrary, by unification it would become more truly itself. As it enters into a relationship of oneness with things that aren't eyeballs — an interconnected and elegant network of optic nerves, muscles, and neurons — it becomes more unique, purposeful, and essential *as an eyeball*. A body is precisely that beautiful kind of unity that enhances, rather than erases, diversity.[21]

It is self-giving that makes for a vigorously healthy body. The eye, in a sense, gives itself to the rest of the body, so that the hand knows to grab the toothbrush and not the toilet brush, and the legs know when to walk and when a train is approaching. This pattern — something giving itself for the good of others and thereby becoming more itself — happens in our bodies every day. The hands serve the mouth by giving it an apple. The mouth serves the digestive system by pureeing the fruit. The digestive system breaks it down, and sends the filtered nutrients to the circulatory system, which, in turn, powers the muscles for even more acts of life-giving service. This is why body is one of Paul's favorite images for the kind of unity God creates in his people.[22] Christians living in community are to exhibit precisely this kind of intricate chain reaction of self-giving that we find in a healthy body. "When each part is working properly," says Paul, Jesus "makes the body grow so that it builds itself up in love."[23] But if I exist only for myself, then I become as strange and lifeless as a severed eyeball on the sidewalk.

Self-giving

The metaphor takes us further. A body can be an elegant system of unity and diversity. But something mysterious happens when a lone body becomes one with a different body. In a good marriage, two very different people become one in an identity-enhancing way. The husband becomes more truly who he is as a husband when he gives himself away to his bride, and vice-versa. That self-giving union may even spark brand-new life into existence.

And so a profound pattern of unity and diversity emerges. By becoming one with something other than itself, an eyeball not only becomes more truly an eyeball, but we also have a more whole body. When a body becomes one with something other than itself, it not only becomes more truly a body, but we have something new and beautiful — a bride. As that bride becomes one with something other than herself, the bride is not only more truly a bride, but we have something new and beautiful — a family. When that family becomes one with something other than itself, it is not only more truly a family, but something new and beautiful comes into being — a community, and eventually a nation. Self-giving has a wonderfully explosive way of causing more life, more beauty, and more love to spring into being.

We become most truly ourselves only when we give ourselves to something other than ourselves.

If self-giving is like a Big Bang expanding outward, making the universe bigger, then self-seeking is a black hole. When we live only for ourselves, we become consumers instead of creators. We take, rather than make, light. In earlier chapters we encountered "the paradox of hedonism," how the most inwardly obsessed people, those most fixated on their own happiness, tend to become the most miserable. We can now appreciate this paradox as something more than a contingent quirk of the human psyche. It is not as if there is some alien world out there where the most self-seeking extraterrestrials happened to evolve as the most happy. The fact that Creatures + Self-seeking = Emptiness is more like the fact that 1 + 1 = 2. It is true from one end of the cosmos to the other, in every possible world. Why? Because it has to do with the very essence of the God who made everything, a God who is and always has been self-giving. C. S. Lewis takes us to the heart of the matter:

> In self-giving, if anywhere, we touch a rhythm not only of all creation but of all being . . . self exists to be abdicated and, by that abdication, it becomes more truly self. . . . This is not a . . . law which we can escape. . . . What is outside the system of self-giving is . . . simply and solely Hell . . . that fierce imprisonment in the self. Self-giving is ultimate reality.[24]

How, then, do we escape the "Hell" of self-seeking? How do we stop brooding alone and find our steps in the "rhythm of all being"? There's no way around it: *we have to give ourselves away*. Given the kind of creatures we are, the kind of creation we inhabit, and the kind of Creator who made it, self-giving is the only road back to reality. Like eyeballs in a healthy body, bodies in a beautiful marriage, members in a good family, or families in a thriving community, we become most truly ourselves only when we give ourselves to something other than ourselves.

It should not surprise us, then, that when the New Testament writers tried to describe what church is supposed to be, they reached for the metaphors of body, bride, family, and nation. In each picture, we find precisely the kind of self-giving that makes us more ourselves. We see beyond the false Either-Ors that leave us lost or lonely. We glimpse the beautiful Both-And, the God of Unity and Diversity, who invites us into the dance. And with the religions of Brahman and Marduk, nations like North Korea and the United States, families like the Smiths and Jones, romances like Mary's and Layla's, and worldviews like Thales's and Anaximander's, isn't that exactly the kind of love we need?[25]

4.4 LOVE'S SECURITY: "I IN THEM"

We may find ourselves in another ancient dilemma. Take the phrase, "You're the first person I have ever told." In two decades of ministry, I have had the privilege of hearing this phrase more than once. With it come telltale non-verbals — slumped shoulders, fidgeting fingers, and evasive eyes. Sometimes the body goes rigid, as if a T-Rex with motion-triggered vision was waiting to pounce from behind the bookcase. If the body language could be translated into English, it would say, "I'm afraid that if you really see me, you'll reject me."

Fear

But when dark secrets first meet daylight, and people are met with love, it is a beautiful thing. The muscles start to thaw, and the oxygen starts to flow. Bright, unforced smiles return. It is like an upside-down version of Plato's most famous allegory. When we descend into the cave, deep below the world of social expectations, with its facade houses, long rows of manicured lawns, self-guarded small talk, and bleached white smiles, and find that there, underground, in reality, we are loved — it is one of the greatest feelings in the world.

There is, however, an almost universal fear that keeps us from making the subterranean venture. It is the fear that revelation and rejection go together, that the deeper we go into reality, the less we will be loved. So we live in the shiny world of forms. We hang pretty self-portraits. We match them with profound/clever/witty placards. Then, visitors can ooh and aww from a safe distance. You're a stand-up comic, supermodel, expert on politics, religion, and the culinary arts? Me too!

To be fair, social media is not the culprit. It is more of a conduit for an impulse as old as Adam. He hid behind pretty bushes in the Garden. We do the same thing with our technology. Behind this impulse lurks that all-too-unquestioned fear that with reality comes rejection. Our dilemma becomes: either be exposed to reality and get rejected or hide in a nonreality where we might win acceptance. It is a dilemma older than Thales and Anaximander. It is our dilemma. It also happens to be a false dilemma.

Again, Jesus' prayer in John 17 frees us from a false Either-Or. Right after he prays for the unity and diversity of his followers, Jesus says to his Father, "you loved them even as you loved me." Read those eight words again slowly. In them we find the solution to Adam's dilemma, to our dilemma: How does the Father love the Son? He loves the Son deeply, happily, unapologetically, irreversibly, infinitely, with the full weight of divine perfection, without reservation, without wavering, without fail. That is how you are loved. Maybe you didn't hear me the first time. *You* are loved deeply, happily, unapologetically, irreversibly, infinitely. *You* are loved with the full weight of divine perfection. *You* are loved without reservation, without wavering, without fail. "You loved them even as you loved me," Jesus said.

The deeper we descend into reality, the deeper we are loved.

After allowing yourself to jump with wild abandon and fall on the ground in a smiling heap of thankfulness [take a moment], focus with me on the word *kathos*. Theologians have long tried to condense the good news of the Bible to a single word, small Greek prepositions like *de, en,* and *uper*. *De* means "but," as in we were spiritually dead *but* God made us alive. *En* means "in" to express all the life and privilege we have *in* Christ. *Uper* means "for" or "in place of," as in Jesus died *for/in place of* sinners. But right along with the good news of But, In, and For we find the gospel of Even As. The little Greek preposition — *kathos* — captures the exhilarating truth that God the Father doesn't merely love us; he loves us *even as* he loves the Son.

This 'Even As' gospel shows how inverted our thinking about love has become. We avoid the depths to seek acceptance on the surface. The truth is that, the deeper we descend into reality, the deeper we are loved. Venture below the social media buzz, below family drama, and even below the voices in your own head. Press on underneath all that is fallen, dysfunctional, and crazed. Go until there is no such thing as deeper. There you behold the most radiant, perfect, and sane Being in existence. His whisper silences all of the jumbled, head-spinning static overhead. He now declares for you all the intimacy, joy, and affection he has been declaring to his Son forever. Philosophers told us there was only a cold black abyss. Gurus told us to expect a grand impersonal energy. Religious zealots had us expecting a white bearded judge poised to crush us with his giant gavel. But, they never hit metaphysical bedrock. There, at the bottom of all things, is Love.

Gifts

In the next breath, Jesus refers to people the Father loves as those "whom you have given me." Giving is the primary love language the Father speaks to the Son throughout the Fourth Gospel. He gives the Son "life in himself," "authority to execute judgment," "sheep," "authority over all flesh," "words," "the name," "glory," and more.[26] One of those gifts, according to Jesus, is people. Anyone who believes in Jesus is a gift to Jesus — an expression of the Father's infinite love.

You could backpack Europe, tour the seminar circuit with celebrity gurus, eat mushrooms and sit in Child's Pose chanting "Om" at a misty mountain monastery, while Deepak Chopra whispers quantum mysteries in your headphones. You could soul search your entire life away and never find a more profound answer to the existential question — Who am I? If you believe in Jesus, then you are a gift. You are not your spiritual awareness, or lack thereof. You are not your love life, social status, religious performance, psychological togetherness, or lack thereof. If you believe in Jesus, then at the bottom of everything, you are a living, breathing "I love you" the Father speaks to the Son.

We are who we are not on the basis of how well we love, but because of how well God loves.

Objectively, two changes occur when we answer the question — Who am I? — in this way. (I say "objectively" because feelings come and go, but these changes remain true of us nonetheless.) First, our identity no longer rests on our performance. Second, our identity can never be lost. We know this because of the way in which Jesus prays for his love-gift. He prays, "Father, I desire that they also, whom you have given me, may be with me where I am, to see my glory."[27] Jesus wants to be with his love-gift forever. He wants them to behold and enjoy him, in all of his weight and radiance, for all eternity. So he asks his Father to make that happen.[28] And because he loves the Son so much, with the full weight of his divine perfections, the Father can, and *will*, make that happen. He happily fulfills his Son's request. In other words, we are who we are not on the basis of how well we love, but because of how well God loves.[29] Our identity rests on his performance, not ours.

Imagine a dad who brews a big case of a rare, delicious beverage to enjoy with his boy. As the father makes his way to his son's apartment, his arms start to burn, so he lightens the case by a few bottles. Then, he trips on a crack and a few more bottles pop and fizzle on the sidewalk. Some neighborhood hooligans harass the old man and steal a few more. By the time he knocks on the front door, only a few bottles remain in the case. The son swings the door open and there stands his blushing father with a half-empty case. Over the father's shoulder, the son spots the sad trail of bottle shrapnel, and brown liquid running into the gutters. Every bottle let go, stolen, or broken is a bottle not enjoyed by the son. The extent to which bottles are lost is the extent to which the father's love has not reached its full, intended expression.

Is the Father so powerless? Could we destroy ourselves and leave him blushing at the Son's doorstep? Could anything prevent the beloved Son from savoring every last drop that the Father wants him to enjoy? No! When Jesus asks for his love-gift to enjoy him and be enjoyed by him forever, the Father delivers.

Security

If only the all-powerful Father held us, that would be enough. But John 6 reveals the Father's will that the Son would "lose nothing of all" that the Father has given him.[30] And Jesus *always* does the Father's will.[31] Doing the Father's will is the primary love-language he speaks to his Father.[32] That is why, when it comes to holding his love-gift secure, Jesus does not say, "I'll *try*," but "I *will* raise him up on the last day."[33] It is why, in John 10, Jesus' love-gifts are given eternal life, will never perish, and cannot be snatched both from the Son's hand and the Father's hand.

The all-powerful Son holds us secure in loving response to his Father's will. The Father wraps his omnipotent fingers around the Son's hand in loving response to his Son's will. Then the Holy Spirit — the third divine person of the Trinity — wraps himself around us as a "guarantee of our inheritance."[34] We are held in the indestructible grip of the loving, Triune God. Here we can let go of all fears. Our destiny does not rest on our own performance, but on the Father's, the Son's, and the Spirit's ability to lovingly carry out one another's wills. You could no more lose yourself, than the Triune God could fail to love himself.

This love between Father, Son, and Spirit holds us secure in ways that no modern love can. We can slip through the fingers of temperamental gods, fallen lovers, or imperfect parents, and shatter on the sidewalk. As Henri Nouwen put it, "As long as we keep running around, anxiously trying to affirm ourselves or be affirmed by others, we remain blind to the One who has loved us first."[35] But when "the One who has loved us first" — the tri-personal God — takes hold of us, we are utterly secure, and that security fundamentally changes all our other relationships. We no longer love others to *become* loved, but *because* we are loved. There is a world of difference between the two. We can love people as ends rather than as means to the end of our own feelings of adequacy and worth. We no longer have to go to desperate measures if they don't make us feel adequate enough. We make no more insecure attempts to determine our love-worthiness. When we go deep to "the One who loved us first," we can forever settle the question — "Am I loved?" — in a way that frees us up to truly love others.

4.5 LOVE'S SOURCE: "FATHER, I ASK"

True love is about unity and diversity. It is also about security. But there is a third thing we learn about true love from John 17. We find it in the most obvious fact of Jesus' prayer — the fact that it is a *prayer*. The implication is that the Father listens and actually answers.[36] God has the power to bring us to love in ways we can't bring ourselves to love. We shouldn't hesitate to ask him to do so.

John 17 is at the crest of a long tradition of such prayers. When the Christians in first-century Thessalonica were exploiting one another for sex and money, Paul prayed, "May the Lord cause you to increase and abound in love."[37] When Augustine faced his personal vices in the fourth century, he asked God to increase his love with his famous words, "Grant what thou commandest." As the African Bishop clarified, "He to whom is given by God the love of God, and the love of our neighbor for God's sake; he indeed, ought to pray insistently that this gift may be . . . increased in him."[38]

In the fifteenth century, Thomas à Kempis had an epiphany that "love is born of God," and so he prayed,

> Expand my heart with love, that I may feel its transforming power, and may even be dissolved in its holy fire! Let me be possessed by thy love, and ravished from myself! Let me love thee more than myself; let me love myself only for thy sake; and in thee love all others.[39]

In the seventeenth century, John Donne came to the same realization in his fourteenth *Holy Sonnet*: "Except you enthrall me, shall never be free. Nor ever chaste, except you ravish me." From the famous *Prayer of Saint Francis*: "Where there is hatred, let me sow love. . . . O Divine Master, grant that I may not so much seek . . . to be loved, as to love." Whenever we ask

God to break some anti-loving habit of our own hearts, heal a marriage racked by selfishness, end a social injustice, or save some lost soul — we step inside the strong flow of that tradition. And they are prayers that God loves to answer.

Years ago I had a student — "Sam" — who forever changed the way I pray. Sam seemed to have a personal rain cloud (like you see in old cartoons). He looked ashamed. He had a hard time with eye contact. I never saw him smile. One day I understood why. In a courageous move, Sam told me about his decade-long struggle against pornography addiction. He explained a terrible loneliness, and how people in real life began to feel more unknowable and two-dimensional — like images on a screen. He hacked his way through Parental Controls. He recruited and then dodged accountability partners. He made bold "Never again!" promises to Jesus until all the exclamation points turned into question marks. Nothing worked.

Had he been one of the many "Sams" I had met in years prior, I would have told him not to give up. Keep up the fight. Try harder. Instead, I encouraged Sam to utterly despair.

"You've been fighting this for ten years, right?"

"Right."

"You've tried all kinds of self-help strategies, right?"

"Right."

"Have you made an inch of progress?"

"It's only getting worse," he replied.

"Then it's time to despair. Totally despair of your own ability to ever conquer your addiction. It's just not going to happen."

There was a long pause. Sam broke the silence.

"Then what?"

"Let's try something drastic," I suggested. "In class we've been exploring, from the Old and New Testaments, how God has the ability to neutralize the anti-love powers in human hearts. We cannot kill the sin in our hearts, but he can. Let's pray together as if that is actually true because it is."

It was a risky proposition. If it failed, like everything else he had tried, then Sam would have reason to write off all the theology we had been learning as useless, spiritual mumbo jumbo.

"Let's ask God to cause you to increase and abound in love," I continued. "Let's ask him to change your heart so that you find him irresistibly sweet and sin repulsive. Let's ask him to recalibrate your affections so that reducing people, who bear his image, to two, soulless dimensions becomes unthinkable to you."

For the following week, Sam and I prayed the same way Paul prayed for those struggling with *porneia* in Thessalonica: "May the Lord cause you to increase and abound in love."[40] We asked God every day to not only eliminate a pornography addiction, but to generate powerful, new love to take its place. We asked for what Thomas Chalmers described so well as "the expulsive power of a new affection."[41]

When Sam entered the classroom the following week, I barely recognized him. The rain cloud was gone. What an old King James Bible would call his "countenance" — the outward appearance of the soul's inner state — changed dramatically. It was like catching a first glimpse of the real Sam, the one who had been trapped inside a walking cadaver, and he was something glorious. I will never forget the way he described it. With a sparkle in his eye, Sam explained, "I'm so filled up to the brim with God's presence and love, that there's just no room left for the pornography." Over the following months and years, I watched Sam's friendships spark to life and flourish. I saw all the external effects you would expect to come from a bona fide internal miracle. I saw what the heart transplant Ezekiel described more than 2,500 years ago — "I will remove the heart of stone from your flesh and give you a heart of flesh"[42] — looks like in a 21-year-old college student. In Paul's words, I watched Sam "increase and abound in love."

Ever since that transformative encounter (transformative for both of us), I have had the joy of meeting new Sams every semester. It is not some secret Voodoo incantation, or magical New Age technique that I offer them. We simply pray together the way Thomas à Kempis, John Donne, Augustine, and Paul prayed — the way Jesus prays in John 17. I have seen it time and again. When we reach the end of ourselves, and learn by experience the utter futility of even our best self-help strategies, and then ask the triune God of love to cause us to increase and abound in love, he answers. Sometimes it is an instantaneous "yes," sometimes an elongated "yeeeeeeeeeeeeeees," but he does answer.

Here we see another way in which Schaeffer's insight — that modern love is not radical enough — holds true. It does not go deep enough to the very Source of love. In Schaeffer's day, "love" was a defining buzzword of the hippie generation that he and his wife Edith warmly welcomed into their Swiss chalet. Love became the synonym for rebelling against the plastic culture, protesting racism, abolishing monogamy, ending the war in Vietnam, taking a psychedelic odyssey toward Oneness, and more. In our day, there are entire religious and political movements (and often religiously political movements) that continue to wave the love banner high. And, of course, "love" is a banner worth waving.

Picture all of these love banners standing like so many trees. If the only roots propping up and nourishing love are our own subjective feelings, or if a warm, tingly sensation in our bellies (or perhaps a few inches lower) is as deep as our love goes, then the tree will flail in the gusts of life and finally buckle. If love only goes as deep as a social construct, a mere byproduct of my biology, or some concept of divinity in which God is not quintessentially and eternally loving, then that love can only go so high until its shallow, metaphysical support structure can no longer sustain it. In short, the height to which love can rise is determined by the depth of its roots.[43]

When Jesus prayed, "that the love with which you have loved me may be in them, and I in them," he was not lifting a flimsy banner. If we really want a sturdy, fruitful, towering kind of love then we need the kind of love Jesus prayed for — a love rooted in "that which has always been," and that grows in and out of us from the triune God himself.

This chapter began with the Bible's first malediction — "it is not good for man to be alone." We were created *for* love by a God who *is* love. Without that God of love there are many ways to end up alone. We either consume other people in the name of unity or lose connection with them in the name of diversity. In either case, we find ourselves alone. We either seek shallow acceptance where the real us remains unknown or go deep only to get rejected. Either way, we end up alone. We either try harder to love only to find our selfishness getting the best of us or give up and resign ourselves to a loveless existence. Again, we are alone. Jesus frees us from all these false dilemmas. The old malediction rings true — it is not good for man to be alone. Thankfully, because of Jesus, we don't have to. Leonardo Boff concludes,

> We need to go beyond the understanding of Trinity as logical mystery and see it as a saving mystery. . . . We are not condemned to live alone, cut off from one another; we are called to live together and to enter into the communion of the Trinity. . . . If the Trinity is good news, then it is so particularly for the oppressed and those condemned to solitude.[44]

A PRAYER TO LOVE

Jesus, it is not good for us to be alone. We need you to pull us out of the shadows and into the rhythm of self-giving community that you have enjoyed since before the world began. Help us to go underneath all the layers of deception and hurt to comprehend just how deep and vast and wide and boundless is the Father's love for us. Cause us to increase and abound in love. Amen.

5

ELEVATE

Mirroring the Saving Grace of Jesus

Jesus cried with a loud voice, "*Eloi, Eloi, lema sabachthani*?" which means, "My God, my God, why have you forsaken me?" . . . And Jesus uttered a loud cry and breathed his last.

— MARK 15:34, 37

> At the center of all religions is the idea of Karma. You know, what you put out comes back to you. . . . And yet along comes this idea called Grace to upend all that. . . . Love interrupts, if you like, the consequences of your actions, which in my case is very good news indeed, because I've done a lot of stupid stuff. . . . I'm holding out that Jesus took my sins on the cross, because I know who I am, and I hope I don't have to depend on my own religiosity.
>
> BONO

To think, feel, act, and love in a Jesus-reflecting way is not challenging; it is impossible. Anyone who thinks otherwise has either laughably overestimated himself, or seriously underestimated Jesus. The distance between him and us is infinite. Thankfully, there is grace.

5.1 MOONJUMPING

Years ago, I was enjoying a meal with some friends at a beach tavern in Dana Point, California. We were seated close enough to the bar for me to overhear a man ordering shot after shot of Bacardi 151 (151 being the proof of the rum, making it a flammable 75.5% alcohol). This was not a typical drink order, unless of course you were looking to forget your own name and unlearn the basic principles of bipedal locomotion. I noticed a unique tattoo on the mysterious rum-shooter's left forearm. There, in English Gothic caps, were the words: GOING TO HELL. I approached and introduced myself. "That's quite a tattoo. What's the story there?" I asked. "Richard" proceeded to tell me his story with the honesty of a man whose entire internal editing department had been evacuated due to rum flooding.

He told me how love from Mom, Dad, and even God was something he could reach only by climbing a thousand-mile-high mountain of rules. Richard had spent his entire childhood climbing, but the peak never got one inch closer. After a few moral rockslides after high school incurred his parents' condemnation, Richard eventually concluded that it made no difference whether he climbed for the next ten years, or simply dove off the mountainside. The peak felt impossibly high. He took a leap and decided to embrace his fate, commemorating his damnation in dark blue ink on his forearm.

By now, Richard was craving nicotine, so I followed him outside. The moon was huge and I proposed a ridiculous game.

"First one to touch the moon wins," I said.[1] Richard's eyebrows drooped in confusion. I explained, "I'm not the most athletic guy in the world, so I run full speed and leap two inches off the pavement. You seem like a smart guy. You run and jump off a car hood and soar eight feet higher than me. Imagine the tavern crowd gets in on the game. Some lady climbs and jumps out of a tree. The bartender leaps off the roof and lands in the bushes. So tell me," I asked, "who wins the game?"

"No one, I guess. No one touched the moon. We all lose," Richard answered.

"That's exactly right," I said. "Some of us may get a few inches or even several feet higher than others, but in the end, we all lose. Trying to leap our way to God by rule keeping is just as hopeless. Some may get an inch off the ground, others a few feet, and some really religious folks may jump off the roof and put us all to shame. But we all lose." Richard was waiting for the point. I explained the good news: God reaches down to helpless moonjumpers like you and me. That's what Jesus is about. Jesus is God traversing all the infinite space we could never cross by our own moral performance and lifting us up to himself. That's what the Bible is getting at when it says, "by grace you have been saved through faith; and that not of yourselves, it is the gift of God; not as a result of works, so that no one may boast."[2] Ajith Fernando echoes:

Religion says, "attain";
    the gospel says, "obtain."
Religion says, "attempt";
    the gospel says, "accept."
Religion says, "try";
    the gospel says, "trust."
Religion says, "do this";
    the gospel says, "it is done."[3]

5.2 PAULS, AUGUSTINES, AND LUTHERS FOR TODAY

One of the strange lessons of history is how much we seem to love our moonjumping games. Indeed, we seem to prefer them to grace. Maybe it is because moonjumping gives us a way to think of ourselves more highly than others. Even if I can't jump to God, maybe I can out jump you. If, however, salvation is by grace, then all our superiority complexes instantly become absurd. Or it could be that we get jittery at the loss of control that comes with entrusting our ultimate fate to someone other than ourselves. Or maybe, as Flannery O'Connor observed, "All human nature vigorously resists grace because grace changes us and the change is painful."[4]

To better understand our vigorous resistance to grace, picture a long line that stretches two thousand years. Above that line is the good news that God's grace saves otherwise helpless moonjumpers. Below the line is the bad news that salvation requires, to some extent, our own moral achievements. In the first half of the first century, Jesus lifted people above that line. This put him at odds with those in the religious establishment who operated below the line. In the second half of the first century, a vocal movement known as the Judaizers claimed to follow Jesus. They taught that getting right with God required a rather inconvenient rite of passage for every non-Jewish male, namely, circumcision. Paul wrote the entire book of Galatians, much of Philippians, and the book of Romans to refute this below-the-line "false gospel," and help people enjoy community with God, and each other, above the line.

Move across the line to the fifth century. Pelagius, a British monk, taught that human willpower is neither morally damaged nor dead, but fully capable of living up to God's moral demands. Pelagius "preached that God commanded nothing impossible, that man possessed the power of doing the good if only he willed."[5] The pope at the time, Zosimus, gave his stamp of approval to Pelagius's moonjumping doctrine. Then a team of African bishops successfully proved to Zosimus that Pelagius had fallen below the line. One of those bishops, Augustine, knew that it was not his own power, but God's grace, that pulled him out of a life of empty fame-seeking and sex addiction. For making too much of human power and too little of divine grace, Pelagianism was rejected and the good news of grace was celebrated at church councils at Carthage in the year 418, Ephesus in 431, and Orange in 529.

Salvation is by God's grace alone through faith alone in Christ alone so that God, and God alone, gets all the glory.

By the time we move into the sixteenth century, much of that same Roman Catholic Church was operating below the line. Leo X — the pope from 1513 to 1521 — helped fund the architectural and aesthetic feat of Saint Peter's Basilica through the indulgence industry. Indulgences were certificates issued by the church to reduce a sinner's time in purgatory. With the help of the itinerant preacher John Tetzel, Leo's passports to heaven were sold throughout Europe with memorable marketing slogans like, "The moment your coin in the coffer rings, the soul from purgatory springs." The sale of indulgences (along with the relic industry that flourished under Leo) implied that we can, by human performance, "merit"[6] our own salvation. It was yet another attempt at moonjumping.[7]

A young German monk named Martin Luther followed these moonjumping strategies to their tragic conclusion. He slept, without a blanket, on the monastery floor in the sub-zero German winter. He gazed upon the relics of dead apostles and saints. He spent hours every day cataloguing his every blunder in the confessional booth. He even took a holy pilgrimage to Rome in hopes of finding relief for his tortured conscience. But, like my friend Richard, all of his self-powered efforts to reach God led Luther, in his own words, "to the very abyss of despair."[8] While GOING TO HELL was not tattooed on Luther's arm, it was certainly tattooed on his agonized psyche.

Then, one day, Luther caught an unexpected glimpse of life above the line and everything changed. While reading Paul's letter to the Romans, Luther learned that the gospel was never about his own power or righteousness. God's power saves and his righteousness becomes ours as we trust Jesus. With this epiphany, Luther said, "I felt that I was altogether born again and had entered paradise itself."[9] The liberated Luther helped catalyze the Protestant Reformation with its rally cry — that salvation is by God's grace alone, through faith alone, in Christ alone, so that God, and God alone, gets all the glory. Many followed Luther from "the abyss of despair" into "paradise," finding life above the line, and Protestantism was born.

Return with me to the present day. Protestants in mainline denominations were asked, "Do you get to heaven by doing good works?" Seventy-three percent said yes. Let that number sink in. Nearly three out of four mainline Protestants have fallen below the line to embrace the very idea that Protestantism was originally protesting! Another survey revealed that 82% of "born-again Christians" marked "God helps those who help themselves" as their personal favorite Bible verse. Seventy-five percent of American teenagers identified "God helps those who help themselves" as the central message of the Bible. A "Jaywalking" sketch, on *The Tonight Show*, asked random people on the street to name one of the Ten Commandments. The most popular response was — you guessed it — "God helps those who help themselves." This motivational catchphrase actually comes from the pen of an obscure political theorist named Algernon Sidney in his 1698 work, *Discourses Concerning Government*. Ben Franklin's *Poor Richard's Almanac* borrowed the phrase in 1736. The same idea shows up in ancient Roman fables and religious texts like the Koran and the Book of Mormon.[10] The one place you will not find it is in the Bible. The Bible is the story of how God helps those who are broken beyond self-help.

So a strange, saw-tooth pattern emerges over the past two millennia:

We slowly drift below the line until someone comes along, reads the Bible, and champions the good news from above the line. Systems of religious manipulation are subverted. Guilty souls are liberated. God's grace is celebrated. But as time wears on, we slide right back down into hopeless rituals of human performance. Then God raises up a new generation of reformers.

If we follow that pattern from the Judaizers, to the Pelagians, Tetzel, and on to the present day, then we are led to an important question: Where are the Pauls, Augustines, and Luthers of the twenty-first century? Who will remind a religiously wearied world that God helps those who *cannot* help themselves? Who will inspire us to give up our senseless moonjumping and surrender our exhausted selves into the sovereign hands of grace? I pray that you — the Pauls, Augustines, and Luthers of the twenty-first century — are reading this book. I pray that there are millions of you.

5.3 THE SELF-SERVING BIAS

If you look at the Pauls, Augustines, and Luthers of history, you will find that, though they were fallible, they shared a clear understanding of three infallible truths. They understood the deep meaning of the cross. They understood the deep meaning of the cross because they understood the depth of their own corruption. They understood the depth of their own corruption because they understood the height of God's perfection. In our day, we will not understand Jesus' crucifixion — just how far down God had to reach — unless we understand just how low we sink on our own. We will not understand our own moral under-achievements unless we see ourselves in light of God's goodness — just how high God really is. Without these three truths, religion in the twenty-first century will be nothing more to us than an absurd game of guilt, self-righteousness, and despair.

However, we face a major obstacle to seeing the cross like Paul, Augustine, and Luther did. We face a phenomenon called "the self-serving bias." The self-serving bias refers to our tendency to exaggerate our strengths and successes while under-emphasizing our flaws and failures. It is one of the most widely documented findings in all of psychology and social science:

- 829,000 high school students were asked: "How do you rate yourself, compared to other students, in your ability to get along with other people? Would you say that you are average, above average, or below average?" 829,000 students out of 829,000 students — 100% — ranked themselves "Above Average." Mathematically, this means that 414,500 students believed themselves to be better than they actually were. One in 4 even ranked themselves in the top 1%.
- Among college faculty, 88% rated their own performance as "Above Average." One in 4 had the humility to rate themselves as "Truly Exceptional."
- A majority of patients, while still in the hospital because of a car accident they caused by their own bad driving, rated themselves as "Above Average" drivers.
- A *USA Today* poll asked people to rate their chances of getting to heaven. Seventy-two percent rated their chances at eternal bliss as good to excellent, while they believed that only 60% of their friends were likely to enjoy everlasting life.
- In a study of people learning about the self-serving bias, 87% were thinking about someone else whom they believed was clearly guilty of this bias, while feeling quite above it themselves.

We often have X-ray vision into the defects of others. But we wear rose-colored glasses when we introspect.

Reinforcing this bias, there is no shortage of voices in the culture telling us how great we are. Self-help programs and school curriculums tell us we are all perfect little snowflakes. Children's shows tell us that we can do no wrong.[11] Pop songs tell us that we are all superstars. Spiritual gurus tell us that "heaven lies within yourself," that "we are as gods and might as well get good at it."[12] Best-sellers by celebrity pastors tell us to "have confidence in yourself. . . . When we believe we have what it takes, we focus on our possibilities. . . . [We] don't do wrong on purpose."[13]

Compare these inspirational voices with the uninspirational words from the ancient Bible authors. According to Jeremiah, "The heart is deceitful above all things, and desperately sick."[14] Solomon says that our hearts "are full of evil and insanity."[15] Paul's self-image was so maladjusted that he referred to himself as a "wretch" and "the chief of sinners."

At times, Paul gets plain offensive, like when he tells us that we were "dead in trespasses and sins."[16]

Why are the self-assessments of Jeremiah, Solomon, and Paul so bleak by twenty-first-century standards? We tend to assess ourselves on a horizontal plane — "I'm a good person compared to those other people." They assessed their moral status vertically — "compared to God, I'm a wretch." Every Reformer in history, from Isaiah to Paul, from Augustine to Luther, moved beyond a horizontal self-image of their own goodness to a vertical perspective where they each, in their own way, found their pride obliterated.[17]

Why should morally self-confident people like us take that vertical perspective seriously? I offer two reasons. First, without it we will fundamentally redefine Jesus, and, thereby, miss out on the joy of knowing the actual Jesus. With no vision of God's goodness, we will go through life with our self-serving bias intact. If we are basically good people then we don't need Jesus as a Savior to take us from Depraved to Saved; we only need him (if at all) as a Life Coach to inspire us from Good to Great.

Second, without a vertical view we tend to unleash hell on earth. Our utopian dreams become dystopian nightmares. To see this point, imagine a big tree that represents the whole human race. Why, we may ask, does the tree bear bad fruit? Why does our species do so many mean things? Why do we hurt ourselves, each other, and the planet? With no concept of God's goodness, sin becomes nothing more than an outmoded superstition to us. We will go right along thinking that we are basically good people. If we're basically good people, if the human tree itself is nice and healthy, then all that bad fruit can't possibly be coming from inside us. If the *tree* is not the problem, then it must be a *soil* problem.[18]

Perhaps, if the human tree were in less religious soil, then the bad fruit would go away. There would be no more close-minded dogmatism or "holy war." So let's replant ourselves in the soil of secularism. But bad fruit grows there too. Just ask the victims of Robespierre's Revolution, visit the Siberian gulags, or walk the killing fields of the Khmer Rouge. "Secular soil's the problem!" "No, religious soil's the problem!" "The Left is the problem!" "No, the Right is the problem!" "Into free market soil!"

say the Capitalists. "Into the soil of Economic Equality!" say the Socialists. "Better government programs!" say the Progressives. "Less government meddling!" say the Conservatives. "Too much machinery and materialism!" say the Hippies. "More technology and prosperity!" answer the Yuppies.

So it goes. Our world has become a long series of failed experiments in gardening. Our every attempt to uproot and replant ourselves in some new soil yields the same result — bad fruit. Yes, soil is important. Some soils are more nourishing while others are toxic and lead to more poisonous fruits. But the empirical fact that bad fruit persists no matter what soil we find ourselves in ought to give us pause to ask: What if the tree itself is sick at its very roots? What if our hearts really are as "desperately sick" as Jeremiah thought, as "full of evil and insanity" as Solomon thought, as "dead in trespasses" as Paul thought? The human heart is, after all, the common denominator in every failed utopia.[19] As Jesus said, a diseased tree cannot bear good fruit.[20]

If we are basically good people then we don't need Jesus as a Savior to take us from Depraved to Saved; we only need him (if at all) as a Life Coach to inspire us from Good to Great.

A vertical view matters, then, because without it we end up with a false Jesus — a Life Coach rather than a Savior — and a false gospel that more religion, science, politics, technology, money, romance, or social engineering can save us.[21]

5.4 THE MULTIFACETED CROSS

We are now in a better place to behold the cross of Jesus in the liberating way that the Pauls, Augustines, and Luthers of history did. Mark's Gospel takes us there: "Jesus cried with a loud voice, 'Eloi, Eloi, lema sabachthani?' which means, 'My God, my God, why have you forsaken me?' . . . And Jesus uttered a loud cry and breathed his last."[22] What happens in those brief passages is so scandalous and profound that the Bible does not limit itself to a single explanation. Dutch theologian Herman Bavinck explains:

REFLECT

The work of Christ is so multifaceted that it cannot be captured in a single word nor summarized in a single formula. In the different books of the New Testament, therefore, different meanings of the death of Christ are highlighted, and all of them together help to give us a deep impression and a clear sense of the riches and many-sidedness of the mediator's work.[23]

"Multifaceted" is exactly the right word for the cross. It brings to mind the image of a giant deep-cut diamond, a unity with a multiplicity of facets, each refracting rays off and through the other.[24] Picture it like this:

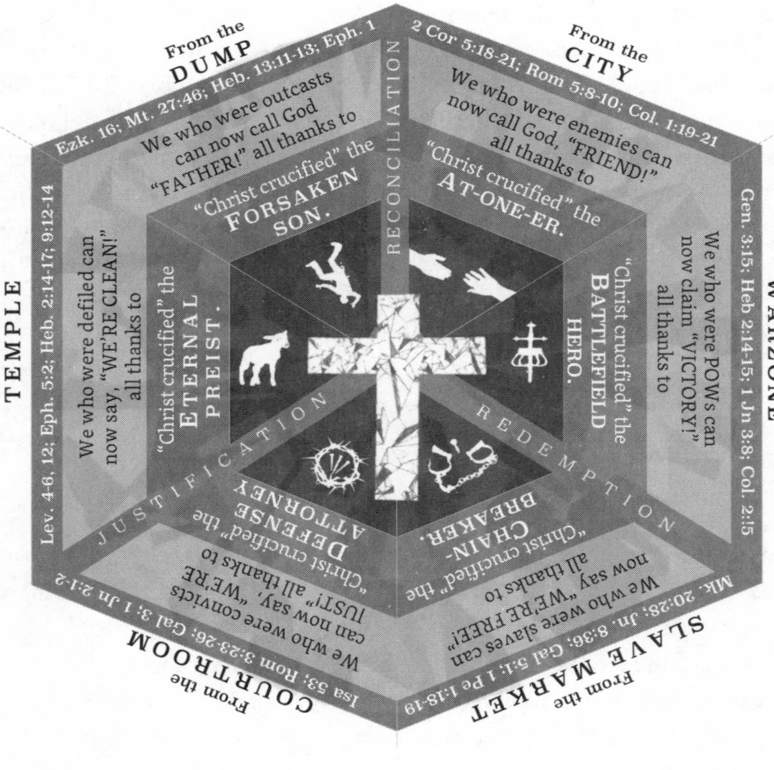

From the DUMP
Ezk. 16; Mt. 27:46; Heb. 13:11-13; Eph. 1
We who were outcasts can now call God "FATHER!" all thanks to
"Christ crucified" the FORSAKEN SON.

From the CITY
2 Cor 5:18-21; Rom 5:8-10; Col. 1:19-21
We who were enemies can now call God, "FRIEND!" all thanks to
"Christ crucified" the AT-ONE-ER.

RECONCILIATION

From the WARZONE
Gen. 3:15; Heb 2:14-15; 1 Jn 3:8; Col. 2:15
We who were POWs can now claim "VICTORY!" all thanks to
"Christ crucified" the BATTLEFIELD HERO.

From the SLAVE MARKET
Mk. 20:28; Jn. 8:36; Gal 5:1; 1 Pe 1:18-19
We who were slaves can now say "WE'RE FREE!" all thanks to
"Christ crucified" the CHAIN-BREAKER.

REDEMPTION

From the COURTROOM
Isa 53; Rom 3:23-26; Gal 3; 1 Jn 2:1-2
We who were convicts can now say, "WE'RE JUST!" all thanks to
"Christ crucified" the DEFENSE ATTORNEY

From the TEMPLE
Lev. 4-6, 12; Eph. 5:2; Heb. 2:14-17; 9:12-14
We who were defiled can now say, "WE'RE CLEAN!" all thanks to
"Christ crucified" the ETERNAL PREIST.

JUSTIFICATION

Let's take one lap around this flawless wonder of the cross.

At-one-er

Behind our first image of the cross is the idea that we are not merely apathetic about God, but we are "hostile" toward him.[25] There is a part of us, deep down, that wants to extend the spiritual middle finger in his face. The irony is that we declare war against the only one who can give us real peace. Hence, our need for what the Bible calls "atonement," someone to bring at-one-ment where two sides are at war, a peacemaker. The Bible also uses the term "reconciliation" — mending a rift, bringing friendship to a hostile situation. The cross is God's decisive way of making this new friendship a reality. "In Christ," says Paul, "God was reconciling the world to himself."[26] It is not us, but God, in Christ, who makes the first disarming move. As 83% of self-identified evangelicals "agree" or "somewhat agree" with the statement that "a person obtains peace with God by first taking the initiative to seek God and then God responds with grace,"[27] we desperately need to recover the true *evangel*, the good news that God and God alone is the great Initiator of peace and salvation for hostiles like us.

A powerful image from the pen of Fyodor Dostoyevsky clarifies the point. In *The Brothers Karamazov*, we meet Ivan Karamazov, a staunch atheist who criticizes his little brother Alyosha's faith. So Ivan tells Alyosha a fictional "poem" about Jesus' return to sixteenth-century Spain. In Ivan's story, "the Grand Inquisitor" arrests Jesus and proceeds to interrogate his prisoner for nearly twenty pages. The verbal slaughter fest concludes with the Inquisitor's verdict: "To-morrow I shall burn Thee." What Dostoyevsky wrote next is one of the most moving moments in the history of literature:

> The Prisoner had listened intently all the time, looking gently in his face and evidently not wishing to reply. The old man longed for him to say something, however bitter and terrible. But He suddenly approached the old man in silence and softly kissed him on his bloodless aged lips. That was all his answer.[28]

Once Ivan finishes his story, intended to make his little brother's Jesus look pathetic, guess what Alyosha does next? Dostoyevsky narrates, "Alyosha got up, went to him and softly kissed him," and the brothers walk out together into the night. What a beautiful picture of Jesus the peacemaker. We mock and wish him dead; he kisses us. The cross is about our At-one-ment, *and more . . .*

Battlefield Hero

In Genesis 3:15 we find a cryptic promise that a Man would one day be born and bruised to fatally stomp on the serpent's head. Later the serpent is described as a vicious dragon, a devouring lion, a murderous thief, and Apollyon, "the destroyer."[29] Jesus appears in first-century Palestine "to destroy the works of the devil,"[30] that is, to crush the serpent, slay the dragon, hunt the lion, catch the thief, and destroy the destroyer. Paul tells us that God, in Christ, "disarmed the rulers and authorities and put them to open shame, by triumphing over them."[31] Just as the captured soldiers of a defeated army were often dragged in chains on a public shame walk, so Jesus shows "the ruler of this world," "the prince of the power of the air," the "strong man, fully armed,"[32] to be powerless.

We were prisoners of war in the death grip of this dark regime. Jesus came so "that through death he might destroy the one who has the power of death, that is, the devil, and deliver all those who through fear of death were subject to lifelong slavery."[33] God "has delivered us from the domain of darkness and transferred us to the kingdom of his beloved Son."[34] The cross is about our Battlefield Hero, and more.

Chain-Breaker

While bringing bondage to the devil, Jesus brings "freedom," pays "the ransom," and offers "redemption" to us.[35] This is the language of the slave market. Some historians estimate that when the New Testament was written, two-thirds of the Roman Empire was enslaved.[36] It is into this shackled empire that the good news comes, "Christ has set us free."[37]

This good news will seem irrelevant if our self-serving bias tells us that we were never slaves in the first place. Years ago, my friend "Mike" told me that he'd "rather reign in hell than serve in heaven!" Mike would serve no one but Mike. It wasn't until years later, while listening to Bob Dylan's Grammy-winning single, "Gotta Serve Somebody," that the problem with Mike's credo became evident. Dylan sings about big-shot politicians, egomaniacal preachers, heavyweight champions, rock stars, warlords, business moguls, network executives, mansion-dwelling fat cats, and more. Dylan, as only Dylan can do, subverts the status quo:

> You're gonna have to serve somebody. . . .
> Well, it may be the devil or it may be the Lord,
> But you're gonna have to serve somebody.

For Dylan, the sultans are the real slaves.[38] Millennia earlier, Jesus told a crowd who believed they were already free that "everyone who practices sin is a slave to sin."[39] We typically think of slavery as being chained by some outside force. Jesus describes a slavery from within. We are not so much held captive *against* our desires, but *by* our desires — not bondage *against* the will, but what Martin Luther called "bondage *of* the will." Francis Turretin clarified with his memorable image of "a prisoner who kisses his chains and refuses deliverance."[40]

We may think that freedom means doing whatever the self-ruling *I* wants, unburdened by any moral judgment. But ask any addict if doing whatever we want is true freedom.[41] Thankfully, through the death of Jesus, God "has delivered us from the domain of darkness." Jesus died "so that we would no longer be enslaved to sin."[42] As Jesus put it, "If the Son sets you free, you will be free indeed."[43] The cross is about our Chain-Breaker, *and more . . .*

Defense Attorney[44]

God makes and enforces laws.[45] It would be a mistake to think of these laws as a killjoy's list of do's and don'ts. They are good laws that flow from God's good nature for our joy and flourishing. But we love ourselves more than our Maker, more than our neighbors, and more than the poor and outcast. This is criminal, and God is a God of Justice.[46]

But God loves criminals.[47] He wants them in his home, around his dinner table, and in his family forever. Since "the wages of sin is death," we need our criminal record expunged, our "not guilty" verdict rendered beyond appeal. So, the Judge sends us a Substitute, someone willing to be "pierced for our transgressions" and "crushed for our iniquities."[48]

In this "wonderful exchange" (as Luther described it), Jesus chooses, at the behest of his loving Father, to stand in the place of lawbreakers to be treated as *the* Lawbreaker. He dons our scrubs and cuffs. He walks the long mile. He offers his veins to accept the syringe. Our death sentence has been served. Justice has been satisfied.[49] No punishment remains — only peace with God. "There is therefore now no condemnation for those who are in Christ Jesus."[50] John Calvin echoes,

> The guilt that held us liable for punishment has been transferred to the head of the Son of God. . . . We must, above all, remember this substitution, lest we tremble and remain anxious throughout life.[51]

If any anxiety remains, the New Testament adds that "we have an advocate with the Father, Jesus Christ the righteous."[52] "Advocate" (from the Greek *parakleton*) pictures the resurrected Jesus as someone zealously pleading our case. If we represent ourselves before the bar of Perfect Justice, then we should tremble. But we have nothing whatsoever to fear because Jesus offers his services to us *pro bono*, and he never loses a case. He has the only fail-proof argument for the Judge to take our side — his own completed death sentence for all of our law breaking.[53] The cross is about our Defense Attorney, *and more* . . .

Eternal Priest

The ancient Jews, like us, did things that polluted their own hearts — worshiping human artifacts, trivializing God's name, dishonoring, exploiting, killing, lying, cheating, stealing, and coveting. How, then, could a self-polluted people enjoy the presence of a pure Being?

The answer to that question moves us into the temple, where priests performed elaborate purification rituals for more than a thousand years. For a purification offering, the priest would lay his hands on a bull, goat, lamb, or bird as a kind of symbolic transfer of impurity, then slay the animal to bring forgiveness to himself and the people.[54] The annual Day of Atonement offering involved two goats.[55] The first goat was killed by the priest and its blood sprinkled to cleanse the most Holy Place, then the Tent, then the Altar. The second, the "scapegoat," would be symbolically loaded up with the collective defilements of the people, and led outside the city to wander alone.[56] "A "paschal offering" was a lamb "without blemish," killed at twilight, its meat eaten, and its blood painted over the doorposts so that "no plague will befall you to destroy you."[57]

Breaking God's rules is a costly and bloody endeavor.[58] Yet animal slayings are hardly a real solution to the problem. So Jesus

> entered once for all into the holy places, not by means of the blood of goats and calves but by means of his own blood, thus securing an eternal redemption. For if the blood of goats and bulls, and the sprinkling of defiled persons with the ashes of a heifer, sanctify for the purification of the flesh, how much more will the blood of Christ, who through the eternal Spirit offered himself without blemish to God, purify our conscience from dead works to serve the living God.[59]

Jesus became "a merciful and faithful high priest in the service of God, to make propitiation for the sins of the people."[60] The cross is about our Eternal Priest, *and more . . .*

Forsaken Son

Exclusion, expulsion, alienation, and forsakenness — these were major themes in the ancient Jewish world. The "impure" could be expelled from the community. The carcasses of sacrificed animals had to be burned outside the camp. The scapegoat was sent out "to a remote area."[61] To be "inside" was to be pure, wanted, loved, at home, and alive. To be "outside" was to be dirty, unwanted, despised, outcast, and left to die. Unwanted babies of the ancient Near East were often left outside the city to die. Ezekiel picks up on this travesty to describe the Jews like a baby "cast out on the open field . . . abhorred on the day [they] were born." God passed by, saw them "wallowing in blood," said to them "Live!" and brought them into his home.[62] (It is hard to imagine a more vivid image than an abandoned infant to show that God helps those who cannot help themselves.)

The New Testament world also had people thrown outside cities to die.[63] Under Roman law, a father — the *paterfamilias* — had the final word on whether to welcome his babies into the home. If you were deemed ugly,[64] or a financial burden, or, most often, if you were a girl, you could to be thrown out like garbage.[65] (As one first-century husband wrote his wife in a letter, "If you are delivered before I come home, if it is a boy keep it, if a girl, discard it.")[66] "The Exposed," as they came to be known, would often die of starvation or hypothermia, be eaten by scavenging dogs, or be picked apart by birds.[67] Then, as if that weren't gut-wrenching enough, there were predators who would often snatch these abandoned children and make them sex slaves.[68]

Ephesus had a mound outside its city gates where those whom society branded unfit for life and love were dumped. Paul opens his letter to this city with an image that would have shocked an Ephesian audience. He tells them that God the Father

> chose us in him [Christ] before the foundation of the world, that we should be holy and blameless before him. In love he predestined us for adoption as sons through Jesus Christ, according to the purpose of his will, to the praise of his glorious grace, with which he has blessed us in the Beloved.[69]

Many of the first people to ever read those words would have been the Exposed — unwanted by their own fathers and raised as slaves in Ephesus. It's hard to imagine them not weeping at the news that God the Father "chose" them. Their own biological fathers considered them too ugly, too burdensome, or too female to deserve love. God the Father rescues them from the dump and calls them "holy and unblemished."

"Among those who saved the lives of abandoned infants most were interested in exploitation more than in rescue,"[70] a fact that the Ephesians knew all too well. Paul is quick to add that the Father's rescue mission is carried out "in love." They are not used and abused as slaves, but adopted and cherished as sons and daughters. While parents could easily discard a biological child in Ephesus, to become an adopted child, under Roman law, meant that you could *never* be disowned. Adoption was an unbreakable, lifelong contract initiated by the parent. To people without a penny from their deadbeat fathers, Paul breaks the news that their real Father has lavished the riches of his grace on them and guaranteed them an inheritance.[71]

The unwanted have become the wanted. Society's blemished have been renamed by God as the unblemished. The fatherless, at last, have a Father — a Father who chose them, who will never abandon them, and who will spend eternity lavishing gifts on them.

This adoption happens "through Jesus Christ," and the cross is there at the center of it all: "In him we have redemption through his blood."[72] The broader context of the Bible shows that Jesus saves outcasts, making their adoption possible, by taking their place and becoming the Outcast. Like the Exposed, "He was despised and rejected by men." "We esteemed him not." He was "taken away" and "cut off out of the land of the living." He "suffered outside the gate in order to sanctify the people through his own blood."[73]

To be forsaken by your own father, and left to die outside the city was a truly horrific fate.[74] "Why have you forsaken me?" could have been the tragic anthem of the Exposed. Jesus took their (our) place and cried those lonely words so that we don't have to. Instead, we find ourselves "crying 'Abba! Father!'"[75] In the words of Joni Eareckson Tada:

> Jesus willingly chose isolation so that you might never be alone in your hurt and sorrow. He had no real fellowship so that fellowship might be yours, this moment. . . . You will never experience isolation or abandonment or dread of being forsaken as did your Lord. Fellowship is yours! . . . And you have it because He didn't.[76]

We have taken our first lap around the massive diamond. What we have seen is not a few scattered images, but overlapping facets of the same Jesus on the same cross. No matter where we stand on the 360-degree circumference, what we see is Jesus doing a work of elevation. He lifts us up from hostility into a friendship with God, up from satanic oppression into victory, up from slavery into freedom, up from condemnation into justice, from filth into purity, from the human dump into God's family. In each case, Jesus does for us what we could never do for ourselves.[77] He elevates us above the line into a friendship, victory, freedom, justice, purity, and family we could never jump to on our own. That is the meaning of grace.

As we have seen, we can all too easily lose sight of this grace, focus on ourselves, and sink below the line. As Corrie Ten Boom observed, "If you look within, you'll be depressed. If you look at God you'll be at rest." How can you keep focused on God instead of yourself? I encourage you to make a habit of preaching grace to yourself every day. Remind yourself often of all the ways that you are elevated in Christ. Thank Jesus that through the cross he is the . . .

. . . At-one-er.
I was hostile to God, but Jesus has made me "at-one" with him, breaking down the wall of division and welcoming me into friendship.

. . . Battlefield Hero.
The forces of fear and evil held me in their oppressive grip, but Jesus, the Warrior-King, has crushed the enemy's head and claimed victory.

. . . Chain-Breaker.
I was a slave to darkness, selfishness, and anxiety, but Jesus is my great Liberator who purchased my freedom and cut my chains.

. . . Defense Attorney.
I broke the laws of an infinitely just Being, but Jesus took my death sentence and now pleads the winning case for my innocence.

. . . Eternal Priest.
I was unclean, but Jesus became my spotless Lamb and serves as my Priest so I can stand confidently in the presence of divine Perfection.

. . . Forsaken Son.
I was left to die at the human dump, but Jesus became Forsaken in my place so that I can enjoy adoption as a cherished son/daughter of God.

Praying through these six biblical images may take six minutes, or it may take sixty seconds. That brief time of preaching the good news to yourself can turn an otherwise anxious day into something worshipful and grace-filled.

5.5 ELEVATION

How might worshiping someone so gracious change us? Trillia Newbell answers, "Our interactions with others would radically change. Why? Because we'd see each other as equally sinful, equally in need of grace, and equally redeemed."[78] In short, as we worship Jesus, we find ourselves becoming far less self-righteous and far more gracious. We become the kind of people who *elevate* enemies, the oppressed, the poor, the guilty, the unholy, and the unwanted. The Bible tells us that . . .

> . . . people who worship the *At-one-er* become people who work toward unity, who invite others into God's family as ambassadors of reconciliation, who break down walls of hostility and work toward racial reconciliation in their communities.[79]
>
> . . . people who worship the *Battlefield Hero* become people who armor up daily to do battle against Satan, who "demolish strongholds of every pretention that set themselves up against the knowledge of Christ," and who seek liberation for those still under oppression.[80]
>
> . . . people who worship the *Chain-Breaker* become people who use their financial and emotional resources to help those in bondage and who serve others in a way that reflects him who "came not to be served but to serve, and to give his life as a ransom for many."[81]
>
> . . . people who worship the *Defense Attorney* become people who "seek justice, correct oppression; bring justice to the fatherless, [and] plead the widow's cause," who "forgive one another, as God in Christ has forgiven [them]," who are willing to be imprisoned crushed, perplexed, and beaten down to bring others joy.[82]

> . . . people who worship the *Eternal Priest* become people who present their bodies as a living sacrifice, the kind of husbands who love their wives "as Christ loved the church and gave up his life for her," who pour themselves out as an offering for others.[83]

> . . . people who worship the *Forsaken Son*, become people who take care of orphans and widows, who are willing to be viewed as "the scum of the world," who are willing to go "outside the camp and bear the reproach he endured," who "endure suffering, [and] do the work of an evangelist."[84]

In other words, because we have been lifted up we lift others up.

*

I close with a few brief examples of what that elevation looks like.

When a deadly plague ravaged the Roman Empire in the second century, most of society abandoned the sick to save their own skins. As the masses ran for the hills, who ran toward the sick and dying, to take care of (and often die with) them? Those who knew that Jesus ran to them and took their sin plague upon himself.

When America and the British Empire were kidnapping people from their African homes, many saw nothing more than a tolerable utilitarian bargain that helped boost the national economy. Frederick Douglass, Harriet Tubman, John Newton, William Wilberforce, and the Clapham sect knew their own enslavement to sin and found their liberator in Jesus. So they freed others and worked to legally abolish human trafficking.

When a malevolent dictator began to systematically target, imprison, and exterminate Jews, gypsies, and homosexuals, many Germans turned their heads, clenched their jaws shut, and went about their business. Not pastors like Dietrich Bonhoeffer, with his scathing pulpit indictments and plots against the Führer. Not college students like Sophie Scholl and her brother Hans, with their White Rose Society, publishing bold underground leaflets to subvert the Third Reich.

These dissidents were all executed in their efforts to save people from a tyrant. They each died worshiping a Jesus who himself endured execution to humiliate the powers of darkness and save the world from satanic tyranny.

Remember those human dumps from back in the first century? When the early church worshiped the Jesus who saved them spiritually from the human trash heap, they became the kind of people who went to the literal human trash heaps and turned society's unwanted into their beloved sons and daughters.[85]

This beautiful tradition is kept alive today in a poor urban neighborhood of Seoul, South Korea, where Pastor Lee Jong-rak and his wife Chun-ja run their Jusarang Community. Unwanted babies are abandoned in Seoul's alleys and dumpsters to die. Pastor Lee built "the Baby Box" on the street-facing wall of his home with a simple sign that reads: "PLACE TO LEAVE BABIES." Instead of dying alone on the streets, hundreds of babies, most of them disabled, have been saved. "The prejudice against disabled people is severe," Pastor Lee lamented in a *Dateline* interview:

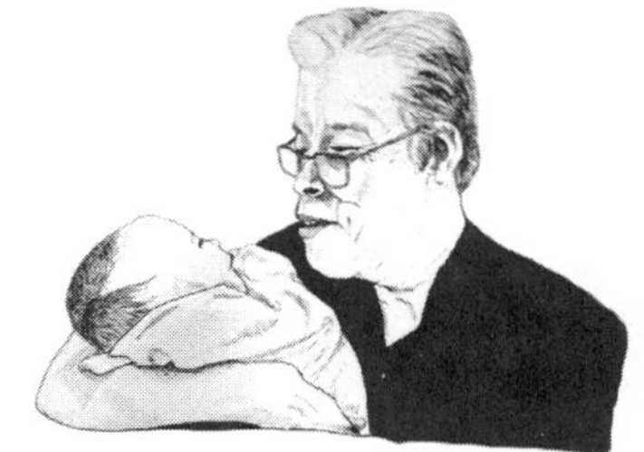

> People neglect them. They find them repugnant. They don't treat them with respect. They don't treat them as human beings. I can see that if these children had gone elsewhere, they would have died.[86]

At the chiming of an electronic bell, the little ones are retrieved through the interior door of the box, and lifted into the gracious arms of Pastor Lee. They are prayed for, cared for, and then connected with families. Pastor Lee and his wife have adopted ten of these children — the maximum allowed by the government — as their own cherished sons and daughters. When asked why he does it all, Pastor Lee answers simply, "God has adopted me." Because we have been so graciously lifted up, we lift up others.

A PRAYER TO ELEVATE

Jesus, you saved us when we could never save ourselves. Thank you for loving us when we were hostile and for making us God's friends. Thank you for triumphing over the enemies of our souls. Thank you for liberating us from chains, for taking the penalty for our crimes and pleading our innocence, for being our perfect Lamb and eternal Priest, for being forsaken so we can enjoy life in your family forever. Help us to elevate our enemies, the oppressed, the poor, the guilty, the unholy, and the outcast. By your grace, make us gracious like you. Amen.

6

CREATE

Mirroring the Artistic Genius of Jesus

On the first day of the week, at early dawn, they went to the tomb, taking the spices they had prepared. And they found the stone rolled away from the tomb, but when they went in they did not find the body of the Lord Jesus.

— LUKE 24:1–3

> He lived serenely, as an artist greater than all other artists, scorning marble and clay and paint, working in the living flesh. . . . Now I say it again — this Christ is more of an artist than the artists — he works in living spirit and flesh, he makes men instead of statues.
>
> VINCENT VAN GOGH

We have seen something of the way in which Jesus reasons, emotes, flips, loves, and elevates us with grace. As Van Gogh came to realize, Jesus is also the great Artist. Since we become like what we worship, the question arises, How might worshiping Jesus make us more creative?

6.1 "HUMAN IN THE FULLEST SENSE"

To many, that is a strange question. Jesus calls us to love our neighbors and make disciples of all nations. He never commanded us to paint our neighbors, or make dancers, sculptors, and musicians of all nations. What, after all, does Jerusalem have to do with New York City's Met, London's Tate, or the Louvre in Paris? Why not leave art to the artists, and get on with the real work of Christian living? Francis Schaeffer counters:

We have tended to relegate art to the very fringe of life. . . . We do not seem to understand that the arts too are supposed to be under the Lordship of Christ. . . . A Christian should use [the] arts to the glory of God — not just as tracts, mind you, but as things of beauty to the praise of God.[1]

Schaeffer loved art at a time when the religious mainstream in America tended to view the arts with either a Platonic apathy that said, "Art is too earthly minded to be any heavenly good," or a puritanical fear that encouraged young people to chuck their Beatles albums into the bonfire. Schaeffer knew that he could not starve his imagination without starving his very humanity. He paced the galleries and feasted alone. Then, on a visit to Amsterdam in 1948, Schaeffer met a young jazz aficionado and Dutch art critic by the name of Henderik R. Rookmaaker. "Fran" and "Hans" stayed up until 4 a.m. celebrating the innovations of black music in America. At last, Schaeffer had found a fellow anomaly, someone else who saw no contradiction between a deep love for Jesus and a deep love for art.

Schaeffer shared Rookmaaker's conviction that Jesus did not come "in order that we might become spiritual ghosts in heaven," but "in order to make us human in the fullest sense, to renew our lives at all levels."[2] Through the 1960s and 1970s, this peculiar duo — a goateed evangelist in his trademark knee-high lederhosen, and a pipe-puffing art professor in a three-piece suit — electrified a generation of young people. Through their books, international lectures, and L'Abri communities in the Swiss Alps (Schaeffer) and the Dutch countryside (Rookmaaker), they transported many disillusioned youth into a wide-open universe where their imaginations could breathe, stretch out, and soar. They did not offer a super-spiritualized Jesus, perched on a faraway cloud with a fishing pole trying to snatch souls out of a hopelessly damned and ugly world. They offered the Jesus of Scripture who involves "the total man in the total world."[3] They offered "true spirituality," which "means the lordship of Christ over the total man."[4] They taught that "the Christian is the one whose imagination should fly beyond the stars,"[5] and many took them up on the interstellar invitation.[6]

Many still do not think that way. I wasted fifteen years of my creative life not thinking that way. Thankfully, with Schaeffer's and Rookmaaker's guidance (along with many who have echoed, deepened, and at times corrected their work),[7] I have slowly come to appreciate the wonderfully diverse ways in which creativity is part and parcel of what it means to bear the Creator's image. As the great culinary artist Robert Farrar Capon says, "We were given appetites, not to consume the world and forget it, but to taste its goodness and hunger to make it great."[8]

We can make new flavor combinations in the kitchen, new sounds on metallic strings stretched over wood, new sights out of pigmented chemicals on flat surfaces, new perspectives by clicking new letter sequences on black keys, and more. The infinity of opportunities to make something of the world can be fun. They can be inspiring, exhausting, and rewarding. But they can also be spiritual. Creativity can be an act of obedience and worship — a way of fulfilling the greatest commandment to love the Creator with our whole being. The God who made the world made us to make something of the world. Creative action, therefore, can be a deeply humanizing action. It can usher us into the daylight, particularly those parts of human nature that have been buried under the pavement of unimaginative modern worldviews and the concrete demands of daily life.

The capital "C" Creator made us — *all* of us — not as creatures of consumption, but to be lowercase "c" creators — active, inspired, outward, inventive, and productive, in short, to multiply the net beauty in the universe. I believe this because the Bible says as much, and my experience confirms it again and again. I do not mean that all of us can make what Michelangelo did with a chisel and a marble block, what Miles Davis did with his lungs and twisted brass, or what contemporary artists like Tim Hawkinson can with a truckload of Home Depot supplies. What I mean is what a silver pony-tailed hippie named "Jasper" taught me nearly a decade ago.

The God who made the world made us to make something of the world.

6.2 WHAT IS "CHRISTIAN ART"?

I had been teaching a series on Christianity and art at a small church community near Los Angeles. There I met Jasper. Jasper was skeptical about the very concept of Christian art for two reasons. First, he believed that he "couldn't draw a stick figure to save [his] life." If there were any truth in the old right brain versus left brain theory, then Jasper's right brain had no more alpha waves than a stuffed turkey. Or so he believed. For a right-brain-dead believer, how could Christianity and art possibly fit together? The second reason for Jasper's skepticism was that he had seen contemporary "Christian paintings," watched "Christian movies," and heard "Christian music."[9] As King's College President Gregory Thornbury quips, "Christianity is the greatest of all nouns, but the lamest of all adjectives."

Jasper and I wondered together, "Is there a way to envision Christian art as something more than misty fairytale cottages, contrived plotlines where typecast God-haters join in a tearful Jesus anthem before the credits roll, or derivative songs that meet a JPM quota (that is, how times you must say Jesus Per Minute to count as a bona fide Christian song)?" Could there be something more to Christian art? In that Sunday morning series, we went back to the Bible to find out.

It struck us that the first time we meet God in the story of Scripture we meet him as an Artist. "Created" is the first verb in the first sentence on the first page of the Bible. Out of the flurry of God's imagination, the heavens and the earth burst into existence and teem with diversity and beauty. This was a countercultural way to look at the world. Most old creation stories traced the world's origin not to a free creative act, but to a destructive showdown between warring gods. To live on earth was to live on a slain deity's corpse. The Bible says that we inhabit the original artwork of a creative Genius, and we inhabit that artwork *as* artwork ourselves.

Next, we mused over the fact that God could have easily spoken a monochrome cosmos into existence. He could have made an all-brown universe — brown planets, brown animals, brown-on-brown rainbows in a brown sky. Even oranges would be called "browns." This Browntopia could have been perfectly efficient and functional from an engineering perspective. Why, then, make our multi-hued universe? Why the color spectrum? Why red strawberries, orange oranges, and yellow lemons? Why mandarinfish, peacocks, and chameleons? Because, as Genesis 1 repeats seven times, "God saw that it was good." God, evidently, cares about more than efficiency and functionality. He also cares about beauty.

James Speigel of Taylor University has made the case that when God said "it was good," he was not making a moral, legal, political, or prudential claim. He was making an aesthetic claim.[10] It is not like saying that the boy who ate all his vegetables "was good" for obeying Mommy, or the Magna Carta "was good" for society, or the Hadron particle accelerator "was good" for quantum research. It is more like beholding a Titian canvas or a sunset over the Pacific and saying, "It was good." Yet God made this aesthetic declaration even before he made Adam and Eve. It follows that beautiful things can be truly beautiful even if there is no human being around to behold and declare it to be so. Beauty, then, is not merely something we as humans dream up (thankfully, we can); it is also something we can discover — something beyond and even before us.[11]

This means that when the Hubble Space Satellite left our atmosphere and started relaying space pictures back to us, there is nothing arbitrary or artificial when we exhale together, "Beautiful!" When human beings over the past thirty years first beheld the sprawling fuchsia clouds of the Orion Nebula, the cobalt pupil and auburn iris of the Helix Nebula, or the somber towering gas pillars of the Eagle Nebula, with their speckles of pink fire and wispy sea-green auras — we did not *fabricate* beauty. We *found* it. They were beautiful long before Hubble left our atmosphere and would stay beautiful even if we all went blind tomorrow.

Why? In a biblical view of the universe, it is because God cares about beauty and declares things beautiful even when we cannot. As Rookmaaker put it, "The original eye for art is in God himself."[12] That is to say, beauty is not merely in the eye of the beholders — us — but in the eye of the Beholder, with a capital "B." From this perspective, we do not enter the world to impose our ever-changing constructs of beauty on some aesthetic void. Beauty is already there, and will impose itself on us and even reconstruct our constructs into something more noble and towering and true, if we dare to let it.

From there, we saw that the very first command from God to a human being in the Bible was to do something creative. "Name the animals" was an invitation to be creative since, as Rookmaaker observes, "one of the functions of poetry is to name things, and by naming things they become important to us."[13] Next come commands to be fruitful and multiply, to fill the earth and steward creation, God's call to make something of the world. We saw how Bezalel and his sons lived within that calling as God's Spirit gave them the aesthetic skill to make tabernacle décor. Israel's God was not worshiped in a drab, hollow cube. We saw invitations to worship the Creative God creatively: "Sing to him a new song, play skillfully on strings, with loud shouts." "Sing praises to the LORD with the lyre, with the lyre and the sound of melody." "Praise his name with dancing."[14]

We noticed that God never limited himself to didactic prose when revealing himself to Israel. He tells multisensory truth — truth with fire cooking meat, blood painted on doorposts, talking asses, vomiting fish, hungry bears, wandering goats, crucified snakes, burning plants, thunder, smoke, rocks, bugs, milk, and honey. He tells truth in vivid images — skeletons coming to life, apocalyptic sea monsters, and menstrual rags. Then there is prophetic performance art. Isaiah wanders naked for three years. Jeremiah invites the prohibitionist Rechabites to a wine-tasting party in God's temple. Hosea marries a well-known harlot.

When we turned to the New Testament, we saw that the masterful Creator we met in Genesis 1 is actually Christ.[15] "All things were made through him."[16] Glowing space nebulae, rainbows, the flavor of watermelon and coffee beans were his idea (in creative collaboration with the Father and the Spirit). The Son took on created flesh. He spent most of his career as a *tekton*, a craftsman who could make both small- and large-scale projects with stone, wood, and metal. Then, when his public ministry started, Jesus taught mostly in parables, painting mental pictures that have lived in our imagination for more than two millennia. We talked about how his greatest commandment — to love God with *all* of ourselves — includes the imaginative and creative parts too (as it most certainly did for him).

What we were doing in that small California church was squinting together toward a vision of how art might take on new light and significance when viewed in light of Christ. We began to see new possibilities for thinking about Christian art.[17] Is that really why Jesus came? After all, we have no record of Jesus setting up easels along the shores of Galilee to host seminars in seascape painting. Was his mission to teach us how to be creative? At first blush, we may say no. But when we step back to take in the overarching storyline of Scripture, it is hardly a stretch to see human creativity among the things that Jesus came to redeem. Recall Rookmaaker's insight that Jesus came, not to make us "ghosts," but "to renew our lives at all levels." The resurrected Lord not only brings life to dead bodies and souls, but to dead imaginations. That is exactly the kind of resurrection I watched happen to my skeptical friend Jasper. It can happen to you too.

To see and experience what that means, we need to ponder the meaning of Jesus' resurrection. It is there, looking deep into the empty tomb, that we see the meaning of true creativity. I offer three prospects for the resurrection of our creative lives from the resurrection of Jesus.

6.3 ART AND THE EMPTY TOMB

The first jolt to our creative lives comes from Luke's account of the first Easter. Jesus' friends "found the stone rolled away from the tomb, but when they went in they did not find the body of the Lord Jesus."[18] Note well, "they did not find the body." It was not merely Jesus' spirit that rose, or his inspirational ethics that live on. The tomb was empty because there was no longer a corpse inside. It was not a ghost that enjoyed a fish breakfast with the disciples. It was not the Golden Rule that offered its scars for Thomas's inspection. Mary Magdalene did not hug a hologram. The New Testament is emphatic on this point. Just as he was born in the flesh, lived in the flesh, and died in the flesh, so Jesus resurrected *in the flesh*. If his body had stayed dead, if Jesus is nothing but dust particles scattered in the Middle East, then Christianity is a con, a bad joke, a total waste of everyone's precious little time on earth.

This is the precise point where many miss the meaning of the empty tomb. There is a widespread belief that Jesus died and rose only so that we can go to heaven when we die. It is as if Jesus lifts our spirits into the clouds to strum harps while God dumps kerosene and turns this whole godforsaken planet to ash.[19] If spirit is all that matters to Jesus, then there is no compelling reason for the tomb to be empty. A spiritual resurrection would have done the trick. Jesus could have bid a forever farewell to material existence and opened a magical portal in the sky so our souls too can escape these carbon and H_2O prisons. It is precisely this attitude — this failure to reckon with the bodily resurrection as a *bodily* resurrection — that inspires so much uninspired Christian art. If God doesn't care about the material world, then why should we bother to make something of it?

The New Testament tells a very different story with far better prospects for our creative lives. It tells us that Jesus came to "reconcile to himself all things, whether on earth or in heaven." Because of him "the creation itself will be set free from its bondage to corruption." Thanks to his resurrection, God will "transform our lowly body to be like his glorious body."[20] Jesus was born, died, and rose in matter because matter matters to him. Back in the eighth century, John of Damascus asked a rhetorical question about the resurrected Jesus: "Is not the body and blood of our Lord matter? Do not despise matter, for it is not despicable."[21]

What are the implications of bodily resurrection for our creative lives? N. T. Wright answers:

> Jesus is raised, so God's new creation has begun — and we, his followers, have a job to do! . . . What you *do* in the present — by painting, preaching, singing, sewing, praying, teaching, building hospitals, digging wells, campaigning for justice, writing poems, caring for the needy, loving your neighbor as yourself — *will last into God's future.*[22]

To see Wright's point, imagine that Wright is wrong. Imagine that Jesus never rose. What then? Atheist Bertrand Russell answers, "All labours of the ages, all the devotion, all the inspiration, all the noonday brightness of human genius, are destined to extinction in the vast death of the solar system."[23] Feel the devastating logical consistency of Russell's point. If there is no God and, therefore, no possibility of resurrection, then, indeed, as Russell says, "the whole temple of Man's achievement must inevitably be buried beneath the debris of a universe in ruins."[24]

A *Time* magazine article entitled "How It All Ends" agrees with Russell's bleak eschatology, that the universe "will become an unimaginably vast, cold, dark, and profoundly lonely place."[25] Assume that Russell and *Time* are right about "How It All Ends." What would it mean to do creative work in that kind of cosmos? It would mean that we are working at cross-purposes with the entire universe. We are on the wrong side of the future. We are polishing brass on the *Titanic*, painting pin-up girls on a falling bombshell, planting flowers at Chernobyl while the reactor core heats up.

If, however, Jesus rose from the dead, then the universe is not destined for extinction but redemption. To work creatively, then, is to step into the forward flow of the universe, to work toward rather than against its final destination. It is to join what Paul calls "a plan for the fullness of time, to unite all things in him, things in heaven and things on earth."[26] The empty tomb teaches us that the material world matters to Jesus and it will *always* matter to him, so it should matter to us.[27]

This is a mark of good art. Look at a Dürer or Rembrandt woodcut. Study the tiny, elegant details in a hand, a beard, a wing, a rhino, a rabbit, or a tree trunk. It is clear that matter mattered to the artists. Listen to Vivaldi's "Four Seasons," the Beatles' "White Album," Radiohead's "O.K. Computer," or Dustin Kensrue and Thrice's "Alchemy Index." Hear the sonic craftsmanship and mastery over their instruments. Matter mattered to these musicians. Taste the edible artwork of a good chef. Savor the care put into each ingredient and the precision at every stage of the cooking process. It is deliciously clear that matter matters to the culinary artist.

Here, frankly, is why a lot of what is marketed as Christian art does not live up to the name. Oftentimes, there is such a rush to get the message out that the medium — the material components of the art — is treated as immaterial, that is, unimportant.[28] The result sends a profoundly anti-Christian message. It does not tell the truth of the empty tomb. It tells the old Gnostic lie that the spiritual trumps the material. We must remember that when Jesus worked as a craftsman, he did not glorify the Father by etching fish symbols into wobbly tables, or chiseling his favorite *torah* verse on crumbling walls. He glorified his Father by making good tables and building sturdy walls.

Jesus describes his own resurrection as an original work of craftsmanship. "Destroy this temple, and in three days I will raise it up."[29] In his bodily resurrection, Jesus launched his most epic building project ever — to renovate, beautify, and ennoble all of creation.[30] Then he invites us into that grand creative work as his apprentices. Where, then, do we start? Start wherever he has positioned you, and with whatever resources he has given you. You can start in the kitchen, the backyard soil, the dirty neighborhood, behind a camera, in front of the piano, or at the blinking cursor on a blank screen. Wherever you are, start living in and toward the new creation. Whatever you have, tell the truth of the empty tomb — the truth that Jesus is Lord of all, and that, therefore, matter matters.[31]

6.4 THE EMPTY TOMB PROTEST

In Luke's narrative, the women are understandably "perplexed" upon discovering the empty tomb. Angels then deliver more perplexing news. "He is not here, but has risen," and they remind the women how Jesus said, "The Son of Man must be delivered into the hands of sinful men and be crucified and on the third day rise."[32] Luke's narrative cuts from news of the empty tomb to a road where two of Jesus' followers walk in despair. Jesus joins their conversation incognito as they voice their dashed hopes. The religious rulers "crucified him. But we had hoped that he was the one to redeem Israel."[33] The mysterious third traveler starts pontificating about the prophetic storyline of the Old Testament, how it was "necessary that the Christ should suffer these things and enter into his glory." The travelers' "hearts burn."[34] That night, over dinner, Jesus opens their eyes and the shock comes. The very man explaining the great hope of the Old Testament *is* the great Hope of the Old Testament, the resurrected Messiah!

What the angels do for the women at the tomb, and what Jesus does for the travelers on the road, is, in the words of John Calvin, to "reveal to us a higher reality than is offered by this sinful world."[35] Except that Calvin was not talking about the first Easter when he said that. He was talking about good art. Herein lies a second insight into the creative life. True creative action has a way of shocking us from despair into a more glowing vision of the world.

One way to get at this insight is to think of the bodily resurrection as, among other things, a form of protest art. "Protest" is a blend of the Latin "before" (*pro*) and "testify" (*testis*). Its basic meaning is "putting truth on display in front of people." Over the centuries (and particularly in the United States) "protest" has come to mean more than putting truth on public display. It is doing so in a way that deliberately challenges the status quo, unmasks its injustices, and calls for a more humanizing way of life. When this is done in a creative, attention-grabbing, and often shocking way, what we have is protest art.

Some of the best protest art I have ever seen was in Berlin. Our sleeper train arrived at 3 a.m., so my wife and I had the whole city to ourselves for a couple hours. We walked the trail where the Berlin Wall once stood, through Check Point Charlie, and the claustrophobic grid of concrete columns that form Berlin's Holocaust Memorial. We found a dark alley that looked like a Hollywood movie set where hooded superheroes pummel street thugs. I took my wife by the hand and we braved our way through trash and busted furniture. Our little adventure led us into a dystopian dream world. There was a rocket ship fuselage propped up on its tail fins. We saw a robot with a propane tank for a torso, scuba gear arms, and mortar shell hands. There was a fence made of brass frames with frayed strings from gutted grand pianos. We saw an armless copper angel, a menorah made of welded bullets, a headless female nude made of chicken-wire and scrap metal, and bodies made of concrete with cracks revealing rebar wire bones. Four welded letters, orange with rust, stood about ten feet tall to spell the word "LUST." My wife pointed up to a black banner stretched between two buildings. It read: "GLOBAL WARNING | Ausstellung | Alex Rodin." We accidentally discovered the outdoor exhibition of a brilliant artist from Belarus named Alexander Rodin.

As the sun rose, we found Rodin himself, covered in chalky debris, hammering away at a plaster statue under a tarp hanging off an old Winnebago. During our brief conversation it became clear. I was speaking to a protest artist, and a masterful one at that. Rodin's art was intended to shock. It turned floodlights on society to reveal something grotesque that we didn't see, or didn't care to see, before — women as headless sex objects, the unholy welding of war and religion, the broken promises of technology, and other dehumanizing side effects of life in the twenty-first century. It is one thing to read about how efficient economic calculus has led to the pruning of music programs from school curriculum. It is another to find yourself fenced in by the stacked skeletons of eviscerated pianos.

Good art does that. It jolts awake something deep inside us that wants to scream, "This is *not* how it should be!" In that protest we find our longings intensified for a better world — for what the Bible calls *shalom*, the way things should be. If good art doesn't leave us longing for *shalom*, it can, at least, put a rock in our shoe. We see or hear or watch something that makes it harder to walk in step with the status quo without feeling uncomfortable, like a grand change is due.

Bob Dylan didn't just call for change by saying, "Racism is bad!" He sang "Oxford Town." Picasso didn't just say, "Booh war!" He painted *Guernica*. Dostoyevsky didn't just say, "Down with Oppressive Religion!" He wrote "The Grand Inquisitor." Emma Sulkowicz didn't just say, "Stop sexual assault!" She hauled the object of her own trauma on her back through public spaces in her "Mattress Performance" entitled "Carry That Weight." Jesus didn't just say, "My kingdom has come." He rose from the dead in a way that jolts us awake to a new and better state-of-being, in Peter's words, "to be born again to a living hope through the resurrection of Jesus Christ from the dead, to an inheritance that is imperishable, undefiled, and unfading."[36]

What, then, did Jesus walking out of the tomb protest? Racism, false religion, war, sexual assault? What kind of world was he beckoning us toward? A world of beautiful diversity, global peace, religious justice, and sexual wholeness? Yes, yes, and yes. All of that and more. To really experience the meaning of what we may call "The Empty Tomb Protest," it helps to view it in the context of the week that led up to it.

On Sunday came the protest piece, "Man on Colt." It was a bustling day in Jerusalem — the first day of Passover week when, every year, the Roman governor made a grand entrance on horseback into Jerusalem, escorted by sword-wielding imperial troops. It was propaganda that said, "Hear ye, tens of thousands of Jews: We are Rome. We are glorious, powerful, and rich. We represent Caesar, the son of the gods. You will bow or be made to bow." As the Roman overlords gallop into Jerusalem from the west, Jesus rides into the holy city from the east on the back of a borrowed colt.[37] Here was a protest against the self-importance and parody of glory that was Caesar's kingdom. Here comes your real Lord not with regal fanfare and implicit death threats, but resolved to die in humiliation for his worst enemies.

The following day, Passover Monday, came "Den of Robbers," Jesus' protest art in the Temple courtyard against the religious establishment. He flipped moneychangers' tables and stood among the scattered shekels to touch and heal the exploited. Thursday came the "Meaning of Power" exhibition in the upper room. Jesus interrupts a dispute over who will be greatest by brandishing a slave's towel and washing everyone's feet. Later that night came "This is my Body," a multisensory exploration of the meaning of sacrifice and vicarious suffering. Then came "Good Friday" — the pièce de résistance against all sin and hell, the public execution of Jesus.

Then comes Easter Sunday. I ask again, what does the bodily resurrection of Jesus protest? Sin and hell? Selfishness? False religious empires? False political empires? The short answer is yes. Jesus' resurrection was his creative subversion of all that is destructive in the universe all at once. It protests what Luke and the New Testament call "the present age." In a biblical worldview, the drama of the entire universe unfolds in two *olams* in Hebrew, two *aions* in Greek, two "ages" in English. There is "the present age" — *ha-olam hazeh* — the long, dark chapter we live in, full of death, social, political, and satanic mayhem. It is the age of groaning, frustration, toiling, warfare, doom, oppression, tragedy, injustice, and heartbreak (basically, everything that people watch cat bloopers, inhale THC, and swallow antidepressants to forget about).

Then there is *ha-olam ha-ba* — "the age to come." This was the great hope that prophets wrote about, psalmists sang and danced about, Jesus told parables about, and that his followers so eagerly wanted him to establish. "The age to come" is the age of *shalom*, of peace with God, peace with one another, peace with ourselves, and peace with the rest of creation. It is the age of the world's best wine,[38] food fit for royalty, abundant life, true justice, and shimmering beauty. It is an age when we are most truly ourselves, where happiness doesn't spike and dwindle in seconds, leaving us shaking for a fix, but crescendos forever. It is the true happy ending that so much great literature, music, painting, choreography, and cinema tries to touch.

Which age, then, are we living in? Sadly, we are languishing in "the present age." But there is a glitch, a cosmic anomaly, a flash from another *aion*. A tomb that, by all the rules of our age, should be occupied is empty.

A body that, by all laws of our age, should be decaying is doing strange things — walking, talking, eating bread and fish — things that no body that has been through rigor mortis should ever do. "The age to come" has broken into (and broken the laws of) the "the present age." The resurrected Jesus is the glitch in our system of death, decay, and despair — a glorious glitch that will eventually bring the whole depressing system of the present age to a crash. To flip the metaphor, the antidote has been injected into a sick and dying cosmos, and is working his way through the whole system putting to death all that puts to death, bringing vim and vigor back to the once terminal universe.

What does this mean for our creative lives? We saw in the previous section that matter matters in good art. Now we may add that, as our creative powers develop, we make matter matter in ways that protest death and "the present age," and beckon us to life, even now, in "the age to come." Like the resurrection, good art shocks us back to life. It is like smelling salts for the unconscious, defibrillator paddles to a cold chest, or flames to Puddleglum's webbed feet.

Granted, that last simile was a little obscure. Puddleglum, for those who have yet to read C. S. Lewis's *Silver Chair*, is a Marsh-wiggle — a tall, froggish humanoid from the land of Narnia. Puddleglum and his human allies, Jill and Scrubb, find themselves in the underground lair of the Green Witch.[39] She fills the room with aromatic green smoke and "thrums" a sweet song on something "like a mandolin." Her smoke and song "made it harder to think." Then she starts in on a seductive line of reasoning. The Witch wants her captives to lose all hope of life beyond her subterranean kingdom. "The sun is but a tale, a children's story," she reasons. "You have seen lamps, and so you imaged a better bigger lamp and called it *the sun.*" The smoke swirls. Thrum — thrum go the Witch's strings. "'Tis a pretty make-believe." Thrum — thrum. "There never was a sun." Puddleglum and the children echo, "No. There never was a sun." Thrum — thrum.

Good art can be the fire to our feet that helps break the enchantment of our age.

It is a testimony to Lewis's creative genius that what seems like disenchantment — curing children from "make-believe" so they can "begin a wiser life tomorrow" — is actually an enchantment, a deceptive spell.

Under that enchantment, it slowly made "very good sense" that "the other world must be all a dream" and that the Witch's "black pit of a kingdom . . . is the only world." Then, a half-dazed Puddleglum does "a very brave thing." He stamps his bare foot into the fire. As Lewis says, "There is nothing like a good shock for dissolving certain kinds of magic." Yes! That is precisely what I mean by protest art, art that administers a "good shock." Jesus, with his news of resurrection, didn't make feet burn in Underland. Luke tells us he made "hearts burn" on the Emmaus road. In doing so, he broke the spell that "the present age" is "the only world."

What we need, then, is art that does what Jesus does. We need art that both disenchants and re-enchants all at once. It can disenchant by breaking the spell that "There is no Narnia, no Overworld, no sky, no sun, no Aslan." In our century it can break the spell that there is no resurrection, no more to existence than what the hard sciences say exist, or no more to human life than what evolutionary psychologists call "the Four F's" — fighting, feeding, fleeing, and . . . well, mating.[40] The Green Witch's music still plays. "You imagined a bigger better Dad and called it *God*." "The cosmos is all there is, ever was, and ever will be." "You Only Live Once." "The only real world of happiness is the one you find within yourself." "There's nothing up there, nothing beyond, nothing more real than your own feelings." Thrum — thrum.

Good art can be the fire to our feet that helps break the enchantments of our age. While disenchanting us, good art also re-enchants our world. Abraham Kuyper makes the point far better than I can:

> Art has the mystical task of reminding us in its productions of the beautiful that was lost and of anticipating its perfect coming luster . . . enabling us to discover in and behind this sinful life a richer and more glorious background. Standing by the ruins of this once so wonderfully beautiful creation, art points out . . . the still visible lines of the original plan, and what is even more, the splendid restoration by which the Supreme Artist and Master Builder will one day renew and enhance even the beauty of His original creation.[41]

6.5 "DISBELIEVING FOR JOY AND MARVELING"

Let's come back down through the atmosphere to our daily world, back to the kitchen, the garden, the neighborhood, the canvas, the keyboard, and the blinking cursor. What would it mean, in our daily creative lives, to make good protest art? How do we make art that both disenchants and re-enchants, and fulfills what Kuyper calls "the mystical task of reminding us of the beautiful that was lost and of anticipating its perfect coming luster"?

To get a realistic sense of what that could look like, consider C. S. Lewis's first encounters with this kind of art. Lewis was just 6 years old when his big brother "Warnie" showed him a toy forest he had crafted inside a biscuit tin lid with moss, twigs, and flowers. For Lewis, this was like his first peek into "the age to come," in Lewis's words, "the first beauty I ever knew . . . Milton's 'enormous bliss' of Eden."[42] His second peek came through Beatrix Potter's description of Autumn in her book, *Squirrel Nutkin.* For Lewis, "It administered the shock. . . . It was something quite different from ordinary life and even from ordinary pleasure: something, as they would now say, 'in another dimension'" (or as we might say in ancient Jewish categories, another *age*).[43] Then there were "the Green Hills" Lewis could view from the windows of his nursery in Belfast. Lewis says that "low line of the Castlereagh hills . . . taught me longing."

Next came three short lines from a Henry Longfellow poem in which Lewis found himself desiring "with almost sickening intensity something never to be described"[44] (reminiscent of 1 Cor. 2:9: "What no eye has seen, nor ear heard, nor the heart of man imagined, what God has prepared for those who love him"). Then came the music of Wagner, the old Norse myths, George MacDonald's *Phantastes* (in which Lewis's "imagination was baptized"), reading G. K. Chesterton's poems in the trenches of World War I, and more. Lewis's inner protestor was learning from these creative luminaries how to cry out for a better world, a restored creation. These artworks, each in its own humble way, became signposts of "the age to come" breaking through into "the present age."

Finally, in 1931, during a Saturday night conversation that turned into a Sunday morning conversation, J. R. R. Tolkien explained to his Oxford colleague and dear friend how "myths have hints of the promise and hope of redemption, of the setting right of all things."[45] As Tolkien later put his ideas to ink in the essay "On Fairy Stories":

> The Gospels contain . . . a story of a larger kind which embraces all the essence of fairy-stories. . . . It is not difficult to imagine the peculiar excitement and joy that one would feel, if any specially beautiful fairy-story were found to be "primarily true," its narrative to be history. . . . The Christian joy, the Gloria, is of the same kind; but it is pre-eminently (infinitely, if our capacities were not finite) high and joyous. Because this story is supreme; and it is true. Art has been verified.[46]

As Lewis came to believe, "the story of Christ is simply a true myth: a myth working on us in the same way as the others, but with this tremendous difference that it *really* happened."[47]

The kind of art that awakens us to the "true myth," the "Christian joy, the Gloria," comes in many shapes, sounds, and sizes. It doesn't have to be a sprawling painting from Genesis to Revelation on a ceiling at the Vatican. It could be a makeshift toy forest in an old biscuit tin, a reflection on Autumn, the shot of a local mountain view, a song, a poem, or a fairy story.

This moves us to a final lesson from Luke's resurrection account for our creative lives. Good art that awakens us to the Gloria is not sentimental. It does not offer us wispy joy untethered from reality. After administering the "good shock" on the Emmaus road, Jesus appeared to his disciples in the upper room and "showed them his hands and his feet." Note the disciples' reaction. John's version has an understated "the disciples were glad when they saw the Lord." Luke uses a strange, psychological turn of phrase — the disciples "disbelieved for joy and were marveling"[48] Commentators take Luke's phrase to say that the sight of Jesus was just too good to be true. It was far too good to be true, hence the disbelief; but it *is* true, hence the joy and marvel.

Contrast that moment in the upper room with a lot of Christian art that tries to evoke joy. Much of it (and I won't name names) makes us yawn. It inspires us not to wonder but to change the station for something more "real." Rap artist Lecrae explains:

Many times, that's how people see Christian art, or Christians making art: They see the art as having an agenda. Christians have really used and almost in some senses prostituted art in order to give answers instead of telling great stories and raising great questions.[49]

For anyone not taken in by its sentimentalism, the kind of "Christian art" Lecrae describes does not seem too good to be true, but too glittery and manufactured to be true. It evokes disbelieving cynicism, not a disbelieving joy.

What the disciples experienced in the upper room was anything but predictable, sentimental, or cynical. There was genuine shock and euphoria. The reason for this is that there is something in Luke's account that is altogether missing from so much of our art. Jesus showed the disciples "his hands and his feet." Why? Because *that's where the scars were*. The glorious truth of the resurrection was not revealed in some dreamy netherworld, outside the context of the deep woundedness of our world.

To press the point further, re-imagine Luke's resurrection narrative like this:

One Sunday morning, after a busy Friday and a restful Saturday, Jesus walked by an open tomb in a garden. He stepped inside. A few moments later he sprung forth and exclaimed, "I'm alive!" with wide eyes and scar-free jazz hands. The disciples turned red.

An exuberant Easter Sunday becomes absurd the minute we leave out the scars of Good Friday and the hopelessness of Black Saturday. Friday, for all the infinite good it brings us, was a traumatizing horror of a day, a day to shudder and weep. Here, on public display, hangs the gruesome reality of sin. On Saturday — what has been branded "Black Saturday" in some church traditions — God seems utterly silent. Had our past few years following Jesus been a total waste? Was he just another false messiah? Will the better kingdom ever come? Will God's will ever be done? The religious and Roman establishment prevailed. Our king is dead. Our best hope has been speared in the heart, wrapped up, and sealed in a tomb to rot to dust. All is lost!

Had Handel been there that Friday or Saturday to lead the disciples in the exuberant "Hallelujah Chorus" in D-major, it would have still been good art from a technical perspective. But it would have been a lie on those days. As the proverb says, singing happy tunes to a heavy heart is pouring vinegar in an open wound.[50] By the following morning, however, the very same Hallelujah chorus would resound truthfully. Friday's vinegar becomes Sunday's wine. Pain and death and silence do not have the final word. Futility and despair were only *temporarily* true. Mix bright yellows into the palette. Let the cymbals crash. Raise the thirds. Clink overflowing glasses from the top shelf bottles. Forget yourself. Sing to each other. Laugh so hard you snort. Whirl like a Dervish. Burn, burn, burn with joy "like fabulous yellow roman candles exploding like spiders across the stars" (to borrow Kerouac's great line from *On the Road*). Disbelieve for joy and marvel. He is risen! Cry out through your quivering windpipes — *Haaaaa-llelujah! Haaaaaaa-llelujah!*

But to be frank, we (myself included) are lousy at artistically expressing that kind of joy.[51] Why? The extent to which we fail to tell gruesome Good Friday truths and shy away from shattered Black Saturday truths is the extent to which our attempts to tell Easter Sunday truths will sound false. As Jesus told the disciples in the upper room, "Christ should suffer and on the third day rise from the dead." As he asked the Emmaus travelers, "Was it not necessary that the Christ should suffer these things and enter into his glory?" The joy of Redemption cannot be detached from the realities of the Fall without ceasing to be joy and becoming an airy, fairy sentimentalism.

To take the thought further, from Fall and Redemption to Consummation, our art must come to terms with the fact that, though Easter Sunday is the glorious launch of "the age to come," it is not its full realization. "The present age," with its angst and depravity, has been undermined, yes, but not yet eradicated. That means that Good Friday and Black Saturday truths still ring true, at least for now. To ignore or caricature those unpleasant truths, to make art that airbrushes the deep gashes in our hearts and our world would not be honest. It would be the artistic equivalent of what theologians call an "over-realized eschatology," pretending we can accomplish *now* what only Jesus will accomplish *then*.[52]

Take one example. A musician friend of mine attended a conference for aspiring artists where a celebrity worship leader shared his secret formula for success — "Never use a minor chord." Major chords, he explained, have that uplifting, sunny-day quality that you want in a good worship set. Minor chords are too dreary, might alienate your audience, and might turn them off to the joy of the gospel. We should worship with party anthems, not a funeral dirge. It should feel like a Southern California beach, not a Seattle cemetery.[53]

What if what alienates the audience is strumming major-chord worship set after major-chord worship set (or should I say "thrumming")? What if it is the happy-clappy anthems themselves, with a refusal to play a true biblical lament, that makes people feel even more alone in their very real woundedness, and makes the gospel feel more like a Hallmark card than the most shockingly good news the world has ever known?

We fail to express real Christian beauty, fail to tell the good news of Easter Sunday and the hope of the coming new creation because we are afraid of minor chords and dissonance, afraid to reckon seriously with the old creation we now inhabit. As Rookmaaker says, "We can never have joy if there are not also tears."[54] Good music has minor and major chords. Good paintings have dark and bright hues. Good movies have real brokenness and real redemption. Good beer has hoppy-ness and maltiness. The good news has death and resurrection. Without the former, the latter becomes inauthentic, contrived, artificial, plastic, kitsch. We must learn how to creatively tell the truth of the gory cross and occupied tomb if we want the good news of the empty tomb, and the new creation it signals, to evoke anything like the joy it should.

At the empty tomb, we learned that matter matters. On the Emmaus road, we learned the power of protest to shock us out of the enchantments of "the present age," and open our eyes to the age that dawned that first Easter. In the upper room, we learned to show the scars if there is to be any true joy and marveling. Those three insights from Luke 24 hold a lifetime of promise for deepening our creative lives.

✶

Before moving on to our final chapter, I have a promise to deliver on. Whatever happened to old Jasper, the skeptic? Something remarkable. After our biblical exploration of creativity, did he unleash his inner Warhol and take the big city art scene by storm? Did he awaken the John Williams within and score Hollywood blockbusters? Did he become the next Banksy, painting striking images of profound questions all over the city? No. Jasper dusted off an old camera and went around town snapping photographs of whatever broken and beautiful things he found. He arranged them into a little cinematic slideshow and wrote a poem to go with it. The photos weren't Ansel Adams, the cinematic work wasn't P. T. Anderson, and the poetry wasn't Emily Dickinson. They didn't have to be. A man who bears God's image, but didn't think he had an artistic bone in his body, a man who spent a half century seeing no connection between creativity and his love for Jesus, took some pictures, made a slideshow, and wrote a poem. And that, in and of itself, is a beautiful story.

A PRAYER TO CREATE

Jesus, you made and sustain the universe and everything beautiful within it. You entered your own artwork, marred as it was by sin. You resurrected and showed us that matter matters and will always matter to you, and that there is more to reality than "the present age." Because you came back to life we can have real joy and hope instead of a sentimental buzz. Help us to mirror your creativity, to make something of the world in ways to point to the real world you inaugurated in your resurrection and will bring to full creative expression at your return. Amen.

7

TRANSFORM

Mirroring Jesus in All of Life

Now the Lord is the Spirit, and where the Spirit of the Lord is, there is freedom. And we all, with unveiled face, beholding the glory of the Lord, are being transformed into the same image from one degree of glory to another. For this comes from the Lord who is the Spirit.

— 2 CORINTHIANS 3:17–18

> We are saved not just in order that we might become spiritual ghosts in heaven. No, Christ came in order to make us human in the fullest sense, to renew our lives at all levels . . . from our thoughts feelings, sex and artworks to our marriages, holidays, and the food we eat. . . . He makes it possible for the totality of a person to be renewed. . . . That's Christianity.
>
> HANS ROOKMAAKER

If you've made it this far then you have taken in something of the profound thinking, just sentiments, upside-down action, radical relationality, saving grace, and artistic genius of Jesus. When I say you have "taken in something," I mean something very, very small. If anything, I have offered you six droplets — hopefully refreshing, life-giving droplets — but droplets nonetheless from an infinite ocean. Jesus is that expansive and deep. There is always more of him to drink in and enjoy.

7.1 TRANSFORMATION

The previous six chapters have spanned a mere week of Jesus' life. On Monday and Tuesday, Jesus engaged the Sadducees on the temple steps and erupted against the religious swindlers in the temple courts. There we saw something of what it means to *Reason* and *Emote* like him. Thursday came the foot washing in the upper room, and Jesus' prayer where we learned to *Flip* our actions into something holy and how to *Love* more radically. Friday was his execution. There, on Skull Hill, we encountered his multifaceted grace and learned to *Elevate* others. Sunday, at the empty tomb, on the Emmaus road, and in the upper room, we learned from the resurrected Jesus what it means to *Create*. Six days and six dimensions of what it means to be robustly human.

And so we reach our final letter of *REFLECT* — T for Transform. How do we actually come to Reason, Emote, Flip, Love, Elevate, and Create like him? What does that change look like? Where does real, lasting transformation come from?

The opening lines of this book were from Psalm 115, in which people worshiped objects that could not speak, see, hear, feel, or walk, and "those who make them become like them." It is an ancient song, not about the *trans*formation but the *de*formation of a human being, how worshiping something dumb, senseless, and heartless will make us increasingly dumb, senseless, and heartless. Here is Emerson's Law — "what we are worshiping we are becoming" — working against us, making us less and less glorious, less weighty and radiant, less human. Having begun with a psalm about deformation, we end with a word on transformation. In a letter to the Corinthians, Paul offers the hopeful antithesis to Psalm 115, a reversal of Emerson's Law so that, as we worship, we become most gloriously ourselves:

> Now the Lord is the Spirit, and where the Spirit of the Lord is, there is freedom. And we all, with unveiled face, beholding the glory of the Lord, are being transformed into the same image from one degree of glory to another. For this comes from the Lord who is the Spirit.[1]

In Paul's words to the Corinthians, we find four insights that prevent us from becoming burned out, self-righteous, over-pious, and spiritually mangled in our efforts to reflect Jesus.

7.2 THE SECRET TO LIFELONG DEPRESSION

As we approach Paul's insights, it must be said that everything up to this point of *REFLECT* could be accurately subtitled, "Becoming Your Worst Self by Trying to Mirror the Greatest Person in History," "The Secret to Achieving

Lifelong Depression," or perhaps, "A Friendly Guide to Total Soul-Crushing Spiritual Implosion." Mirroring Jesus is not difficult; it is impossible.

Imagine that we resolve to really reason like Jesus. We pour loads of mental energy into sharpening our biblical acumen. We invest years nose-deep in good books, honing our logical thinking skills, and boosting our worldview awareness. Imagine that you and I were able to chart real growth in the each of the nine dimensions we observed from Jesus' intellectual life. As our theological IQ soars, we could very easily find ourselves emotionally jumbled.

We resolve together to move beyond the R in *REFLECT*, and focus more energy on emoting like Jesus. We quickly realize the vast difference between his just sentiments and our own, often wacky, emotions. We get to work on our guts to feel what Jesus feels, but are soon struck with the dreadful realization that we are lagging light years behind Jesus in the ways we pursue holy action, the ways we love and elevate others, and in our creative lives. We move on to the FLEC part of *REFLECT*, only to find our abilities to reason and emote begin to atrophy. This whole "becoming like Jesus" endeavor turns out to be far more complicated, draining, and joyless than we first imagined. Instead of finding ourselves coming to life, taking on his gravitas and glow, we find that we are collapsing in on ourselves. As theologian Joanne Jung notes, "Living the facade of the Christian life is tiring; pseudo-transformation is far from the sustainable life of impact for which we were created."[2]

If our pursuit of Jesus is "from the Spirit," then there will be something immensely liberating about the whole process.

This book would indeed be about "pseudo-transformation," about "Becoming Your Worst Self," if we ignored Paul's words: "Where the Spirit of the Lord is, there is freedom." If our pursuit of Jesus is "from the Spirit," then there will be something immensely liberating about the whole process.[3] According to Jung, God's

goal is to make us like Christ. The power to accomplish this is the abiding presence of his Spirit. When we understand that almighty God is at work in us for our spiritual formation, we may feel that a huge weight has been lifted from us.[4]

But if our efforts to become like Jesus are from ourselves they lead us only into bondage and despair. Corrie Ten Boom concludes, "Trying to do the Lord's work in your own strength is the most confusing, exhausting, and tedious of all work. But when you are filled with the Holy Spirit, then the ministry of Jesus just flows out of you."[5]

7.3 THE FIRST THING

Paul continues, "And we all, with unveiled face, beholding the glory of the Lord . . ." Real transformation does not occur in the first-person singular — the capital "I" burrowing deeper into itself for answers. It occurs in the first-person plural — when "*we* all . . . behold the glory of the Lord." Paul is, after all, writing to the *church* in Corinth. In the words of Thabiti Anyabwile, "The apostles did not preach so that there simply would be a new me, but so that there would be a new we."[6] It is within community that real transformation happens. A community can reflect Jesus far more radiantly than any lone soul.

Note well what that "we" does. It does not stare into the mirror to "oooh" and "awww" at its own image. When a community becomes enamored with itself — its slick name brand, celebrity poster boys, or swelling numbers — it is only a matter of time until that community turns dark and destructive. Real transformation happens when people come together for the chief purpose of "*beholding the glory of the Lord.*" It is not about overanalyzing ourselves and masterminding the success of our own programs. It is in fixing our eyes on someone infinitely more interesting than ourselves, marveling together at Jesus as we meet him in Scripture every week, that our communities take on supernatural gravitas and glow. As Richard Sibbes says: "The very beholding of Christ is a transforming sight . . . it is a transforming beholding. . . . A man cannot look upon the love of God and of Christ in the gospel, but it will change him to be like God and Christ."[7]

This is the very point where we often behold Jesus all wrong. We look not *at* him but *through* him, not as the End, but as the means to our own ends. One dead giveaway that we have been duped by a false Christianity is that it treats Jesus not as an intrinsic good, but as an instrumental good. It sees Jesus as desirable only insofar as he helps us get something we want more fundamentally than we want him. When we want health and wealth, we look to a Mercedes-driving, Rolex-bestowing, private Jet-flying Jesus as the means to the end of opulence. When we want higher self-esteem, we look to a Life Coach Jesus who high-fives our efforts, tickles our ears, and enlarges our sense of self-importance. When we want our political agenda to prevail, we put Jesus on an elephant's back to promote our Republican causes, or saddle him on a donkey to champion our Democratic policies.

Even when we focus on biblical themes like forgiveness and eternal life, we can still reduce Jesus to a means rather than the End. Francis Chan makes the point:

> The Good News — the best news in the world, in fact — is that you can have God himself. Do you believe that God is the greatest thing you can experience in the whole world? Do you believe that the Good News is not merely the forgiveness of your sins, the guarantee that you won't go to hell, or the promise of life in heaven? . . . Are we in love with God or just his stuff?[8]

In the context of this book, the question becomes: Are we in love with Jesus because he can help us reason, emote, flip, love, elevate, and create, or are we in love with Jesus himself? The best news is not that we can have a more profound intellectual life, more just sentiments, more holy actions, and so on. The best news in the universe is that we can have Jesus himself.

Recall Lewis's distinction between first and second things. If we make reason, emotion, holiness, love, grace, or creativity into first things we will not only lose those things, we will lose out on Jesus, which is infinitely worse. If Jesus is our First Thing, if glorifying and enjoying him is our chief end, then those second things will become more true of us. Sadly, our twisted hearts want second things more than the First Thing. We want gifts more than the Giver. Such inverted affections are why real transformation must come from beyond us, "from the Spirit."

7.4 UP OR DOWN?

What can we realistically expect to happen to us while "beholding the glory of the Lord"? Paul answers, we are "being transformed into the same image from one degree of glory to another." There is an upward and a downward reading of this text. One reading will transform and the other deform us.

On the upward reading, transformation "from one degree of glory to another" means becoming more "heavenly" and less "earthly." To understand this reading, consider a competition that broke out between some Protestants and Catholics in sixteenth-century Europe. It was not a competition for converts, or land, or political power. It was a contest over who could use less soap, yes, who could use *less* soap. Charles Panati's *Extraordinary Origins of Everyday Things* offers a fascinating history of hygiene, revealing, in grimy detail, a close correlation between stink and spirituality in the sixteenth century.[9] The less you bathed, the thinking went, the less you were fixated on the trifles of bodily existence. The more odorous your filth, the more amorous your faith. Why? Because your stench reveals your zeal for what really matters — the spiritual world — and your carelessness for what doesn't matter — the material world.

This prejudice against the world God made and called "good" has nothing in common with Paul (or Jesus). It was Plato who famously argued that "the noblest and the highest" form of inspiration is a state in which one "stands apart from worldly interests and is fastened upon the divine, careless of the world below"[10] (though it is doubtful whether the great Athenian pondered the pungent implications of his philosophy). Such an upward vision of glory would later inspire such Western ascetics as Simeon Stylites the Elder, who spent thirty-seven years on a pillar in the Syrian desert. Then there was Alypius, who stood atop a pillar for fifty-three years before his legs gave out. Then he laid there another fourteen years until his death.[11] The East also has a tradition of celebrity *sadhus* ("holy men"), men like India's Lotan Baba, known for eating grass, standing on one foot for a year, and rolling hundreds of miles in the dirt. What connects the pillar-sitters of the West and the holy rollers of the East? They all took their actions to be profoundly spiritual, moving "from one degree of glory to another."

But Jesus, in his topsy-turvy way, turns such spirituality on its head. He reveals the profound spirituality of all of life, how even the most mundane and material of actions can be acts of worship. Whether he was fixing tables, finishing dinner, or fishing with friends, Jesus was spiritual. It is Jesus, not Plato or the Eastern gurus, who shaped Paul's view of glory. We are better off, then, with a downward reading of "being transformed into [his] image," a reading more compatible with what N. T. Wright calls "God's new project not to snatch people away from earth to heaven but to colonize earth with the life of heaven."[12]

A downward reading of what it means to be transformed first struck me in the dairy box of a local supermarket. I was working the graveyard shift. Around 3 a.m. the big rig would pull up with pallet after pallet of cheese — Goat, Cow, Blue, Brie, American, Swiss, Colby Jack, Monterey Jack, Pepper Jack, hard, soft, shredded (you come to appreciate how many shapes, sizes, and styles of glorious cheese exist working in a dairy box). As the city slept, we began our nightly ritual known to my crew as "throwing cheese." We would slide the boxes down waxed floors, tear into them with box-cutters, and begin the tedious task of placing each of the thousand-and-one cheeses under the right tags.

One night, a few blocks into the cheddar section, an old quote (falsely attributed to Martin Luther) popped into my hazy head. It was something to the effect of how a widow sweeping her floor to the glory of God can be every bit as worshipful as a clergyman doing his "spiritual" work. If she can sweep floors to God's glory, why not throw cheese for the same reason? Having long associated worship with singing in church on Sunday morning, I wasn't quite sure what worshiping in the cheese aisle at 3 a.m. on a Tuesday should look like. I prayed very simply, "Jesus, I don't know what it means to throw cheese for your glory right now, but, please, somehow be glorified in this."

Kraft mild cheddar, medium, sharp. *Oh Lord my God . . .* Tillamook mild, sharp, extra sharp. *When I in awesome wonder . . .* Shredded mozzarella, thick cut, deli-cut. *Consider all the worlds Thy hands have made . . .* Daisy sour, extra sour. *Then sings my soul, my Savior God to Thee . . .* Gouda, Feta, Gorgonzola. *How Great Thou Art . . .* Muenster, Provolone, Havarti. *How Great Thou Art!*

It wasn't that my body went on autopilot while my soul focused on Jesus. It wasn't a matter of worshiping *and* throwing cheese, but worshiping *as* throwing cheese. There was no Platonic split between the spiritual and the material.

If we who are "spiritual" try to explain the emergence of the materialism that eats away the soul of our culture, then look no further than the matter-defying asceticism of our own traditions. ("Every action has an equal and opposite reaction" is as much of a social law as it is a physical law.) We must recover our vision, not of Plato's demiurge cursing creation, but of Jesus who made and blessed, entered, died, rose within, and will one day liberate and glorify creation. This biblical vision frees us up from trying to jump through the clouds. As Luther says in *The Freedom of a Christian*, "Our heavenly Father has in Christ freely come to our aid, we also ought freely to help our neighbor *through our body and its works*."[13] We are "transformed into his image from one degree of glory to another" down here, in everyday life, in cheese aisles, freeway traffic, gardens, sanctuaries, classrooms, bedrooms, DMV lines. We need the same breakthrough that Irish poet Evangeline Paterson experienced:

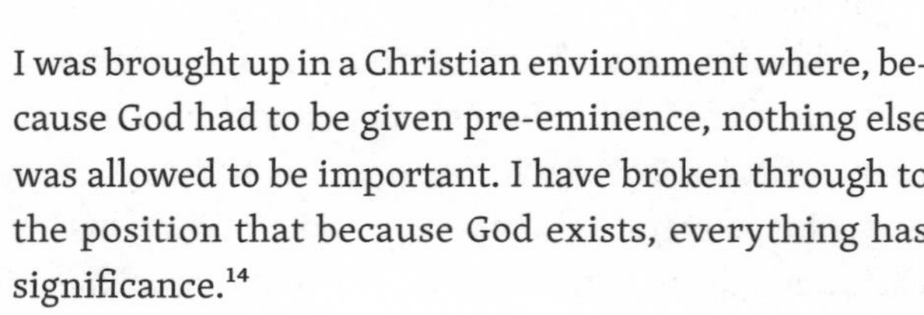

> I was brought up in a Christian environment where, because God had to be given pre-eminence, nothing else was allowed to be important. I have broken through to the position that because God exists, everything has significance.[14]

7.5 "CHRIST WILL SHINE ON YOU"

How do we experience Paterson's breakthrough? How do we come to see everything in light of God's existence? How do we live out the fact that, in Abraham Kuyper's famous words, "There is not a square inch in the whole domain of our human existence over which Christ, who is Sovereign over all, does not cry: 'Mine!'"[15] Paul answers, "This comes from the Lord who is the Spirit." Because it "comes from the Lord," transformation can never be codified into a legalistic list of *do's* and *don'ts* so we can check more boxes and feel superior to others. Because real transformation "comes from the Lord," he gets all the credit. Notice that Paul does not say that we transform, but that in beholding Christ we are "being transformed." The voice of that verb marks the line between Christianity and every hopeless spiritual technique that masquerades as Christianity. Paul uses the passive voice — "being transformed" — because we are not the prime actors but the acted upon. We do not transform ourselves. Paul knew his Old Testament in which we are the heart patients and God the Surgeon; we the skeletons, God the Life-breather; we the slaves, God the Liberator; we the abandoned newborns, God the Rescuer; we the pots, God the Potter.

How, then, can we tell the difference? How do we know if we are experiencing real transformation or trying to transform ourselves? There are many questions we could ask to expose the source: Do we feel superior to others? Do we really love people, especially the hard-to-love? Have our spiritual lives become a tired formula? Are we enjoying or merely appeasing God? Do we crave the spotlight? Do we need to be thought of as spiritual superstars? Do we tell other people about Jesus, and, if so, is it out of duty or delight? Are we any more like Jesus this year than we were last year? Do we love him for his own sake, or for what we want him to give us?

Those are helpful questions. But there is one more question, rarely asked, that reveals whether we are self- or Spirit-transformed. Before this question can make sense, it is important for us to see that Jesus is not merely a sum of parts. It is not as if you add reason to emotion, then throw in holiness, love, grace, and creativity and, after some basic metaphysical arithmetic, it all equals Jesus. It is not like this:

Reason + Emotion + Holiness + Love + Grace + Creativity = Jesus

Jesus is not a sum; he is a fully integrated Person. Every one of his attributes can be used as an adjective or adverb to describe any other attribute. Jesus is not merely reasonable. He is *reasonably* emotional. He is not merely emotional. He is emotional in a reasonable, holy, loving, gracious, and creative kind of way. His love is a reasonable, emotional, holy, gracious, and creative love, and so on. Each attribute is not *added to* but *multiplied to the power of* every other attribute:

(*A whole lot more*) = Jesus
Reason
Emotion
Holiness
Love
Grace
Creativity

As we behold this fully integrated Jesus, and become more like him, we gradually become more integrated ourselves. When the Holy Spirit transforms us "into the same image from one degree of glory to another" we come to reason more lovingly. We create more graciously. We emote with more holiness, and so on. If we find ourselves pulling apart at the seams, our heads unraveled from our hearts and hands, then we are not becoming more like Jesus. We are being self-deformed, not Spirit-transformed. Our question then is this: Are we becoming more or less integrated?

Because Jesus is not a fragmentary human but a fully realized human, it stands to reason that, as we reflect him, we become most fully ourselves. This is not assimilation into a race of clones. There is no one else in the history of the world who can reflect Jesus in the unique rays and colors of your God-given personality. Reflecting him makes you more vividly and irreplaceably *you*. Of course, we are all still fragmented and underdeveloped, shadows of ourselves, on this side of the new creation. "For now we see in a mirror dimly, but then face to face."[16] Because our *beholding* is now limited, so is our *becoming*. Yet there is hope because "we know that when he appears we shall be like him, because we shall see him as he is."[17] To fully behold him is to become most fully ourselves.

Who or what else could possibly warrant that kind of hope for becoming our full and radiant selves? Recall from the Introduction that an object that truly deserves our worship is more like a sun than a spotlight. It does not illuminate one or two parts of our humanity and banish the rest of us to the dark. If we stroll together through the twenty-first-century pantheon, we see the gods of Romance, Wealth, and Fame. Behold, a statue to the god of Government, the god of Religion, the gods of Sex and Serotonin Rushes. Take it all in and ask yourself, "What object of worship offered by our world is not, in the final analysis, a mere spotlight?"

Jesus is the Sun. He is the most reasonable, passionate, holy, loving, gracious, creative, and transformational being in existence. He has enough radiance to illuminate and enough weight to integrate our whole selves. As the ancient church sang: "Awake, O sleeper, and arise from the dead and Christ will shine on you."[18]

*

Finishing this book is not quite like finishing some great biography, like David Donald's celebrated *Lincoln*, or Taylor's Branch's Pulitzer-winning *King Trilogy*. Those books are not only critically acclaimed, unlike this book. They are also about dead people. You are not only reading a book about someone who is alive, you are reading in his living presence. And so, I leave you with a plea and a prayer.[19] First a plea:

> What is there that you can desire should be in a Savior, that is not in Christ? . . . What is there great or good . . . which is not found in the person of Christ? . . . You need not hesitate one moment; but may run to him, and cast yourself upon him. You will certainly be graciously . . . received by him.[20]

Then a prayer:

A PRAYER TO TRANSFORM

Jesus, we run to you. We cast ourselves on you. Receive us graciously. We don't want the bondage of self-help, we want the freedom of the Spirit. We can't change ourselves. We ask to "be transformed." We don't want you as a means to our self-fulfillment. We want you. As we worship you as our First Thing, make us be like you and, therefore, be most truly ourselves. Transform us to reason, emote, flip, love, elevate, and create like you, not in the clouds but in everyday life. We ask this "from the Spirit" and for your glory. Amen.

REFLECTion LOG

What follows is a small aid to help you reflect Jesus. Of course, there is infinitely more to him than what is listed in the following log (or captured in an acrostic).

Here is how it works. In the left column, take a couple of minutes to write down ways that you are reflecting Jesus. Then in the right column list ways you are *not* reflecting him. Keep in mind that we often wear primrose glasses when we introspect, so it may be worth praying with the psalmist, "Search me, O God, and know my heart! Try me and know my thoughts! And see if there be any grievous way in me, and lead me in the way everlasting!" (Ps. 139:23–24). Once you have filled both columns as honestly as possible, pray your way down the left column. Thank God for any ways that you are Reasoning, Emoting, Flipping, Loving, Elevating, Creating, and being Transformed like Jesus. Recognize that any ways in which you actually reflect Jesus (even as mere flickers compared to the Sun) are not from your own willpower or spiritual savvy. They are gifts from God's grace, so he gets the praise and thanks. Then pray down the right column, confessing any sin and asking God to transform you into Christ's image "from one degree of glory to another."

That's it. It takes a few minutes and can be done weekly, monthly, annually (or whenever) to gauge your progress over the years. (I have found it immensely helpful over the past ten years.) I am not offering some new, secret formula for achieving enlightenment. And I am certainly not offering an alternative to the tested and true methods for reflecting Jesus, for example, praying continuously, reading Scripture often, and contributing to the life of a healthy, biblical church. It is a supplement, not a substitute, to help you become yourself by mirroring the Greatest Person in History.

[A free PDF of the following REFLECTion Log can be downloaded for on-going use at www.thaddeuswilliams.com.]

REF LECT

Log Date: ___|___|___

	How I am **REFLECT**ing	How I am *not* **REFLECT**ing
Reason Am I mirroring the profound thinking of Jesus, reasoning more biblically, logically, factually, creatively, and relationally, pursuing all truth as Christ's truth for the glory of God?		
Emote Am I mirroring the just sentiments of Jesus, feeling rage at the mockery of God and exploitation of his image-bearers, compassion toward the suffering, and my deepest joy in God?		
Flip Am I mirroring the upside-down action of Jesus, using my power to empower others, pursuing pleasure by questing for their good, and finding purity that only comes from God?		

Love Am I mirroring the radical relationality of Jesus, giving my self to others not to *become* loved but *because* I am loved, and not from my strength but from God who makes me "abound in love"?		
Elevate Am I mirroring the saving grace of Jesus, lifting enemies, the oppressed, poor, guilty, unholy, and unwanted into friendship, victory, freedom, justice, purity, and family?		
Create Am I mirroring the artistic genius of Jesus, showing that matter matters, protesting "the present age," and inspiring joy and hope of "the age to come" in the things I make?		
Transform Am I mirroring Jesus in all of life, being transformed in daily life by the Spirit so that, as I behold Christ in Scripture and in community, I am becoming more truly myself to God's glory?		

APPENDIX A

The Secret to Becoming Irrelevant (Spend All Your Time Trying to Be Relevant)

The Peace and Love Hippie Hostel is one of Paris's most budget-friendly, a dingy sanctuary for under-showered backpackers. It was there that I met "Derrick." Derrick didn't believe in organized religion. Derrick didn't believe in unorganized religion. Derrick believed in marijuana, and that marijuana alone gave life meaning. One factor that drove Derrick to find meaning in chemicals rather than Christ was, quite frankly, Christ's people — the church. In Derrick's own words, "Whatever the world can do, Christians can do ten years later and worse." He went on to cite Christian music, movies, literature, and church trends that struck him as derivative, contrived, inauthentic, shallow, and kitsch. The big irony was how so many of these Christian endeavors were aimed precisely at being relevant to guys like Derrick. The harder the church tried to be relevant, the more irrelevant it became.

THE RELEVANCE QUESTION

Behind this irony lies a question that is both good and dangerous. It is what we may call the "Relevance Question," which asks: *What would it look like for us, as believers, to be relevant to unbelievers?* We don't want the Derricks of the world to see us as a quirky tribe of xenophobes. So in answering the Relevance Question we usually come up with a projection of what we think those unbelievers out there are like. Once we think we've got a good grip on the tastes and preferences of our unbelieving target demographic, we take the Relevance Question further: we reinvent how we do Christianity so that what we're selling coincides with what they're buying. As perceived demand shapes what we supply, innovative church models begin to emerge. We make Jesus relevant again. Or do we?

Not according to Derrick and the many like him. With the Relevance Question as the first step in our journey, our final destination is irrelevance. Sure, the Relevance Question has its place (for example, Paul didn't speak Hebrew on Mars Hill or cite the Stoic philosophers in the synagogues). The Relevance Question is a good question; it is just not to be the *first* question. When relevance is our first priority, we end up powered not by the Spirit of Christ, but the spirit of the age. There is a more fundamental question we must face squarely together. Before asking what relevance looks like to this or that culture (or subculture), we must first ask, Who is the Jesus we exist to reverently worship and reflect with our lives? Let us call this the Reverence Question.

WHEN RELEVANCE TRUMPS REVERENCE

I briefly highlight four effects of putting the Relevance Question ahead of the Reverence Question:

1. *We alienate anyone who doesn't fit the bill.*

If we start with a drive to be relevant to postmoderns, then we become instantly irrelevant to anyone who still puts faith in science, still values logical propositions, or still holds out hope for objective truth. If we assume that postmodernism is in the oval office of ideas in Western culture (and that's debatable), there are still protesters in the streets who voted for the other guy. *Don't all these people need the gospel too?*

2. We play a never-ending game of follow the leader.

Like every other "ism" created by human minds, postmodernism's days are numbered. One day the polls will come in and some new "ism" will be sworn into office — post-postmodernism. Eventually we will realize that our postmodern church is yesterday's news, ask the Relevance Question all over again, and dream up a post-postmodern church. In this train-of-thought, the church has made itself the caboose, always trailing distantly behind culture. What's even more of a problem is that culture itself has become the engine, pulling the church caboose along. *Shouldn't Jesus be our engine, and his Word the tracks we follow into the future?*

3. We present a torn portrait of Jesus to the world.

Postmoderns, so we are told, value the image over the word, mystery over certainty, questions over answers, the relational over the rational. So the relevance-driven church follows suit. If post-postmodernism one day swings the pendulum back toward reason and objectivity, then what happens to the relevance-driven church? She packs her candles and icons in storage, swaps out storytelling time with serious study time, and replaces open questions with closed answers. Yet Christ is simultaneously relational *and* rational. He used words *and* images, mysteries *and* certainties, questions *and* answers. When we begin with the Relevance Question, we allow cultural trends to determine which few aspects of our multidimensional Christ the church expresses. *Shouldn't we be displaying a wider spectrum of Jesus' radiance to the watching world?*

4. We lose sight of the chief end of everything.

The chief end not only of man, but of *everything* — waterfalls, education, subatomic particles, romance, art, science, food, sleep, golfing, mountains, humor, and tears — is to glorify God. Driven by the conviction that "the aim and final end of all music is none other than the glory of God," Johann Sebastian Bach created some of the most original, powerful, and beautiful music ever composed. Imagine, however, if he saw the "aim and final end of all music" as being relevant to a culture that likes music. What if the primary factor determining where Bach's dots fell on the score sheet was not glorifying an infinite God, but merely making something that people would like? Do you think that his music would have been as powerful? Me neither. There is a profound difference between the art motivated by adoration for God and that motivated by the approval of people. *Shouldn't worship be the deepest motive behind every thought we think, word we speak, and sound we make?*

BECOMING TRULY SEEKER-SENSITIVE

In sum: live a life of authentic reverence for Jesus and you become relevant to the watching world. Live your life to become relevant and you become both irreverent to Jesus and irrelevant to the watching world. Let me say again, the Relevance Question *is* a good question, it is just not to be the *first* question. Before we ruminate on how to reach seekers, we must focus on how to revere the Great Seeker, the God who seeks worshipers who worship him in spirit and in truth (John 4:23). You exist "to the praise of his glory" (Eph. 1:12b, 14b) "so that the name of our Lord Jesus may be glorified in you" (2 Thess. 1:12a), that your life and mine would shout together Paul's anthem "to him be glory forever" (Rom. 11:36b).

APPENDIX B

Doing Our Theology as if It Is Actually True (Because It Is)

I recently watched a disturbing video. A camera caught the head of a certain political organization; we'll call him "Lucius." He was attempting to convince a packed auditorium about the reality of moral law. Specifically, Lucius appealed to a real moral law above and beyond culture to argue against a right to homosexual marriage. What struck me most was less of what he said and more how he said it. Lucius taunted the crowd relentlessly, hurling insults like hand grenades.

People often argue against moral reality by appealing to moral reality (for example, there can't be absolutes because look at out how absolutely wrong the crusades and inquisitions were!). But there is an equal and opposite inconsistency, namely, arguing for moral reality while breaking the very morality we are defending (for example, real morals like "love your neighbor" exist, you ignoramus!). In other words, Lucius's problem was that he did not argue his worldview as if his worldview were actually true. No matter what he said, the way in which he said it made it seem like morals like love and respect were not to be taken seriously after all. The medium refuted the message.

A WINSOME RESONANCE

I pray for Lucius and those like him, and I have certainly been guilty of the same self-refuting dissonance between what I say and how I say it. As God moves to mortify the theological bully in my heart and conform me more and more to the image of his Son, I find myself bumping into the same truth: that, as Christians, there ought to be a beautiful consistency, a kind of winsome resonance between what we say and how we say it. In short: we ought to do our theology as if our theology is actually true (because it is).

Let me clarify: I believe at my core that Jesus is supremely reasonable, that as "the Truth" and the incarnate *Logos*, his intellect is something worth mirroring. I also believe that Jesus is supremely passionate, not like those whom C. S. Lewis described as "men without chests," but having a sizeable and strong-beating heart, full of what Lewis called "just sentiments," emotions of joy, outrage, sorrow, and compassion that were in perfect sync with reality. I also believe Jesus to be supremely holy, with a unique moral splendor about him; and supremely loving, enjoying a constant and intimate connection with his Father and painfully committed to maximizing the joy of others; and full of grace, bestowing undeserved favor on those who despised him; and the Masterful Artist who thought up poetic parables, pink sunsets, different skin colors, the sublime spectrum of glowing gases in a space nebulae, and the marble patterns in a human iris.

If I believe theologically that Jesus is all of those things (and more!), then the question is this: Do I do my theology reasonably, passionately, morally, relationally, graciously, and artistically? Is there that winsome resonance between *what* I believe and *how* I express those beliefs? Do I do my theology as if my theology is actually true?

THE SECRET TO C. S. LEWIS'S SUCCESS

Oftentimes I don't. I have a hard drive full of theological work that might reflect something of the reasonableness of Jesus, but with all the grace of an inquisitor, the love of a pit bull, and the creativity of a monkey. The extent to which my theology is not reasonably, passionately, morally, relationally, graciously, and artistically expressed is the extent to which, no matter what I'm saying, the way I'm saying it conveys on some primal level that I don't really appraise those attributes of Jesus with enough worth to imitate them. When there is such dissonance between what is being said and how it's being said, we appropriately cringe, like when an off-pitch note turns a beautiful song into a sonic train wreck.

However, when that beautiful harmony hangs between our medium and our message, it can trigger not our gag reflex but our tear ducts. I think of Dr. Philip Johnson debating God's existence with a famous atheist. Every time Dr. Johnson made a point of contention, the atheist pushed a button pulling up a PowerPoint slide of a giant cartoon bull, informing the audience that Dr. Johnson's point was bull. Did Dr. Johnson return insult for insult? No. Right in the middle of the debate Dr. Johnson paused to pray publicly and passionately for his atheist opponent's sad battle with cancer.

Dr. Johnson was not only saying that a God of grace, forgiveness, love, and power exists, he was saying it in a way that was beautifully compatible with that God's existence. We can hear the same compelling harmony in much of the Puritan literature that is all at once poetic and persuasively reasoned. This harmony between what is said and how it's said explains much of the profound and enduring impact of C. S. Lewis. The way Lewis wrote reflected consistently the reason, passion, love, creativity, and grace of the God Lewis was writing about. Lewis's message shaped his medium, and hence his momentous impact.

YOU ARE WORTH IT!

Like these great theologians we must let the truth of what we're saying infuse how we say it. Perhaps Johnson, the great Puritans, and Lewis thought very consciously about harmonizing what they said with how they said it. But I think there is something deeper going on too. The harmony of *what* was being said and *how* it was being said was in large part reached because of *who* was saying it. In other words, there was something irrefutably Christlike in the characters of Johnson, the great Puritans, and Lewis that perhaps even subconsciously permeated how they said what they said. The *who* will, for better or worse, shape both *what* we say and *how* we say it.

This means that character formation and doing good theology cannot be compartmentalized. The more and more we are conformed to the image of Jesus, in whom we find the most praiseworthy integration of reason, passion, holiness, love, grace, and creativity, the better and better we will become in expressing a theology worthy of him. Putting the cart before the horse, however, seeking first and foremost to write good theology papers, preach good sermons, do good ministry, and the like, we quickly become living contradictions to our own theology. The cultivation of Christlike character becomes the essential premise of writing, preaching, and modeling good theology. And, oh, don't we all need more grace and character-shaping Spirit-power in that department! Would you join me in praying?

> *Sovereign God, make us more like Jesus in* ***who*** *we are so that a beautiful harmony can be heard between* ***what*** *we say and* ***how*** *we say it. Make us the kind of theologians who express what we believe about you as if it's actually true because it is, and you are worth it! Amen.*

ACKNOWLEDGMENTS

My name should not be on the cover of this book. *REFLECT* is the product of my wife Jocelyn's love and support; the daily joy and comic relief of our kids — Gracelyn, Holland, Harlow, and Hendrik — who kept me sane and smiling after long writing days; the unwavering encouragement of my parents — Russ and Judy — who have been right behind me from Day 1 (of both of my births); the ongoing encouragement from great friends — Aron McKay, Uche Anizor, Sean Maroney, Gabe Fluhrer, Brian Mattson, James Petitfils, Yara Brighton, Suresh Budhaprithi, Andrew Deloach, Joe Mellema, Chris Poblete, Mark Chepel, and Thom Goldstein; the wisdom of mentors and colleagues — Milan Yerkovich, Erik Thoennes, J. P. Moreland, Peter Jones, Myron Steeves, Barry Corey, Douglas Huffman, Clint Arnold, John Lunde, Ken Berding, and, of course, Hendrik Vroom; the sharp editorial eyes of Taylor Landry and Maria denBoer; the stellar design work of Alexander Bukovietski and Frank Gutbrod; the integrity, faith, and vision of Jim Weaver; the generous support of the Kern Foundation; the gracious grunt work of my trusted TAs — Brandon Hurlbert, Derrick Dallmeyer, Bradley Watts, Ryan Hacker, and Taylor Harmon; the inspiration from my beloved Biola students, the thoughtful Guinea pigs for nearly all the content of this book. Paul said it best:

> I thank my God in all my remembrance of you . . . because of your partnership in the gospel from the first day until now. . . . It is right for me to feel this way about you all, because I hold you in my heart, for you are all partakers with me of grace. (Phil. 1:3, 5, 7)

NOTES

HOW TO MEET YOUR FUTURE SELF

1. These words are attributed to Ralph Waldo Emerson in multiple works, including the Unitarian Universalist Hymnal.

2. David Foster Wallace, "This Is Water," commencement speech, Kenyon College, May 21, 2005. The great Russian storyteller and skilled excavator of human nature Fyodor Dostoyevsky also found that "man has no more constant and agonizing anxiety than find as quickly as possible someone to worship." Dostoyevsky voices this observation through the mouthpiece of "The Grand Inquisitor" in *The Brothers Karamazov,* vol. 1, trans. David Magarshack (New York: Penguin, 1978), 297–98.

3. Bob Goudzwaard, *Aid for the Over-Developed West* (Toronto: Wedge, 1975), 114–15. See Romans 1:18–24.

4. Alexander Solzhenitsyn, "An Interview with Malcolm Muggeridge" (May 1983), in *Chosen Vessels,* ed. Charles Turner (Ann Arbor, MI: Servant, 1985), 186.

5. Roger Trigg notes, "Religion is always a target of totalitarian regimes. . . . Dangerous for would-be dictators, is the appeal to transcendent norms, and a supernatural authority beyond this life" (*Equality, Freedom, and Religion* [Oxford: Oxford University Press, 2012], 29).

6. G. K. Chesterton, *Christendom in Dublin,* in *G. K. Chesterton: Collected Works,* vol. 20 (San Francisco: Ignatius, 2001), 57.

7. Charles Darwin, *The Life and Letters of Charles Darwin,* vol. 1, ed. Francis Darwin (New York: D. Appleton, 1896), 65.

8. Charles Darwin, "A Personal Letter to W. D. Fox," November 28, 1864 in *The Life and Letters of Charles Darwin,* vol. 1, 303.

9. John Crosby, *Sons and Fathers: Challenges to Paternal Authority* (New York: Routledge, 2014), 58.

10. Charles Darwin, *The Autobiography of Charles Darwin,* ed. Nora Barlow, in *The Works of Charles Darwin,* vol. 29 (New York: New York University Press, 1989), 158.

11. *The Autobiography of Charles Darwin,* 158.

12. *The Life and Letters of Charles Darwin,* vol. 1, 269.

13. See Perry Miller, *Jonathan Edwards* (Lincoln: University of Nebraska Press, 2005), 225. According to the *Stanford Encyclopedia of Philosophy,* Edwards "is widely acknowledged to be America's most important and original philosophical theologian." See http://plato.stanford.edu/entries/edwards/, retrieved May 30, 2016.

14. See Jonathan Edwards, *Personal Narrative* in *Jonathan Edwards: Representative selections,* ed. Clarence H. Faust and Thomas H. Johnson (New York: American, 1935), 12.

15. In Edwards's words, "The noun (*kavod*) signifies gravity, heaviness, greatness, and abundance" (*The End for Which God Created the World,* in *The Works of Jonathan Edwards,* vol. 1 [Peabody, MA: Hendrickson, 2000], 116).

16. See Isaiah 17:4; 40:5–8, 15; and 41:29.

17. See 2 Corinthians 4:17, emphasis added. See also Psalm 63:5.

18. Isaiah 60:19; emphasis added. See Ezekiel 10:4.

19. C. S. Lewis, "First and Second Things," in *God in the Dock: Essays on Theology and Ethics* (Grand Rapids: Eerdmans, 1994), 280.

20. Wallace, "This Is Water."

21. See 2 Kings 17:15.

REFLECT OVERVIEW

1. "Yale's first and foremost child prodigy" is a title supplied by his alma mater. See http://je.yalecollege.yale.edu/about-us/history, retrieved May 30, 2016.

2. George Marsden, *Jonathan Edwards: A Life* (New Haven, CT: Yale University Press, 2003), 206, 220.

3. Marsden credits him as inspiration behind Mount Holyoke Seminary. Other examples include Yale University's first residential college as well as Nashville's Jonathan Edwards Classical Academy and Trinity International University's Center for Jonathan Edwards. For fields of study that have sprouted from Edwardsian thought, see *Jonathan Edwards*, 498–502.

4. *Jonathan Edwards*, 500–501. The disproportionate success of Edwards's descendants earned him a spot in *Ripley's Believe It or Not*.

5. Jonathan Edwards, *Resolution* 53, July 8, 1723 in *The Works of Jonathan Edwards*, vol. 1 (Peabody, MA: Hendrickson, 2000), xxiii.

6. Edwards, *Personal Narrative*, 7, 12. Biographer Iain Murray agrees that the young Edwards's *Resolutions* are "the key to understanding his whole life and future ministry" (*Jonathan Edwards: A New Biography* [Edinburgh: The Banner of Truth Trust, 1987], 44).

7. Jonathan Edwards, "The True Christian's Life: A Journey Towards Heaven," in *The Works of President Edwards*, vol. 4 (New York: Leavitt & Allen, 1852), 575.

1. REASON: MIRRORING THE PROFOUND THINKING OF JESUS

1. Matthew 22:37.

2. Jonathan Edwards, "The Excellency of Christ," in *The Works of Jonathan Edwards*, vol. 1 (Peabody, MA: Hendrickson, 2000), 682.

3. Josephus, *Antiquities of the Jews*, 18.1.4, in *Josephus: Complete Works*, trans. William Whiston (Grand Rapids: Kregel, 1982), 377.

4. Matthew 22:23–27.

5. Matthew 22:28.

6. This section, in particular the logical breakdown of the Sadducees' argument, is highly indebted to the work of my colleague Douglas Groothuis of Denver Seminary.

7. *Antiquities of the Jews*, 377.

8. Matthew 22:30.

9. Matthew 22:31–32.

10. See Matthew 22:34.

11. See Matthew 22:33.

12. Dallas Willard, "Jesus the Logician," *Christian Scholar's Review*, vol. 28, no. 4 (1999): 605–14.

13. Stuart Ewen, "Leo Burnett: Sultan of Sell," *Time*, December 7, 1998; see http://content.time.com/time/magazine/article/0,9171,989783-2,00.html, retrieved May 30, 2016.

14. Stephen Leacock, *The Garden of Folly* (Whitefish, MT: Kessinger, 2004).

15. Burnett had no small part to play in the fact that, according to *Time*, "an informed public, once a cherished cornerstone of democracy, may be passing into oblivion."

16. Rodney Clapp, "The Theology of Consumption and the Consumption of Theology," in *The Consuming Passion: Christianity and Consumer Culture*, ed. Rodney Clapp (Downers Grove, IL: InterVarsity, 1998), 188.

17. Lexus, for example, has advertised four thousand pounds of moving metal with the slogan, "Whoever said money can't buy happiness isn't spending it right." With such ads, it is not reason that pushes people to the car dealer.

18. We could also list entertainment among the forces stupefying our intellects. Who knows how many brain cells are spent passing levels in the virtual worlds of video gaming, or how many of our great ideas get swept away with the endless flow of streaming movies and viral videos?

19. Luke 10:25–37.

20. Mike Featherstone, "Perspectives on Consumer Culture," *Sociology*, vol. 24 (February 1990): 7. The technical term for this phenomenon is "associative advertising."

21. See Douglas Groothuis, *On Jesus*, Wadsworth Philosophers Series (Florence, KY: Wadsworth, 2003); and Garrett DeWeese, *Doing Philosophy as a Christian* (Downers Grove, IL: IVP Academic, 2011), 108–12.

22. Matthew 22:41–46.

23. John 7:21–24 and Matthew 7:11.

24. Matthew 11:2–6.

25. John 1:1–3.

26. Willard, "Jesus the Logician," 614.

27. Dallas Willard, *The Great Omission: Reclaiming Jesus' Essential Teachings on Discipleship* (San Francisco: Harper, 2006), 183.

28. See 1 Corinthians 15:1–11.

29. Second Peter 1:16.

30. See N. T. Wright, *The Resurrection of the Son of God* (Minneapolis: Fortress, 2003); and Gary Habermas and Michael R. Licona, *The Case for the Resurrection of Jesus* (Grand Rapids: Kregel, 2004).

31. Richard Rorty, *Philosophy and the Mirror of Nature* (Princeton, NJ: Princeton University Press, 1979), 176. If Rorty's colleagues would not let him get away with his sophistic view of truth (and many didn't) does his view, therefore, cease to be true by Rorty's own standards?

32. *Finding God at Harvard: Spiritual Journeys of Thinking Christians*, ed. Kelly Monroe (Grand Rapids: Zondervan, 1996), 17.

33. John 18:37–38.

34. See Rodney Stark, *The Victory of Reason: How Christianity Led to Freedom, Capitalism, and Western Success* (New York: Random House, 2005). Given the Reformation's emphasis on *sola scriptura* and its impact on education it may be said that, in many cases, inerrancy has been the father of literacy.

35. Carl Sagan, "The Harmony of Worlds," in *Cosmos* (New York: Random House, 1980), 51.

36. There is also the man whom Neil deGrasse Tyson considers the greatest physicist in history — Sir Isaac Newton — the devout theist and English polymath who invented integral and differential calculus before his twenty-sixth birthday and discovered the laws of optics, motion, and gravitation.

37. Such erudite ignorance can happen in the other direction too. Imagine a scientifically curious Junior whose every question about what lawnmowers are made *of* is met with some profound insight into the meaning of lawnmowers. Eventually he earns a Ph.D. in Lawnmower Teleology. Then comes time to cut the grass. Junior stares blankly at the lawnmower, not sure which button to push or lever to pull. Ignorant of lawnmower mechanics, the renowned scholar of lawnmower teleology watches his yard slowly become a dark Amazonian jungle from which housecats never return.

38. As atheist Thomas Nagel argues, "Whatever one may think about the possibility of a designer, the prevailing doctrine — that the appearance of life from dead matter and its evolution through accidental mutation and natural selection to its present forms has involved nothing but the operation of physical law — cannot be regarded as unassailable. It is an assumption governing the scientific project rather than a well-confirmed scientific hypothesis"

(*Mind and Cosmos: Why the Materialist Neo-Darwinian Conception of Nature Is Almost Certainly False* [New York: Oxford University Press, 2012], 11).

39. Richard Lewontin, "Billions and Billions of Demons," *The New York Review of Books*, January 4, 1997, 31.

40. Loyal D. Rue, "The Saving Grace of Noble Lies," address, American Academy for the Advancement of Science, February, 1991.

41. Philip Yancey, *The Bible Jesus Read* (Grand Rapids: Zondervan, 1999), 214, 219.

42. As Colin Gunton notes, "The realms of science, ethics, and art are understood in radically different ways and that the very possibility of a universe of meaning, a world and experience making overall unified sense, is lost to view. . . . There is modern fragmentation in a nutshell." He then points to the Christian alternative in which "it is not therefore something which holds things together, but someone" (*The One, The Three, and the Many: God, Creation and the Culture of Modernity* [Cambridge: Cambridge University Press, 1993], 115–16, 178).

43. John Updike, *Self-Consciousness: Memoirs* (New York: Random House, 2012), 216.

44. Psalm 139:17.

45. Plato, "Phaedrus," in *The Dialogues of Plato,* vol. 1, trans. B. Jowett (New York: Random House, 1937), 249. Such holy madness was Americanized during the Second Great Awakening of the early nineteenth century. As one eyewitness recalled: "[Many] professed to fall into trances and see visions . . . they would prophesy under the pretense of Divine inspiration. . . . It made such an appeal to the ignorance, superstition, and credulity of all the people" (Peter Cartwright, *Autobiography of Peter Cartwright, The Backwoods Preacher* [London: Arthur Hall, Virtue,, 1862], 16).

46. One Christian leader, claiming to relay a message from God, tells us, "The Lord is saying, 'I'm bypassing your mind and going straight to your heart' [because] the heart is what matters to the Lord" (Lindell Cooley, "1997 Conference on the Ministry" brochure [Grand Rapids: First Assembly of God, 1997]).

47. Mark Noll, *The Scandal of the Evangelical Mind* (Grand Rapids: Eerdmans, 1994), 137.

48. See, for example, Daniel 12:2–3; Job 19:25–27; and Isaiah 26:19.

49. Josephus, *Antiquities of the Jews*, 377.

50. As Michael Anthony puts it, "Because Jesus had this unique ability to discern the hearts of those in his audience, he was able to direct his teaching

with pinpoint accuracy to their greatest need" ("Christology and Christian Education," in *A Theology for Christian Education*, ed. James Estep, Michael Anthony, and Gregg Allison [Nashville: B & H Academic, 2008], 1124–46, 1137).

51. Dallas Willard adds, "This understanding only comes from the inside, from the understandings one already has. It seems to 'well up from within' one. Thus [Jesus] does not follow . . . the method that characterizes most teaching and writing today. That is, he does not try to make everything so explicit that the conclusion is forced down the throat of the hearer. Rather, he presents matters in such a way that those who wish to know can find their way to, can come to, the appropriate conclusion as something *they* have discovered — whether or not it is something they particularly care for" ("Jesus The Logician," 183; emphasis in original).

52. John 8:29.

53. As Ernest De Witt Burton puts it, "God entered into covenant relation with Abraham, Isaac, and Jacob . . . he affirmed that he could never cease to love those of whom he said, 'I am their God.' But if so, then it is impossible that these men should cease to be" ("Jesus as a Thinker," *The Biblical World*, vol. 10, no. 4 [October 1897]: 245–58, 254).

54. Matthew 3:17.

55. Matthew 22:29.

56. George Gallup and James Castelli, *The People's Religion* (New York: Macmillan, 1989), 60.

57. See www.barna.org.

58. Luke 2:46, 52.

59. *The Works of President Edwards*, vol. 1 (New York: Robert Carter and Brothers, 1881), 4.

60. As Edwards warned, "It is possible that a man might know how to interpret all the types, parables, enigmas, and allegories in the Bible, and not have one beam of spiritual light in his mind" (*Religious Affections* [Carlisle, PA: The Banner of Truth Trust, 1997], 204).

61. John 5:39–40.

62. See Acts 17:11.

63. See Psalm 119:18.

64. See James 1:22–25.

65. Rosaria Champagne Butterfield, *Openness Unhindered: Further Thoughts of an Unlikely Convert on Sexual Identity and Union with Christ* (Pittsburgh: Crown and Covenant, 2015).

2. EMOTE: MIRRORING THE JUST SENTIMENTS OF JESUS

1. "The Cost of Freedom: How Disagreement Makes Us Civil," a dialogue with Cornel West and Robert George at Biola University, La Mirada, California, April 30, 2015.

2. See Charles Taylor, *A Secular Age* (Cambridge, MA: The Belknap Press of Harvard University Press, 2007), 473–504.

3. Plato, *Republic*, 402 A.

4. Aristotle, *Nicomachean Ethics*, 1104 B.

5. *The Green Book* is *The Control of Language* by Alec King and Martin Ketley (London: Longmans, 1939).

6. C. S. Lewis, *The Abolition of Man* (New York: HarperOne, 1974), 4.

7. Aquinas called this deep level of awareness about nonphysical realities our "synderesis" or our Deep Conscience. See Aquinas, *Treatise on Law*, trans. Richard J. Regan (Cambridge: Hackett, 2000); and J. Budziszewski, *What We Can't Not Know: A Guide* (San Francisco: Ignatius, 2003).

8. Celine, *Journey to the End of Night*, trans. Ralph Manheim (New York: New Directions, 1983), 291.

9. Herbert Muller quips, "To say that a man is made up of certain chemical elements is a satisfactory description only for those who intend to use him as fertilizer" (*Science and Criticism* [New Haven, CT: Yale University Press, 1943], 107).

10. In the words of Carl Becker, "We regard him as little more than a chance deposit on the surface of the world, carelessly thrown up between two ice ages by the same forces that rust iron and ripen corn. . . . Man is but a foundling in the cosmos, abandoned by the forces that created him" (*The Heavenly City of the 18th Century Philosophers* [New Haven, CT: Yale University Press, 1932], 14).

11. Colin Campbell expounds, "The 'self' becomes, in effect, a very personal god or spirit to whom one owes obedience. Hence 'experiencing,' with all its connotations of gratificatory and stimulative feelings becomes an ethical activity, an aspect of duty. This is a radically different doctrine of the person, who is no longer conceived of as a 'character' constructed painfully out of the unpromising raw material of original sin, but as a 'self' liberated through experiences and strong feelings from the inhibiting constraints of

social convention" (*The Romantic Ethic and the Spirit of Modern Consumerism* [Oxford: Basil Blackwell, 1987], 285–86.

12. David F. Wells, *No Place for Truth: Or Whatever Happened to Evangelical Theology?* (Grand Rapids: Eerdmans, 1993), 61–63.

13. We become like the men Alexis de Tocqueville observed on his famous tour of America, "Each one of them, withdrawn into himself, is almost unaware of the fate of the rest. He touches them but feels nothing. He exists in and for Himself" (*Democracy in America*, trans. Henry Reeve, ed. Bruce Frohnen [Washington, DC: Regnery, 2002], 268). This is the mad self-imprisonment of life in the postmodern feeling room.

14. Lewis, *The Abolition of Man*, 14–15.

15. William Barclay, *The Mind of Jesus* (New York: Harper & Row, 1961), 190.

16. That's not to mention the mandatory temple tax of roughly two days workers' wages for every freeborn Jewish man, only acceptable in kosher coins.

17. It is little wonder that when Crassus plundered the temple in 53 BC he left Jerusalem about four-and-a-half million dollars richer.

18. Matthew 21:12.

19. See Acts 3:2.

20. Richard Bauckham, "Jesus' Demonstration in the Temple," in *Law and Religion: Essays on the Place of the Law in Israel and Early Christianity*, ed. B. Lindars (Cambridge: James Clark, 1988), 72–89, 76.

21. See Isaiah 56:1–8.

22. See Jeremiah 7:1–12. See N. T. Wright, *Jesus and the Victory of God*, Christian Origins and the Question of God, vol. 2 (Minneapolis: Fortress, 1996), 412.

23. See Proverbs 14:31.

24. Gloria Copeland, *God's Will Is Prosperity* (Tulsa, OK: Harrison House, 1978), 54.

25. Lynda Simmons, Senate Finance Committee, Minority Staff Review of EAGLE MOUNTAIN INTERNATIONAL CHURCH d/b/a KENNETH COPELAND MINISTRIES, 2008, 19. The full report can be viewed at https://cbsdallas.files.wordpress.com/2011/01/emic-copeland-01-5-11.pdf.

26. A boost in third-world giving could also help fund the upkeep on one of televangelists Jesse Duplantis's, Jerry Savelle's, or Mark Bishop's Cessna-500

jets (1.25 million dollars each), or one of Fred Price's, Creflo Dollar's, or Benny Hinn's Gulfstream-2s (4.5 million dollars each).

27. See Ephesians 4:26.

28. Aristotle, *Nicomachean Ethics* (Hertfordshire, UK: Wordsworth, 1996), 64.

29. A Jewish *Midrash* on Psalm 91 described the temple as the place where "one prays before the throne of glory; for there is the gateway of heaven and the open door to the hearing of prayer."

30. Matthew 21:14. It is little wonder that the children in the temple weren't afraid of the man who had just violently flipped tables. In Matthew's account they sang and praised him (21:15–16). Children, with their finely tuned emotional radars, detected the gentle compassion behind Jesus' aggressive rage.

31. N. T. Wright argues that Jesus' table-flipping in the temple would have stopped the flow of temple sacrifices for a short while, prophetically previewing the total destruction of the temple to come in AD 70 and hailing his role as the ultimate Sacrifice. See *Jesus and the Victory of God*, 420–27.

32. There is an increasing trend among scholars to see Jesus' attack on the temple as the point of no return toward his execution.

33. There are approximately 24 unique events where Jesus' emotions are explicitly recorded for us in the Gospels. Of those 24 instances, compassion is used 7 times, in comparison with sorrow (4), gratitude (4), anger (4), love (3), and joy (2). Five of those 7 occurrences feature the term *splanchnizomai*, making it the most common term the Gospel authors used to describe Jesus' emotional state.

34. See Matthew 15:32 (cf. Mark 8:2); Matthew 14:14; Matthew 20:34; Luke 7:13; and Matthew 9:36 (cf. Mark 6:34).

35. See Luke 10:30–33.

36. See Luke 15:20.

37. See Matthew 22:1–4.

38. See Matthew 11:19.

39. See Warfield, "The Emotional Life of Our Lord," https://www.monergism.com/thethreshold/articles/onsite/emotionallife.html, retrieved July 19, 2016.

40. C. S. Lewis, *The Weight of Glory* (New York: HarperOne, 1949), 26.

41. See Matthew 8:20.

42. This description is found in Psalm 16, which Acts 2:25-31 applies to Jesus.

43. See John 15:11; 16:24; cf. Matthew 13:44. David Brainerd, "Detached Papers," in *The Works of Jonathan Edwards*, vol. 2 [Peabody, MA: Hendrickson, 2000], 441.

44. Edwards, *Personal Narrative*, 7.

45. Says Van Til, "It is . . . God's comprehensive interpretation of the facts that makes the facts what they are" (*Christian Apologetics* [Phillipsburg, NJ: P & R, 1976], 7). See chapters 3–5.

46. Francis Turretin, *Institutes of Elenctic Theology*, vol. 2, ed. James Dennison (Phillipsburg, NJ: P & R, 1994), 523.

47. Edwards recounts: "Before, I used to be uncommonly terrified with thunder . . but now, on the contrary, it rejoiced me. I felt God. . . . Another Saturday night (January 1739) I had such a sense, how sweet and blessed a thing it was to walk in the way of duty . . . that it caused me to break forth into a kind of loud weeping, which held me some time, so that I was forced to shut myself up, and fasten the doors. I could not but, as it were, cry out, 'How happy are they which do that which is right in the sight of God! They are blessed indeed, they are the happy ones!'" (*Personal Narrative*, 7, 33).

3. FLIP: MIRRORING THE UPSIDE-DOWN ACTION OF JESUS

1. Fyodor Dostoyevsky, *Memoirs from the House of the Dead* (London: Oxford University Press, 1965), 331.

2. In Nietzsche's words, "Faith is always coveted most and needed most urgently where will is lacking. . . . Once a human being reaches the fundamental conviction that he must be commanded, he becomes 'a believer'" (*The Gay Science: With a Prelude in Rhymes and an Appendix of Songs* [New York: Vintage, 1974], 347).

3. In Kevin Bacon character's defense, there is a moving scene in which he proves to the town pastor that dancing is actually biblical.

4. This section is heavily indebted to the superb work of Andy Crouch on the meaning of power, which I was introduced to at the 2014 Acton University Conference in Grand Rapids and the Christian Legal Society Conference in Boston, and in conversations with Andy.

5. Nietzsche asks, "Do you want a name for this world? This world is the will to power — and nothing besides! And you yourselves are also this will to power — and nothing besides!" (*The Will to Power* [New York: Vintage, 1968], 550).

6. Michel Foucault, *The History of Sexuality* (New York: Pantheon, 1978), 95.

7. *The Will to Power*, 550.

8. Think of Nebuchadnezzar (see Daniel 4:28-37).

9. John 13:3a.

10. John 13:4.

11. On the towel (or *chiton* in Greek) as the slave's uniform during meal times, see Luke 12:37 and 17:8.

12. John 13:5.

13. Andy Crouch, "It's Time to Talk about Power: How to Recognize and Use the Gift That Most Eludes the Church," *Christianity Today*, October 6, 2013, 32.

14. John 13:13.

15. Crouch, "It's Time to Talk about Power," 32.

16. See Revelation 4:11.

17. Suetonius, *Suetonius*, vol. 2 (Cambridge, MA: Harvard University Press, 1914).

18. See John 13:2, 11, 18–30.

19. As Augustine puts it, Jesus "did not esteem it beneath His dignity to wash also the feet of one whose hands He already foresaw to be steeped in wickedness" (*Homilies on the Gospel of John* in *Nicene and Post-Nicene Fathers*, vol. 7, ed. Philip Schaff [New York: Cosimo, 2007], 301). Jesus also knew Peter would deny him three times that night, and that all the rest of his disciples would scatter the following day when he died. And, one by one, Jesus washes their feet anyway.

20. C. S. Lewis, "First and Second Things," in *God in the Dock: Essays on Theology and Ethics* (Grand Rapids: Eerdmans, 1994), 280.

21. Wallace, "This is Water."

22. As Montana so eloquently restates Nietzsche's doctrine of the will to power, "The only thing in this world that gives orders is balls. Balls. You got that?"

23. The brilliant philosopher spent his final years in an insane asylum.

With his mind tragically broken and his body riddled with syphilis, Nietzsche signed his last cryptic letters in his own blood as "The Crucified One," under the delusion that he was the Christ. While some credit Nietzsche's insanity exclusively to his syphilis, many see his own philosophy as a contributing factor. For anyone interested, MIT Press has published a fascinating piece from this perspective by George Bataille and Annette Michelson titled "Nietzsche's Madness" in the journal *October* (Spring 1986).

24. John 1:1-3. See also Colossians 1:15–17 and Hebrews 1:8–13.

25. Calvin DeWitt explains, "Genesis 2:15 conveys a marvelous teaching. Here, God expects Adam to serve the garden and to keep it. The Hebrew word for serve (*'abad*) is translated as till, dress or work in most recent translations of the Bible. Adam and his descendants are expected to meet the needs of the garden so that it will persist and flourish. But how on earth can we serve creation? Shouldn't creation serve us instead? God also expects us, as Adam's descendants, to keep the garden. This word 'keep' is sometimes translated 'end, take care of, guard, look after.' The Hebrew word on which these translations are based is the word *shamar*. And *shamar* indicates loving, caring, sustaining type of keeping" (*Earthwise: A Biblical Response to Environmental Issues* [Grand Rapids: CRC, 1994], 40).

26. Satan had to convince Adam and Eve that God did not want them to become "like him," that the Creator would somehow be threatened if his creatures exercised power. This was terrible theology. Adam and Eve were *already* "like him." They were already made in God's image and commanded to exercise great power, to fill, and rule, and tend, and steward the earth.

Once he had misrepresented the Creator as scared of losing a monopoly on power, Satan could misrepresent God's creation. An expanding universe where power increases by multiplication could look like a zero-sum universe where addition requires subtraction. This bad theology and warped cosmology made the first lie about power seem plausible. It is the lie about power that every totalitarian kingdom since has been built on. It is the lie that every bad leader in history has made his life creed. It is the same lie that we believe every time we push others down to lift ourselves up, the lie that power comes by taking someone else's fruit rather than by being fruitful.

27. Though there is another sense in which God's law functions as schoolmaster, it is intended to bring us to the end of our power, to expose our powerlessness, so we seek grace and tap into an infinite power Source.

28. He commands us to express our sexuality in a faithful marriage covenant because he knows that infidelity takes away our power to love, and be trusted, and be credible or admirable in the eyes of children.

29. Psalm 115:6–8.

30. In fact, all of God's commands can be better seen as exercises of divine power aimed at multiplying rather than diminishing human power.

31. Blaise Pascal, *Pensees and Other Writings*, trans. Honor Levi (Oxford: Oxford University Press, 1995), 51.

32. John 13:17.

33. "What to Do When There Are Too Many Product Choices on the Store Shelves?" *Consumer Reports*, March 2014.

34. In the ahead-of-its-time book, *The Invisible Religion*, sociologist Thomas Luckmann noticed this rising trend back in the 1960s. "The individual," says Luckmann, "is left to his own devices in choosing goods and services, friends, marriage partners, neighbors, hobbies and . . . even 'ultimate' meanings in a relatively autonomous fashion. The consumer orientation, in short, is not limited to economic products but characterizes the relation of the individual to the entire culture" (*The Invisible Religion* [New York: Macmillan, 1967], 98). This is what C. S. Lewis described as "the fatal superstition that men can create values, that a community can choose its 'ideology' as men choose their clothes" ("The Poison of Subjectivism," in *Christian Reflections*, ed. Walter Hooper [Grand Rapids: Eerdmans, 1967], 73).

35. "NCHS Data Brief, no. 76," October 2011.

36. Psychologist Barry Schwartz sees the irony of it all: "We have more choice, and thus more control, than people have ever had before. . . . [This] might lead you to expect that depression is going the way of polio, with autonomy and choice as the psychological vaccines. Instead," Schwartz laments, "we are experiencing depression in epidemic numbers" (Barry Schwartz, *The Paradox of Choice* [New York: HarperCollins, 2003], 109-110).

37. For an eye-opening look into this phenomenon, see Malcolm Gladwell's fascinating piece on Paco Underhill entitled "The Science of Shopping," in *Signs of Life in the U.S.A.*, 4th ed., ed. Sonia Maasik and Jack Sololom (New York: St. Martin's, 2003), 403–409.

38. We could add that a quest is not option maximizing like shopping. It is often profoundly option-limiting. We are *bound* to a quest. Barry Schwartz comments: "To be someone's friend is to undertake weighty responsibilities

and obligations that at times may limit your own freedom. The same is true, obviously, of family. And to a large extent, the same is true of involvement with religious institutions. Most religious institutions call on their members to live their lives in a certain way and to take responsibility for the wellbeing of their fellow congregants. So, counterintuitive as it may appear, what seems to contribute most to happiness binds us rather than liberates us" (*Paradox of Choice*, 107-108).

39. John 13:13–15.

40. See John 15:12–13; cf. 1 John 3:16; 4:11.

41. Dietrich Bonhoeffer, *The Cost of Discipleship* (New York: Macmillan, 1963), 99.

42. Is the literal act of dying the only action Jesus offers questers? In that case, the command could only be obeyed one time per person. Jesus, having just washed the disciples' feet, says to "do as I have done for you." It is important that we see what he had just done (that is, the foot washing) for what it is — a clue, a pointer, a signpost to something more, what scholars often call "an acted parable." What if *that* is what we're supposed to do as Jesus did, not one isolated act, but a pattern of life in which we engage daily in "acted parables" that point beyond themselves to the cross? Examples emerge all over the New Testament. There are obvious examples like eating and drinking at the communion table or baptism. Eating, drinking, and dunking (just like foot washing) burst forth with all new meaning when seen in light of the cross. So does marriage. Husbands are called not just to love their wives, but to love them in a way that reflects Jesus giving himself up for the church (Eph. 5:25–27). Those in charge are to serve those under their charge in a way that reflects Jesus, who "came not to be served but to serve, and to give his life as a ransom for many" (Mark 10:45). Good workers enduring bad treatment are to become living proof of the fact that "Christ also suffered" (1 Pet. 2:21–25). All of life becomes an imitation of the one who "humbled himself by becoming obedient to the point of death, even death on a cross" (Phil. 2:5–11).

43. Wallace, "This Is Water."

44. This cross-taking has a remarkable effect on our happiness. Instead of the shopping's unrealistic and ultimately futile goal of avoiding pain at all costs, questing now enlarges the meaning of happiness, making it big enough to include the inevitable pains of life. It fills pain up with redemptive meaning. Being hurt and being happy are no longer mutually exclusive.

45. Hebrews 12:2.

46. So many great quests point beyond themselves to the meaning of the cross: Aslan being slain to free Edmund from the White Witch's ownership; Pinocchio giving his life to save Geppetto from Monstro; Neo freeing humanity from our computerized captors; Anna saving Arendelle from an endless winter.

47. As Alexander Solzhenitsyn put it in his famous Harvard commencement speech: "[Our] task on earth . . . cannot be unrestrained enjoyment of everyday life. It cannot be the search for the best ways to obtain material goods and then cheerfully get the most of them. It has to be the fulfillment of a permanent, earnest duty so that one's life journey may become an experience of moral growth, so that one may leave life a better human being than one started it" ("A World Split Apart," Harvard University, News Office, 1978) 14-15.

48. John 13:8.

49. Darrin McMahon, *Happiness: A History* (New York: Atlantic Monthly, 2005), 263–64.

50. McMahon notes Lequinio's indebtedness to Christian thought. See *Happiness*, 263–64.

51. *Happiness*, 263–64.

52. The man who has told a big hurtful lie, for example, might seek purity by being genuinely remorseful, confessing his wrongdoing, paying whatever debt his dishonesty has incurred, restoring relationships severed by his deception, and getting back in the right. If he doesn't seek purification in those ways, Budziszewski argues, the liar isn't magically relieved of his need to feel clean. That irrepressible need will come out somehow. Rather than let himself feel remorse, he might be sure to always hold some glowing screen in his field of vision so he never has to look face to face at the deceiver in the mirror. Rather than pay the actual price incurred by his lie, he may punish himself in other ways. Rather than restore deception-broken relationships, he might seek out the company of other liars so that his own dishonesty seems normal. Rather than become just, he may justify himself by inventing fanciful stories and self-deceptive rationalizations about why his original deception was necessary and perhaps even noble. See chapter 7 of Budziszewski, *What We Can't Not Know* (Charlotte, NC: Ignatius Press, 2011).

53. This game could go on. Charlie Manson thinks he's not so bad as Jeffrey Dahmer, who thinks he's not so bad as Hitler, who thought Stalin was the

real monster, and on it goes. As much as we might hope for a world in which no such demonic evildoers exist, perhaps some part of us secretly needs them to justify our cherished belief that we're really angels after all.

54. Tom Segev, *Soldiers of Evil: The Commandments of the Nazi Concentration Camps,* trans. Haim Watzman (New York: McGraw-Hill, 1987), 80.

55. While the Nazis are easy targets for critique, we all invest words with new conscience-soothing definitions. "The seven hour season streaming binge? I'm not lazy; I'm just resting up for a productive tomorrow. Dishing all of your friend's very personal problems to other people? I'm not a gossip; I'm sharing 'prayer requests.' That tirade against the child, the spouse, the clerk, the liberal, the conservative? Someone needs to set them straight, and I may be just the brave lover of truth to do it! I'm not a jerk; I'm honest. That's not evil. It's for God! It's for scientific progress! It's freedom of choice!"

56. If blame-passing, comparison, and redefinition aren't enough of a morphine shot to our consciences, then there is always the social justification game. In the history of Christian theology justification refers to (among other things) the moment that God declares a sinner "not guilty!" God is the Judge, Satan is "the accuser," and Jesus is our Defense Attorney who never loses a case. He appeals to his own already served death sentence so we can be declared not guilty. But if we leave God out of the process of living free from guilt, then where do we turn for that authoritative declaration? We turn to society. The media, the law, education — we must get everyone in unison to declare us "Not Guilty!" and anyone who fails to acknowledge and celebrate our guiltlessness must be demonized and finally silenced.

57. Michel Foucault, preface to Gilles Deleuze and Felix Guattari's *Anti-Oedipus*, in *The Essential Works of Foucault,* vol. 3, *Power,* ed. James Faubion (New York: New York Press, 200), 108.

58. See Galatians 6:14.

59. See John 3:3.

60. See Ezekiel 36:26–27.

61. Martin Luther King Jr., *Strength to Love* (Minneapolis: Fortress, 2010), 16.

62. Galatians 5:24. See also Colossians 3:9–10.

63. Romans 8:13.

64. John Owen, *The Mortification of Sin in Believers* in *Overcoming Sin*

and Temptation, eds. Kelly Kapic and Justin Taylor (Wheaton, IL: Crossway, 2006), 48.

65. Leviticus 20:26 and 1 Peter 1:16.

4. LOVE: MIRRORING THE RADICAL RELATIONALITY OF JESUS

1. Though sung by the Man in Black for his 1980 album *Rockabilly Blues*, "Without Love" was originally composed by Cash's son-in-law Nick Lowe.

2. Johnny Cash with Patrick Carr, *Cash* (San Francisco: Harper, 1997), 170–71.

3. This letter is reproduced in Jon Krakauer's *Into the Wild* (New York: Villard, 1996), 57.

4. I owe this insight to R. C. Sproul.

5. Love dwarfs all other creative themes. The lyrical climax of Clapton's "Wonderful Tonight" is not "the wonder of it all is that you just don't realize how much I logically contemplate you." The Beatles never sang the anthem "All you need is reason, do do do do do." Elvis's rewrite — "Think me Tender" — would have never made the pop charts.

6. Richard Putnam, *Bowling Alone: The Collapse and Revival of American Community* (New York: Simon & Schuster, 2000), 331; emphasis in original.

7. Lisa Berkman and Leonard Syme, "Social Networks, Host Resistance, and Mortality: A Nine-Year Follow-up Study of Alameda County Residents," *American Journal of Epidemiology*, vol. 109 (1979): 186–204.

8. I owe this insight to my colleague at Biola University, Fred Sanders.

9. John 14:11.

10. John 17:24.

11. William Shedd adds, "Here is society within the Essence, and wholly independent of the universe; and communion and blessedness resulting there from. But this is impossible to an essence without personal distinctions. Not the singular Unit of the deist, but the plural Unity of the Trinitarian explains this. A subject without an object . . . could not love. What is there to be loved?" (preface to Augustine, *City of God*, 15).

12. Francis Schaeffer, *The God Who Is There* (Downers Grove, IL: InterVarsity, 1968) 97.

13. *The God Who Is There*, 97.

14. Dostoyevsky, *The Brothers Karamazov*, vol. 1, 297, 302.

15. As I explain (with Dostoyevsky's help) elsewhere, "Like an oscillating universe, millions of people doing their own thing expand outward from one another in growing alienation and social entropy. As society turns colder and sparse, it eventually hits a critical point when the innate longing for something more meaningful and fulfilling than self-created subjective values kicks in. Society then begins rapidly collapsing back in on itself toward a point of singularity; that is, toward an all-absorbing state. The Big Bang of autonomy, sprawling outward in all directions, is followed by a Big Crunch toward a liberty-consuming centralized authority. As Dostoevsky's Shigalev observed in *The Possessed*, 'Starting from unlimited freedom I arrive at unlimited despotism.' The end result is that "One-tenth enjoys absolute liberty and unbounded power over the other nine-tenths. The others have to give up all individuality and become, so to speak, a herd." . . . the growing mass of self-glorifying supermen eventually reach the end of themselves, finding their own willpower to be an inadequate and ultimately unsatisfying object of worship. They finally return on all fours like a herd seeking a Great Shepherd. Enter the State, enlarged to meet an intense demand for transcendent meaning that it helped to create" ("Beyond Capes and Cowbells: How a Christian Approach to Law and Virtue Transcends Both Autonomy and Authoritarianism," *Journal of Christian Legal Thought*, vol. 4, no. 2 [Fall 2014]: 4–11, 8, 9).

16. This alienation has been reinforced by the legal redefinition of freedom offered by Justice Anthony Kennedy in the famous 1992 Supreme Court Case, *Planned Parenthood v. Casey*. Kennedy defined freedom as "the right to define one's own concept of existence, of meaning, of the universe, and of the mystery of human life."

17. Bukkyo Dendo Kyokai, *The Teachings of Buddha* (New Delhi: Sterling, 2004), 36.

18. Siddhartha, *The Dhammapada* XVI, 211. The Buddha is also credited with saying, "Those who have a hundred dear ones have a hundred woes; those who have ninety dear ones have ninety woes; . . . those who have one dear one have one woe; those who hold nothing dear have no woe" (Udana 8:8). This problem finds poignant expression in the story of Sangamaji as recorded in the Pali canon of Buddhist Scriptures. After abandoning his wife and child to pursue a life of meditation (as Siddhartha, the Buddha, had done before him), Sangamaji is approached by his wife, who lays their small daughter in

his lap as he meditates. The wife's repeated plea, "Nourish us," goes unacknowledged by the meditating husband. Disheartened, she leaves with her daughter. Siddartha then says of Sangamaji, "He feels no joy when she comes, no sadness when she goes — a true Brahman released from prison" (Udana 1:8 Pali Canon 2:7). Here detachment trumps love as the mark of the enlightened.

19. Michael Reeves explains, "The Father, then, is the Father of the eternal Son, and he finds his very identity, his Fatherhood in loving and giving out his life and being to the Son. . . . If there were once a time when the Son didn't exist, then there was once a time when the Father was not yet a Father. And if that is the case, then once upon a time God was not loving since all by himself he would have nobody to love. . . . Thus it is not as if the Father and Son bumped into each other at some point and found to their surprise how remarkably well they got on. The Father is who he is by virtue of his relationship with the Son. . . . And the Son would not be the Son without His Father" (*Delighting in the Trinity: An Introduction to the Christian Faith* [Downers Grove, IL: InterVarsity, 2012], 27, 34).

20. Colin Gunton, *The One, The Three, and the Many: God, Creation, and the Culture of Modernity* (Cambridge: Cambridge University Press, 1993), 214.

21. This should not be taken to imply partialism, that the Father, Son, and Holy Spirit are merely parts that put together make up God. Each member of the Trinity is fully, not partially, God. I use the body metaphor here to explain, like Paul, the kind of unity and diversity the Triune God brings about in his church.

22. See 1 Corinthians 12. It's the same reason in Ephesians 2:19–22 that Paul could describe Christians as a building, that is, a brick unified with the structure of some towering cathedral becomes more, not less, of a brick.

23. Ephesians 4:16.

24. C. S. Lewis, *The Problem of Pain* (New York: Macmillan, 1961), 140.

25. If you're looking for a concrete next step toward experiencing this kind of true love, I have a bit of friendly advice: find a church that worships God the Father, Son, and Spirit, and start giving yourself away.

26. See John 5:26–27; 10:29; 13:31–32; 17:2, 8, 11–12, 22, 24.

27. John 17:24a.

28. The Father does not fail to give the Son any of the other gifts mentioned in the Fourth Gospel: for example, "life in himself" (5:27a), "authority" (5:22, 27b; 17:2); "words" (17:8), "the name" (17:11-12); "glory." Are we to believe

that the Father's love-gift of people is the one exception to this rule because those people have autonomous God-resisting power?

29. This point is reinforced in John 6:37, where Jesus reveals, "All that the Father gives me will come to me." The Father "gives" in the present tense. People "will come" in the future tense. Grammatically, this is like saying, "All the majority *votes for* (present tense) *will sing* (future tense) in the next round," or "All the governor *pardons* (present) *will enjoy* (future) freedom from death row." The present-tense verb is why the future-tense verb happens. The vocalist has the voting majority to thank for her singing in the next round. The convict has the governor to thank for his freedom. You have the Father to thank for your coming to the Son. We don't believe in Jesus to *become* love-gifts; we believe *because* we are love-gifts. For further insight see part 3 of Thaddeus Williams, *Love, Freedom, and Evil: Does Authentic Love Require Free Will?* (Leiden: Brill, 2011).

30. See John 6:38–40.

31. If God's will to the Son is that he lose not a single love-gift (6:38–40) and we have the autonomous power to lose ourselves, then we can, in effect, keep the Son from perfectly fulfilling his Father's will. What happens, then, to the beautiful substitution that happened at the cross? Biblically, the cross is where the Son who perfectly fulfilled his Father's will takes the place of those who fall short of such perfect will-keeping. Not only does our egregious will-breaking (and the awful consequences it entails) become his; but the Son's perfect will-keeping (and the extravagant rewards it entails) becomes ours. If, however, we can say 'no' to Jesus, shatter our salvation, break off the relationship with self-condemning finality, then we can prevent the Son from fulfilling his Father's will that "none" of the love-gift "would be lost." The cross would then become a place where we exchange our filthy rags for another set of soiled clothes. Imperfection is substituted for yet another imperfection. The Son's failure to keep the Father's will that "none would be lost" would be a failure credited to our account. It follows that if one love-gift is lost, then all love-gifts are lost. Why? Because the cross work of Christ only succeeds in saving anyone if there is not a single slip of will-keeping on Christ's part. John's Gospel does not lead us to such hopeless conclusions. The Son says "I love you" to his Father through a track record of impeccable obedience.

32. As Jesus says in John 14:31, "I do as the Father has commanded me, so that the world may know that I love the Father." On keeping the Father's will

as the Son's primary love language in John's Gospel, see also John 12:49–50; 15:10; and 17:4.

33. John 6:44; emphasis added.

34. See Ephesians 1:13–14.

35. Henri Nouwen, *Turn My Mourning into Dancing*, ed. Timothy Jones (Nashville: Thomas Nelson, 2001), 32.

36. As Bible scholar Raymond Brown comments on John 17, "Any approach that places the essence of unity in the solidarity of human endeavor is not really faithful to John's insistence that unity has its origins in divine action. The very fact that Jesus prays to the Father for this unity indicates that the key to it lies within God's power" (*The Gospel According to John XIII–XXI,* The Anchor Bible, vol. 29A [New York: Doubleday, 1970], 776).

37. First Thessalonians 3:12, NASB.

38. Augustine, *On Psalm 118*, 17th 3:4, cited in Thomas Hand's *Augustine on Prayer* (New York: Catholic Book Publishing Co., 1986), 35.

39. Thomas à Kempis, *The Imitation of Christ*, trans. John Payne (Boston: Gould and Lincoln, 1856), 175–76, 177.

40. First Thessalonians 3:12.

41. Thomas Chalmers, *The Works of Thomas Chalmers*, vol. 3 (Bridgeport, CT: M. Sherman, 1829), 64.

42. Ezekiel 36:26.

43. John Jowett articulates the same principle in an upside-down way: "The force of love always depends on its height. We find the analogy in water. The force of falling water is determined by its height. . . . There is a type of love which has no vigor because it has no height. It is a weak, sickly sentiment that just crawls about you. It is low and therefore it has no enlivening force" ("Illimitable Love," *The Methodist Review,* vol. 35 [January 1919]: 106–11, 108).

44. Leonardo Boff, *Trinity and Society* (Maryknoll, NY: Orbis, 1988), 158.

5. ELEVATE: MIRRORING THE SAVING GRACE OF JESUS

1. I first heard a version of this moon-jumping illustration used by Greg Laurie at a Harvest Crusade in Anaheim, California, in the 1990s.

2. See Ephesians 2:8–10.

3. Ajith Fernando, *The Supremacy of Christ* (Wheaton, IL: Crossway, 1985), 144.

4. Flannery O'Connor, *The Habit of Being* (New York: Farrar, Straus, and Giroux, 1979), 307.

5. Adolf Harnack, *History of Dogma*, pt. 2 (Amazon Digital Services), 174.

6. This is the language of the Council of Trent, Session VI. See Decrees on Original Sin, on Justification, and on Penance.

7. The Roman Catholic Church is not completely Pelagian, but semi-Pelagian in its view of salvation. In this system we retain the ability (albeit a wounded ability) to choose God, a premise that found exaggerated emphasis in the sixteenth century. For analysis of Cassian's thought and Roman Catholicism, see Rebecca Harden Weaver, *Divine Grace and Human Agency: A Study of the Semi-Pelagian Controversy* (Mercer, GA: Mercer University Press, 1998), 122.

8. Martin Luther, *Luther's Works*, vol. 33 (Minneapolis: Fortress, 1972), 189.

9. *Luther's Works*, vol. 34, 336–37.

10. Surah 13:11 of the Koran reads, "Indeed, Allah will not change the condition of a people until they change what is in themselves."

11. For example, an episode titled "We're All Potatoes at Heart" from the animated Disney Jr. show *Small Potatoes* concludes with a talking potato telling a vast audience of impressionable minds, "I think it's great to be different and unique because then everyone has their own different way of doing things and there's no wrong or right answer for doing something."

12. Swami Vivekenanda, *The Complete Works of the Swami Vivekananda*, vol. 1, Mayavati Memorial, 2nd ed. (Amora, Himalayas, 1915), 30, 33; Stewart Brand, *Whole Earth Discipline: An Ecopragmatist Manifesto* (New York: Viking, 2009), 20.

13. Joel Osteen, *Becoming a Better You: 7 Keys to Improving Your Life Every Day* (New York: Free Press, 2007), 56, 87, 91, 129. Osteen is far from alone in this conviction. Historically, we can trace the staggering confidence in man's moral abilities from Pelagius in the fourth century, to Erasmus in the sixteenth century, to Charles Finney in the nineteenth century, and to many Christian pastors in our day. In Pelagian thought, "Human nature is uncorrupted, and the natural will competent to all good . . . and salvation is essentially a work of man" (Philip Schaff, *History of the Christian Church*, vol. 3 [Grand Rapids: Eerdmans, 1985], 815). For Erasmus, "It is in the power

of every man to keep what is commanded" (*Diatribe Concerning Free Will*, cited in Martin Luther, *Bondage of the Will* [St. Louis: Concordia, 2012], 171). For Finney, "men have power or ability to do all their duty" (*Finney's Systematic Theology*, 3rd ed., ed. Dennis Carroll [1878; Minneapolis: Bethany, 1994], 307). For the contemporary church, see R. C. Sproul, "The Pelagian Captivity of the Church," *Modern Reformation*, vol. 10, no. 3 (2001): 22–29.

14. Jeremiah 17:9.

15. Ecclesiastes 9:3b, NASB.

16. Ephesians 2:1.

17. This is precisely what happened to Isaiah when he encountered the "holy, holy, holy" God in his temple. Isaiah's self-serving bias was instantly incinerated at the sight of real holiness. See Isaiah 6.

18. One of the architects of modern thought, Jean-Jacques Rousseau, famously put it this way, "Man is naturally good. . . . It is by our institutions alone that men become wicked." See *Letters to Malesherbes*, in *The Collected Writings of Rousseau*, vol. 5, ed. Christopher Kelly (Hanover, NH: University Press of New England, 1995), 575; *Oeuvres Complètes*, vol. 1, ed. Bernard Gagnebin and Marcel Raymond (Paris: Gallimard, Bibliothèque de la Pléiade, 1995), 1136.

19. Atheist Michael Ruse adds, "I think Christianity is spot on about original sin. How could one think otherwise, when the world's most civilized and advanced people (the people of Beethoven, Goethe, Kant) embraced that slime-ball Hitler and participated in the Holocaust? I think Saint Paul and the great Christian philosophers had real insights into sin and freedom and responsibility, and I want to build on this rather than turn from it" ("Darwinism and Christianity Redux: A Response to My Critics," *Philosophia Christi*, vol. 4 [2002]: 192).

20. Matthew 7:18.

21. We might add that a vertical view of God's goodness matters because it also happens to be true.

22. Mark 15:34, 37.

23. Herman Bavinck, *Reformed Dogmatics*, vol. 3, *Sin and Salvation in Christ* (Grand Rapids: Baker, 2006), 383–84.

24. The trick to a theology of the cross, then, is not to stay in the same place forever fixated on a single image, mesmerizing though it may be. A better way to "survey the wondrous cross" and experience it as a treasure that

"demands my soul, my life, my all" (in the words of the old hymn) is to stay in motion. Walk its circumference. Marvel for a while from one angle, then move on to watch how one facet catches new rays of light when viewed through the other facets.

25. See Romans 8:7 and Colossians 1:21–22.

26. Second Corinthians 5:19a. Elsewhere Paul expands: "For in him all the fullness of God was pleased to dwell, and through him to reconcile to himself all things, whether on earth or in heaven, making peace by the blood of his cross. And you, who once were alienated and hostile in mind, doing evil deeds, he has now reconciled in his body of flesh by his death, in order to present you holy and blameless and above reproach before him" (Col. 1:19–22; see also Rom. 5:8–10).

27. LifeWay Research, "2016 State of American Theology Study: Research Report," 2016. See http://thestateoftheology.com/, retrieved October 14, 2016.

28. Dostoyevsky, *The Brothers Karamazov,* vol. 1, 308.

29. Revelation 12:9; 1 Peter 5:8; John 8:44; and Revelation 9:11.

30. First John 3:8.

31. See Colossians 2:15.

32. See Luke 11:21–22; John 12:31; 14:30; 16:11; Ephesians 2:2; and 1 Corinthians 15:25.

33. Hebrews 2:14–15.

34. Colossians 1:13. See also 2 Timothy 2:26; and Galatians 1:4; 4:3.

35. See Ephesians 1:7; Colossians 1:14; Hebrews 9:12; 1 Corinthians 6:20; and Galatians 3:13.

36. Margaret Killingray adds, "Only around one to two percent of the population of a Roman town would be genuinely comfortably off. The vast majority would be the destitute poor" ("The Bible, Slavery, and Onesimus," *ANVIL*, vol. 24 no. 2 [2007]: 85–96, 89). In the ancient world, there were three ways to become someone's property: you could be taken captive by some enemy force, you could dig yourself so deep in debt that you or your loved ones ended up in chains, or you could be born into slavery. All three (we must say with twisting guts) still occur in today's world, where an estimated 27 million people are victims of human trafficking. And just as there are sex slaves in our day, and house slaves, and coco-bean slaves, and carpet loom slaves, so in the ancient world there were human beings forced to do unspeakable sex acts with strangers, treated like property rather than persons in homes, and

exploited for the economic prosperity of others. See Kevin Bales, *Disposable People: New Slavery in the Global Economy* (Oakland: University of California Press, 2012).

37. Galatians 5:1. Jesus understood himself to be on a rescue mission to "Give his life as a ransom for many" (Mark 10:45). See also 1 Peter 1:18–19.

38. Nineteen centuries earlier, the apostle Paul, like Dylan, tried to jolt people with "a knowledge of the truth [so] they may come to their senses and escape from the snare of the devil, after being captured by him to do his will" (2 Tim. 2:25b–26).

39. John 8:34.

40. Francis Turretin, *Institutes of Elenctic Theology*, vol. 1, ed. James Dennison (Philipsburg, NJ: P & R, 1992), 671.

41. As Paul says, sin can "reign in your mortal body, to make you obey its passions" (Rom. 6:12). We can believe we are in charge when we are actually obedient slaves under the dominion of our own disordered and self-destructive passions. For parallels between ancient slavery and spiritual slavery, see James Montgomery Boice, *Foundations of the Christian Faith* (Downers Grove, IL: InterVarsity, 1986), 327–28.

42. Hebrews 2:15; Colossians 1:13; and Romans 6:6b.

43. John 8:36.

44. See John 3:16–17; Romans 5:16, 18; 1 Peter 2:23; and 1 John 2:1. The view of atonement that I merely sketch here is known as "penal substitutionary atonement." For a more biblically detailed defense, see J. I. Packer, "What Did the Cross Achieve?" in *Celebrating the Saving Work of God: Collected Shorter Writings of J. I. Packer*, vol. 1 (Exeter, UK: Paternoster, 1998); Bavinck, *Reformed Dogmatics*, vol. 3, 162–63, chapter 7; and Adam Johnson, *Atonement: A Guide for the Perplexed* (New York: Bloomsbury, 2015).

45. Derek Rishmawy puts it well: "Given this, forgiveness cannot be a simple affair of 'letting it go,' or passing it over for God. His own character, his holiness, his righteousness, his justice means that he cannot treat sin as if it did not happen. And it bears repeating that *we don't want him to*. We honestly don't want a God who looks at sin, idolatry, murder, oppression, racism, sexism, rape, genocide, theft, infidelity, child abuse, and the thousand dirty 'little' sins we'd like to sweep under the rug, and just shrugs his shoulders and *lets it go*" ("The Beauty of the Cross: 19 Objections and Answers on Penal Substitutionary Atonement," derekrishmawy.com, posted on October 23, 2014).

46. Herman Bavinck clarifies: "Retribution is the principle and standard of punishment throughout Scripture. . . . All this is grounded in the fact that God is the God of justice and righteousness, who by no means clears the guilty, yet is merciful, gracious, and slow to anger, and upholds the rights of the poor and the afflicted, the widow and the orphan (Exod. 20:5–6; 34:6–7; Num. 14:18; Ps. 68:5; etc.). He, accordingly, threatens punishment for sin (Gen. 2:17; Deut. 27:15–26; Pss. 5:5; 11:5; 50:21; 94:10; Isa. 10:13–23; Rom. 1:18; 2:3; 6:21, 23; etc.) and determines the measure of the punishment by the nature of the offense" (*Reformed Dogmatics*, vol. 3, 162–63).

47. Mark Galli clarifies, "This is not the behavior of a God who stands aloof in a huff, waiting for propitiation before he'll have anything to do with us" ("The Problem with Christus Victor," *Christianity Today*, April 7, 2011). Rather, "In this is love, not that we have loved God but that he loved us and sent his Son to be the propitiation for our sins" (1 John 4:10). Paul echoes, "God shows his love for us in that while we were still sinners, Christ died for us" (Rom. 5:8).

48. See Isaiah 53.

49. It would be a mistake to understand anger as God's emotion toward Jesus on the cross. Calvin clarifies, "Yet we do not suggest that God was ever inimical or angry toward him. How could he be angry toward his beloved Son, 'in whom his heart reposed' [cf. Matt. 3:17]? How could Christ by his intercession appease the Father toward others, if he were himself hateful to God? This is what we are saying: he bore the weight of divine severity, since he was "stricken and afflicted" [cf. Isa. 53:5] by God's hand, and experienced all the signs of a wrathful and avenging God" (*Institutes*, I.xvi.11). See also Thomas McCall, *Forsaken: The Trinity and the Cross, and Why It Matters* (Downers Grove, IL: InterVarsity, 2012), 13–47.

50. Romans 8:1.

51. John Calvin, *Institutes of the Christian Religion*, vol. 2, ed. John T. McNeill (Louisville, KY: Westminster John Knox, 1960), 509–10.

52. First John 2:1b. See also Romans 8:34 and Hebrews 7:25.

53. As John declares in the very next breath: "He is the propitiation for our sins, and not for ours only but also for the sins of the whole world" (1 John 2:2). According to Paul, God has "forgiven us all our trespasses, by canceling the record of debt that stood against us with its legal demands. This he set aside, nailing it to the cross" (Col. 2:13b–14).

54. Read Leviticus 4–6 for more detail.

55. Read Leviticus 16 for more detail.

56. J. I. Packer sees this as "an illustrative device to make plain to God's people that their sin really has been taken away" ("Sacrifice and Substitution," in *Celebrating the Saving Work of God: Collected Shorter Writings of J. I. Packer*, vol. 1 [Exeter, UK: Paternoster, 1998], 130).

57. Read Exodus 12:1–28 for more detail.

58. See Bavinck, *Reformed Dogmatics*, vol. 3, 332–37.

59. Hebrews 9:12–14. See also John 1:29; Revelation 5:6, 12; and 17:14.

60. Hebrews 2:17b. See also Ephesians 5:2.

61. Leviticus 16:20–22.

62. See Ezekiel 16.

63. According to W. V. Harris, "infants were usually, it seems, abandoned outside towns or villages" ("Child Exposure in the Roman Empire," *Journal of Roman Studies*, vol. 84 [1994]: 1–22, 9).

64. According to the Twelve Tables of Roman Law, "Deformed infants shall be killed." Soranus of Ephesus wrote a first-century guide to gynecology, obstetrics, and pediatrics with a list of physical conditions that "indicate the infant not worth rearing."

65. "Child Exposure in the Roman Empire," 11–12.

66. Cited in Naphtali Lewis, *Life in Egypt Under Roman Rule* (Durham, NC: American Society of Papyrologists, 1999), 54.

67. According to Philo, "Others carry them to a deserted place, exposing them, so they claim, to the hope of safety, but in reality to the most dreadful misfortunes, for animals and birds come to devour them" (*On Special Laws*, iii.1 10–19). According to historian A. R. Colón, "An infant could be abandoned without penalty or social stigma for many reasons, including an anomalous appearance, being an illegitimate child or grandchild or a child of infidelity, family poverty, parental conflict (*ob discordiam parentum*) or being one of too many children. Sometimes they were given to friends, but more often than not they were abandoned to the elements, and death resulted from hypoglycemia and hypothermia. Sometimes the infant was devoured by the dogs that scavenged public places. It was likely however, that the *expositi* were rescued from these fates and picked up by slavers" (*A History of Children: A Sociocultural Survey Across Millennia* [Westport, CT: Greenwood, 2001], 104–105).

68. Harris notes, "Enslavement was much the commonest fate of foundlings" ("Child Exposure in the Roman Empire," 3–4, 9).

69. See Ephesians 1:4–6.

70. Harris, "Child Exposure in the Roman Empire," 3–4, 9.

71. Ephesians 1:8, 11, 14.

72. Ephesians 1:7a.

73. Isaiah 53:3, 8; Hebrews 13:12.

74. This is not to imply that the Trinitarian relationship was broken on the cross. It wasn't. See also McCall, *Forsaken*, 13–47.

75. Galatians 4:6–7.

76. Joni Eareckson Tada, *31 Days Toward Overcoming Adversity* (Colorado Springs, CO: Multnomah, 2006), 15–16.

77. In this sense we could say that substitution runs through all six images. As John Stott says, "So substitution is not a 'theory of the atonement.' Nor is it even an additional image to take its place as an option alongside the others. It is rather the essence of each image and the heart of the atonement itself. None of the . . . images could stand without it" (*The Cross of Christ* [Downers Grove, IL: InterVarsity, 1986], 202–3).

78. Trillia Newbell, *United: Captured by God's Vision for Diversity* (Chicago: Moody, 2014).

79. See 2 Corinthians 5:16–21 and Galatians 3:28.

80. See 2 Corinthians 10:3–5; Ephesians 6:10–20; 2 Timothy 2:24–26.

81. See Philippians 4:14–20 and Mark 10:45.

82. See Isaiah 1:17; 2 Corinthians 4:8–12; Matthew 16:24; and Philippians 2:5–11.

83. See Romans 12:1; Ephesians 5:25–27; and Philippians 2:17.

84. See James 1:27; 1 Corinthians 4:13; Hebrews 13:12–13; and 2 Timothy 4:5.

85. John Eastburn Boswell notes, "No pre-Christian moral system consistently opposed it, however, and the most common range of feeling seems to have spanned a relatively small distance from resignation to mild embarrassment" ("*Expositio* and *Oblatio*: The Abandonment of Children and the Ancient and Medieval Family," *American Historical Review*, February 1, 1984, 10–33, 28). According to Harris, "denunciations of child-exposure became habitual in Christian literature" ("Child Exposure in the Roman Empire," 7).

86. David Brill, SBS *Dateline*, May 4, 2013. As Biola University student, advocate for the disabled (and a brilliant young theologian), David Chung

adds, “We have to move from the notions of curse, cure, and care as the common defaults of viewing disabilities. I think the word ‘honor’ does it justice because it implies treating someone like royalty, and we are royal because we are God’s children” (personal interview, April, 15, 2016).

6. CREATE: MIRRORING THE ARTISTIC GENIUS OF JESUS

1. Francis Schaeffer, *Art and the Bible* (Downers Grove, IL: InterVarsity, 1973), 13–14, 17.

2. Hans Rookmaaker, “The Westminster Discussions: Faith, Art, Culture, and Lifestyle,” in *The Complete Works of Hans R. Rookmaaker*, vol. 3, ed. Marleen Hengelaar-Rookmaaker (Carlisle, UK: Piquant, 2003), 429.

3. *Art and the Bible,* 89.

4. *Art and the Bible,* 16.

5. *Art and the Bible,* 1.

6. For the many who flourished in the professional art world under Rookmaaker’s influence, see chapter 8 of Laurel Gasque’s *Hans Rookmaaker: An Open Life*, in *The Complete Works of Hans R. Rookmaaker*, vol. 6, ed. Marleen Hengelaar-Rookmaaker (Carlisle, UK: Piquant, 2002), 384–412.

7. Jonathan Anderson, William Dryness, Dan Siedell, and Andy Crouch to name a few. In particular, Schaeffer and Rookmaaker are often criticized for making sweeping and unwarranted negative appraisals of modern art, based, at times, on superficial and/or uncharitable readings of particular artworks. For helpful correctives, see Daniel Siedell, *God in the Gallery: A Christian Embrace of Modern Art* (Grand Rapids: Baker, 2008), as well as Jonathan Anderson and Williams Dyrness, *Modern Art and the Life of a Culture* (Downers Grove, IL: InterVarsity, 2016).

8. Robert Farrar Capon, *The Supper of the Lamb: A Culinary Reflection* (London: Macmillan, 1989), 189.

9. We could add Christian merchandise to the list. There are T-shirts of a famous Peanut Butter Cup logo where “Reese’s” becomes “Jesus,” the scribbled “Mossimo” logo modified into “Messiah,” a Jesus silhouette sprawled through the air like Michael Jordan slam-dunking the earth under the tagline, “Air Jesus: The Ultimate High.” Bob Dylan sang it best: “They make everything

from toy guns that spark to flesh colored Christs that glow in the dark/It's easy to see without looking too far that not much is really sacred."

10. James Speigel, "Aesthetics and Worship," *Southern Baptist Journal of Theology*, vol. 6 (Winter 1998): 40–56, 41–42.

11. As Hans Rookmaaker put it, "Imagine that every human eye were closed and every human ear stopped up, even then the beautiful remains, and God sees and hears it" ("God's Hand in History and the L'Abri Lectures," in *The Complete Works of Hans R. Rookmaaker*, vol. 6, ed. Marleen Hengelaar-Rookmaaker, [Carlisle, UK: Piquant, 2002], 263).

12. "God's Hand in History and the L'Abri Lectures," 263.

13. Rookmaaker, "The Westminster Discussions," 409.

14. See Psalm 33:3; 98:5; and 149:3a.

15. See John 1:3; Colossians 1:15–17; and Hebrews 1:8–13.

16. John 1:1–3.

17. By Christian art I do not mean "art made by Christians" over and against "art made by secularists." Just as I argued in chapter 1 that all truth is Christ's truth, so all beauty is Christ's beauty, whether we see it in a Rembrandt canvas or hear it in a Ramones song. In his book, *Imagine*, London-based poet Steve Turner describes how liberating this truth was when he first encountered it as a young artist. Raised in a Christian environment that drew a sharp, thick line between Christian and non-Christian culture, Turner was exposed to the work of Hans Rookmaaker. Rookmaaker suggested that the question — "Is the artist saved?" — is the wrong question. Is this piece of work technically excellent? Is it a valid expression of the artist's view of the world? Are form and content well integrated? Is truth communicated? These were the questions Rookmaaker was asking. "The effect was liberating," says Turner. Rookmaaker's perspective "confirmed what I had instinctively felt for some time — that a lot of art created by Christians was bad and a lot of art created by non-Christians was good" (*Imagine: A Vision for Christians in the Arts* [Downers Grove, IL: InterVarsity, 2001], 11–12). Abraham Kuyper echoes that "all liberal arts are gifts which God imparts promiscuously to believers and to unbelievers, yea, that, as history shows, these gifts have flourished in a larger measure outside the holy circle. These radiations of Divine Light shone more brilliantly among unbelieving people than among God's saints" (*Lectures on Calvinism* [Grand Rapids: Eerdmans, 1999], 271).

18. Luke 24:2–3.

19. Robert Farrar Capon counters, "The Bible is concerned with the perfecting of what God made, not with the trashing of it — with the resurrection of its native harmonies and orders, not with the replacement of them by something alien" (*The Parables of the Kingdom* [Grand Rapids: Eerdmans, 1985], 16).

20. Colossians 1:20; Romans 8:21; and Philippians 3:21.

21. John of Damascus, *Defense of Icons*, trans. Mary Allies (London: Thomas Baker, 1898), 16–17.

22. Notice that Wright doesn't say those creative acts will hasten or bring God's future, but will last into God's future. Only Jesus can bring the New Heavens and the New Earth. See N. T. Wright, *Surprised by Hope: Rethinking Heaven, the Resurrection, and the Mission of the Church* (New York: HarperCollins, 2008), 193.

23. Bertrand Russell, *Mysticism and Logic* (London: Longman's, Green, 1925), 47–48.

24. *Mysticism and Logic*, 48.

25. Michael D. Lemonick, "How It All Ends," *Time*, June 25, 2001.

26. Ephesians 1:10.

27. As Abraham Kuyper says, "If nothing of all that developed in this temporal life passes over into eternity, then this temporal existence leaves us cold and indifferent. . . . By contrast, if that rich and variegated development of our human life contains something that passes over into eternity, then the temporal obtains abiding significance" (*Common Grace*, ed. Jordan Ballor and Stephen Grabill, trans. Nelson Kloosterman and Ed M. van der Maas [Bellingham, WA: Lexham, 2016], 543).

28. Art professor Deborah Sokolove relays the story of young art student in her course who wanted to work in stained glass. The student, inspired by Amos 5:24 — "Let justice roll down like waters, and righteousness like an everlasting stream" — made several attempts at turning his complicated drawings into a stained glass reality. He failed again and again and was finally told that "glass could not always be made to do what you wanted to do. You had to work with its properties." Then came the student's epiphany: "I was oppressing the glass . . . trying to make it accept my own agenda." The professor comments, "When he worked with the properties of the glass with respect, something else emerged — a remarkable combination of symbols and designs, drawn from Amos but taking a fluid flowing shape." See Deborah Sokolove, *Sanctifying*

Art: Inviting Conversations between Artists, Theologians, and the Church, Art for Faith's Sake series, vol. 9, ed. Clayton Schmit and J. Frede Jasper Davison (Eugene, OR: Cascade, 2013), 90.

29. John 2:19. Scripture describes the Father and the Holy Spirit as raising Jesus from the dead, just as it describes the creation of the universe as a Trinitarian act. True creativity happens in community.

30. See John 14:3.

31. Robert Farrar Capon says it far better in a toast he loved to give at parties: "The road to Heaven does not run *from* the world but *through* it. The longest Session of all is no discontinuation of these sessions here, but a lifting of them all by priestly love. It is a place for men, not ghosts — for the risen gorgeousness of the New Earth and for the glorious earthiness of the True Jerusalem. Eat well then. Between our love and His Priesthood, He makes all things new. Our Last Home will be home indeed" (*The Supper of the Lamb: A Culinary Reflection* [London: Macmillan, 1989], 180-81.

32. See Luke 24:4–7.

33. Luke 24:20b–21a.

34. See Luke 24:26, 32.

35. This thought is attributed to Calvin by Kuyper in *Lectures on Calvinism*, 93.

36. First Peter 1:3–4.

37. As Zechariah, the prophet, said, "Shout aloud, O daughter of Jerusalem! Behold, your king is coming to you; righteous and having salvation is he, humble and mounted on a donkey" (Zech. 9:9).

38. See Abraham Kuyper's brilliant argument for the best wine in "the age to come" from Jesus' claim, "I tell you I will not drink again of this fruit of the vine until that day when I drink it new with you in my Father's kingdom" (Matt. 26:29) in chapter 66 of *Common Grace*, vol. 1, 579–87.

39. All quotes from this section are taken from chapter 12, "The Queen of Underland," in C. S. Lewis, *The Silver Chair* (London: Grafton, 2002), 137–47.

40. We might add a fifth F that humans have evolved to need in the early twenty-first century — "Facebook Likes."

41. Kuyper, *Lectures on Calvinism*, 155. What Kuyper describes as art's "mystical task" in "enabling us to discover in and behind this sinful life a richer and more glorious background" is one reason the sky has been one of the most celebrated artworks in human history. Its aesthetic power challenges

our self-fixation. I can't count how many times I've been driving home from a long day at the office, stuck in my own head, over-analyzing the day's events, when the Southern California sky breaks through, reaches through the windshield, takes me by the shoulders, and shakes me out of dazed introspection. This week it was a rainbow with a humbling reminder that there's real beauty beyond a drab little cell of self, beauty that exists in all of its fire and majesty and color, regardless of how good or dull I think that lecture went, or how the presentation goes tomorrow, or whether that deadline is met.

42. C. S. Lewis, *Surprised by Joy*, in *The Inspirational Writings of C. S. Lewis* (New York: Inspirational Press, 1994), 7.

43. *Surprised by Joy*, 11.

44. *Surprised by Joy*, 11.

45. Jerram Barrs, *Echoes of Eden: Reflections on Christianity, Literature, and the Arts* (Wheaton, IL: Crossway, 2013), 93.

46. J. R. R. Tolkien, "On Fairy Stories," in *Essays Presented to Charles Williams* (London: Oxford University Press, 1947), 83–84.

47. C. S. Lewis, "Letter to Arthur Greeves, October 1, 1931," in *Collected Letters, Vol. 1: Family Letters 1905–1931*, ed. Walter Hooper (San Francisco: Harper San Francisco, 2004), 976–977.

48. See Luke 24:40–42.

49. Emma Green, "Christians Have Prostituted Art to Give Answers," *The Atlantic*, October 6, 2014. Building on Lecrae's point, art that is too heavy-handed with its agenda tends to be very thin art, single-dimensional, uninspiring, and overwrought. Rowan Williams explains that good art has to do with "the configuration of sound or shape which *requires* attention and development from the artist. In the process of that development, we find meaning we had not suspected; but if we try to begin with the meanings, they will shrink to the scale of what we already understand" ("Making It Strange: Theology in Other(s') Words," in *Sounding the Depths: Theology through the Arts*, ed. Jeremy Begbie [London: SCM, 2002], 226). We can't bypass that creative process, which, as good artists will tell you, is often a series of false starts, flops, and frustrations, each one essential to making something honest and worthwhile. When we short-change that process our art can have the ironic side effect of conveying the very opposite of what we set out to say. In a Christian context, a lot of art that tries to express the majesty of Jesus ends up making Jesus seem trite, which is to say, the art tells a lie.

50. See Proverbs 25:20.

51. As musician Sufjan Stevens put it: "On an aesthetic level, faith and art are a dangerous match. Today, they can quickly lead to devotional artifice or didactic crap. This would summarize the Christian publishing world or the Christian music industry. If you are an artist of faith (a Methodist or a Jew), then you have the responsibility to manage the principles of your faith wisely lest they be reduced to stereotype, which is patronizing to the church and to the world, and, perhaps, to God. . . . I've written songs about stalkers. Is that any less religious than a song about an ordained pastor? No way." ("An interview with Sufjan Stevens," September 26, 2006, http://www.adequacy.net/2006/09/interview-with-sufjan-stevens/, retrieved July 19, 2016).

52. As Robert Farrar Capon puts it, "When the church . . . implies that its primary mission is to make history smooth here and now — in fails both its Lord and the world. It fails the Lord, because it is trying to do something Jesus in the end neither said nor did; and it fails the world, because it is offering a false hope" (*The Parables of Judgment* [Grand Rapids: Eerdmans, 1989], 180–81).

53. I can imagine one of history's most prolific worship songwriters — King David — squirming in his conference chair. He wrote such upbeat hits as "Why Have You Forsaken Me," with inspirational hooks like "O my God, I cry by day, but you do not answer, and by night, but I find no rest," "I am a worm and not a man," and "you lay me in the dust of death" (Psalm 22:1-2, 6, 15).

54. *The Complete Works of Hans R. Rookmaaker*, vol. 3, 418.

7. TRANSFORM: MIRRORING JESUS IN ALL OF LIFE

1. Second Corinthians 3:17–18.

2. Joanne Jung, *Knowing Grace: Cultivating a Lifestyle of Godliness* (Downers Grove, IL: InterVarsity, 2011), 7.

3. This is not to be confused with the freedom of our day, the freedom to define your own reality, yielding to no authority higher than your own feelings. That is, we have seen, its own form of bondage. Today's freedom *of* the self turns out to be imprisonment *within* and *by* your self. What Paul describes, by contrast, is the kind of freedom that is enjoyed only when we no longer white-knuckle the steering wheel of our own lives, only when our Lord is not the Self, but the Spirit.

4. *Knowing Grace*, 6.

5. Corrie Ten Boom, *Tramp for the Lord: The Story That Begins Where* The Hiding Place *Ends* (Fort Washington, PA: CLC, 1974), 63.

6. Thabiti M. Anyabwile, *The Life of God in the Soul of the Church: The Root and Fruit of Spiritual Fellowship* (Fearn, Scotland: Christian Focus, 2012).

7. Richard Sibbes, "A Description of Christ," in *The Works of Richard Sibbes*, vol. 1 (Edinburgh: James Nichol, 1862–64), 14.

8. Francis Chan, *Crazy Love: Overwhelmed by a Relentless God* (Colorado Springs: David C. Cook, 2008), 62.

9. Charles Panati, *Extraordinary Origins of Everyday Things* (New York: Harper & Row, 1987), 202.

10. Plato, *Phaedrus*, in *Selected Dialogues of Plato*, trans. Benjamin Jowett (New York: Random House, 2000), 148, 149. Plotinus, the third-century father of Neo-Platonism, likewise urged people "to separate yourself from your body and very earnestly to put aside the system of sense with its desires and impulses and every such futility" (*The Essence of Plotinus*, trans. Stephen Mackenna [New York: Oxford University Press, 1948], V, iii, 161).

11. Twelfth-century Bishop of Chartres John of Salisbury set "sensual pleasure itself" in his crosshairs, "which is illicit, wallows in filthiness . . . and that God without doubt condemns" ("The Natural Inferiority of Women," comp. Tama Starr [New York: Poseidon, 1991], 46). Sermons from around 1700 warn us "to treat one's body as a sworn enemy" and that "if you want not to be damned everlastingly but to be happy for ever in heaven, then you must renounce the world entirely and bid it an eternal farewell" (Jean Delumeau, *Sin and Fear*, trans. Eric Nicholson [New York: St. Martin's, 1990], 437; Jean Delumeau, *Catholicism Between Luther and Voltaire* [London: Burns and Oats, 1977], 44).

12. Wright, *Surprised by Hope*, 293.

13. Martin Luther, *The Freedom of a Christian*, in *Luther's Works*, vol. 31, ed. Jaroslav Jan Pelikan, Hilton C. Oswald, and Helmut T. Lehmann (Minneapolis: Fortress, 1999), 367–68; emphasis added.

14. Joy Alexander, "In Conversation with Evangeline Paterson," *Journal of the Irish Christian Study Centre*, vol. 4 (1989): 42.

15. *Abraham Kuyper: A Centennial Reader*, ed. James D. Bratt (Grand Rapids: Eerdmans, 1998), 488.

16. First Corinthians 13:12.

17. First John 3:2b.
18. Ephesians 5:14.
19. And also, for the imaginative, a poem:

A Scholar,
A heart Surgeon,
A foot-washing Slave,
A radically beloved Son,
An unblemished Substitute
A scarred, bread-breaking Shock
Here and now from the age to come.
Present with a pulse, weighty and radiant.
Fixate so long you forget yourself, and Behold.
As from the smoky shadow of the silver cube
Rising joyful to greet you, being Transformed
With room-shaking gravitas in each step,
And a face that glows with gold Sunrays
A Shock to our enchanted present age
A liberated Slave, a pardoned Sinner
A prized Son, a dancing Daughter
With a hand-washed heart
Recovered cardiac patient,
Full of Truth and Love
The real you.

20. Jonathan Edwards, "Glorying in the Savior," in *The Works of Jonathan Edwards: Sermons and Discourses 1723–1729*, vol. 14, ed. Kenneth Minkema (New Haven, CT: Yale University Press, 1997), 686, 687.

GENERAL INDEX

SCRIPTURE INDEX

Old Testament

ABOUT THE AUTHOR

Thaddeus Williams (Ph.D., Vrije Universiteit, Amsterdam) loves enlarging students' understanding and enjoyment of Jesus at Biola University in La Mirada, California, where he serves as assistant professor of systematic theology for Talbot School of Theology. He has also taught philosophy and literature at Saddleback College, jurisprudence at Trinity Law School, worldview studies at L'Abri Fellowships in Switzerland and Holland, and ethics for Blackstone Legal Fellowship and the Federalist Society in Washington, DC. His previous books include *Love, Freedom, and Evil: Does Authentic Love Require Free Will?* (Leiden: Brill, 2011). He resides in Orange County, California, with his wife and four children.

Connect with Thaddeus at:
website: www.thaddeuswilliams.com
facebook: www.facebook.com/thaddeus.williams.568
twitter: @thaddeuswill